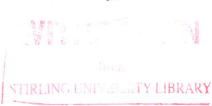

Forensic Aspects of Sleep

Forensic Aspects of Sleep

Edited by

Professor Colin Shapiro
Professor of Psychiatry, University of Toronto, Canada

and

Professor Alexander McCall Smith
Professor of Medical Law, University of Edinburgh, UK

JOHN WILEY & SONS
CHICHESTER · NEW YORK · WEINHEIM · BRISBANE · SINGAPORE · TORONTO

 National   01243 779777
 International (+44) 1243 779777
 e-mail (for orders and customer service enquiries): cs-books@wiley.co.uk
 Visit our Home Page on http://www.wiley.co.uk
        or http://www.wiley.com

Other Wiley Editorial Offices

John Wiley & Sons, Inc., 605 Third Avenue,
New York, NY 10158-0012, USA

Weinheim · Brisbane · Singapore · Toronto

Library of Congress Cataloging-in-Publication Data
Forensic aspects of sleep / edited by Colin Shapiro and Alexander McCall Smith.
     p.   cm.
   Includes bibliographical references and index.
   ISBN 0-471-96998-2 (alk. paper)
   1. Sleep disorders.   2. Medical jurisprudence.   I. Shapiro, Colin
M.   II. McCall Smith, R. A.
   [DNLM: 1. Sleep Disorders.   2. Crime.   3. Sleep Deprivation.
4. Forensic Medicine.   5. Automobile Driving.   WM 188 F715 1997]
RA1170.S54F67   1997
614'.1–dc21
DNLM/DLC
for Library of Congress   96-48755
                                                                CIP

British Library Cataloguing in Publication Data

A catalogue record for this book is available from the British Library

ISBN 0-471-969982

Typeset in 10/12pt Palatino from the author's disks by Servis Filmsetting Limited
Printed and bound in Great Britain by Bookcraft (Bath) Ltd, Midsomer Norton, Somerset
This book is printed on acid-free paper responsibly manufactured from sustainable forestation, for which at least two trees are planted for each one used for paper production.

Contents

Contributors

Roger J. Broughton
Division of Neurology, Ottawa General Hospital, 501 Smyth, Ottawa, Ontario, Canada K1H 8L6

Aileen Brunet
University of Toronto, Toronto, Ontario, Canada M5S 1A8

Eva Chow
Department of Psychiatry, University of Toronto, Toronto, Ontario, Canada M5S 1A8

Peter Collins
Forensic Division, The Clarke Institute of Psychiatry, 250 College Street, Toronto, Canada M5T 1R5

J. Paul Fedoroff
Forensic Division, The Clarke Institute of Psychiatry, 250 College Street, Toronto, Ontario, Canada M5T 1R8

Larry J. Findley
Aspen Medical Center, 1808 Boise Avenue, Loveland, CO 80538, USA

Jonathan A.E. Fleming
Vancouver Hospital and HSCH, UBC Pavilions, 2211 Wesbrook Mall, Vancouver, British Columbia, Canada, V6H 2B5

Carla Granger
Department of Psychiatry, University of Toronto, Toronto, Ontario, Canada M5S 1A8

A. McCall Smith
Faculty of Law, University of Edinburgh, Old College, South Bridge, Edinburgh EH8 9YL, UK

Merrill M. Mitler
Scripps Clinic and Research Foundation, 10666 North Torrey Pines Road, La Jolla, CA 92037, USA

Allan I. Pack
Center for Sleep and Respiratory Neurobiology, 991 Maloney Building, Hospital of the University of Pennsylvania, 3600 Spruce Street, Philadelphia, PA 19104-4283, USA

Stephen J. Pakola
Department of Ophthalmology, University of Pennsylvania Medical Center, Philadelphia, PA 19129, USA

J. Steven Poceta
Scripps Clinic and Research Foundation, 10666 North Torrey Pines Road, La Jolla, CA 92037, USA

Colin M. Shapiro
*The Toronto Hospital – Western Division, Sleep and Alertness Clinic, 399 Bathurst Street, Fell 6-108, Toronto, Ontario, Canada M5T 2S8
Phone: 416-603-5273
Fax: 416-603-5036
Email: cshapiro@torhosp.toronto.on.ca*

Tetsuo Shimizu
Department of Neuropsychiatry, Akita University School of Medicine, 1-1-1 Hondo, Akita City, Akita 010, Japan

Daniel W. Shuman
Southern Methodist University, School of Law, PO Box 750116, Dallas, TX 75275-0116, USA

Eileen P. Sloan
The Toronto Hospital – Western Division, Sleep and Alertness Clinic, Fell Pavilion 6-108, 399 Bathurst Street, Toronto, Ontario, Canada M5T 2S8

Valerie Woods
Ministry of the Solicitor General & Correctional Services, Probation & Parole, 2265 Keele Street, Toronto, Ontario, Canada

Introduction

C.M. Shapiro* and A. McCall Smith‡

University of Toronto and ‡University of Edinburgh

SLEEP LAW: A NEW CHALLENGE IN LAW AND MEDICINE

The study of sleep and its disorders is a relatively new branch of medical science. Over recent decades, considerable progress has been made in our understanding both of sleep and of the effect of sleep disorders in daytime functioning. Alongside this increased knowledge there has been a growing awareness of the economic and social consequences of sleep deprivation, which affects, to a chronic degree, around one in seven people. The legal consequences of this phenomenon have also been the subject of increased attention, and it is this aspect of sleep disorders with which this book is concerned.

The impact that sleep disorders have on the general population is illustrated by the following figures. About 30% of the population experiences insomnia in any year, with one third of that figure describing the problem as severe. Between 4% and 8% of males suffer from obstructive sleep apnoea, a condition which can lead to a range of serious symptoms, including cognitive impairment and chronic fatigue. Approximately 3% of adults and 15% of children are affected by parasomnias, phenomena which not only involve sleep disruption but may also entail a risk of harm to self or to others.

These conditions not only affect the quality of life of those who suffer from them but also have a major impact on the economy. In the case of the United States, the estimated annual cost to the economy of sleep problems has been estimated at some $16 000 million, although this figure has been contested.

Sleep medicine is not only concerned with the treatment of those conditions that prevent people from achieving the amount of sleep which they

Forensic Aspects of Sleep. Edited by C.M. Shapiro and A. McCall Smith.
© 1997 John Wiley & Sons Ltd.

require, but also sets out to further our knowledge of how sleep disorders affect performance and alter levels of alertness. These are questions of considerable interest to the law, which may be called upon to deal with situations in which a drowsy or even a sleeping person has caused damage to others. This occurs in both civil and criminal contexts. For the civil courts, the issue may be that of compensation in a case where a defendant has been unaware of a risk of drowsiness on the grounds of the failure of a doctor to issue a warning that drowsiness may be caused by medication. In the criminal courts, the matter may be one of the liability of a person who, in a state of somnambulism, has assaulted or even killed another person, or of a defendant who has gone to sleep at the wheel of a vehicle. Such cases raise profound questions of moral and legal responsibility, and have recently been the subject of considerable attention following upon exceptional criminal cases in both Canada and the United Kingdom.

The law concedes the non-responsibility of the unconscious actor. This would appear to exonerate the somnambulist, but the position is less clear in relation to those whose consciousness may be said to have been impaired, or whose awareness is in some sense diminished. In particular, the problem of dissociation is one with which the criminal courts seem to be unwilling to grapple. A person acting in a state of dissociation shares at least some features of the somnambulist, and yet in many systems is treated differently from the point of view of criminal liability. Similarly, the semi-automatic states in which sleep-deprived people drive vehicles reveal some of the features of somnambulism, but do not lead to a defence of automatism. All of these cases demonstrate the difficulties inherent in defining consciousness and in basing a theory of responsibility on the presence or absence of consciousness. Consciousness is not an all-or-nothing state; it is more a spectrum, with a high degree of awareness at one end and none at the other.

For the law, the question of liability is often phrased in a dichotomous way, although the issue that is being addressed is often a continuous variable. The criminal law asks: Was the conduct of the accused *voluntary* or *involuntary?* Alternatively, metaphors of control may be used, and the question becomes: Did the accused have *control* over his actions or were they beyond his control? At the present time, these issues of the subsystems within the brain controlling behaviours are not sufficiently well understood to allow for such clear reductionism. This applies with regard to a variety of behaviours, such as memory (the issue of false memory being one such example), alertness and consciousness. In the absence of clear medical and scientific information, the law proceeds to apply a lay perspective as to how these matters should be dealt with, sometimes leading to conclusions that seem irrational, especially when relatively similar phenomena are disposed of in quite different ways. For example, a person who causes harm while in an automatic state associated with concussion may be acquitted of a criminal charge while one who does a similar act as a result of an epileptic seizure will be dealt with as an insane offender and subjected to hospital detention and concomitant restrictions.

This dichotomous approach flows from a simplistic view that behaviours have an on/off type of quality, rather than a rheostat-type gradation. There are situations in which the law recognises this gradation but imposes a dichotomous standard. For example, in the assessment of responsibility in the case of the intoxicated driver there is a clear recognition that blood alcohol level has considerable bearing on the degree of impairment, and a standard is applied which is differently set in different jurisdictions and without reference to neurophysiological measure of impairment of performance. The introduction of measures of blood alcohol level has led to an enormous behavioural shift in terms of drivers' inclination to drive under the influence of alcohol. It is widely recognised that sleepiness while driving has become a major cause of accidents, and of those accidents involving a driver who fell asleep at the wheel an extremely high percentage result in death. These accidents commonly involve only a single vehicle, but when multiple innocent victims are involved there are considerable legal ramifications. To date there is no objective measure that can be easily and quickly applied which assesses the level of alertness or the level of sleepiness of a driver. If such a measure were to be introduced – by way of a test analogous to the blood alcohol measure – then the issue of the sleepy driver and the concern this raises for society could be as important and as charged an issue as the drunken driver has been over the past decade.

In establishing such a measure, there needs to be a clear recognition that sleepiness and alertness are not reciprocal states of mind. There are situations in which an individual with a specific sleep disorder can show profound sleepiness but may be able to perform in an alert fashion, given sufficient environmental cues or self-motivation. There are other situations where sleepiness and alertness run *pari passu*. In some circumstances, treatment may improve daytime alertness without affecting daytime sleepiness. Hitherto, it has been unusual for sleep researchers and sleep clinicians to measure these functions independently, and the means with which to do so are still rudimentary. This situation may well change in the next few years. We have some initial information that a population of patients attending sleep clinics will make distinctions between fatigue, anergy, consciousness, energy and sleepiness on a scale (FACES) which attempts to tease out these distinctions. These distinctions have perhaps not been sufficiently well explored in individuals who are sleep-deprived, and the literature is replete with examples showing the mismatch of subjective and objective assessments. This further emphasises the need for a multi-dimensional approach in assessing states of sleepiness and alertness.

A new technique (the alpha attenuations task) for the objective assessment of levels of sleepiness, which can be carried out quickly and easily, has recently been described and has been shown to distinguish between patients with a disorder of excessive sleepiness and normal controls. Furthermore, this technique has promise in distinguishing treated and untreated states in patients with disorders of excessive sleepiness. Other techniques are currently being explored. When these techniques become generally validated, their use in a forensic context is likely to follow. It is possible to envisage the roadside testing of drivers for levels of alertness, as currently occurs in alcohol screening. The impact of this on road safety would be immense, and yet one can anticipate policy difficulties with such a programme. While the public generally accepts the rationale of testing drivers for blood alcohol, it could be much more difficult to persuade people of the need for alertness testing. The intoxicated driver is generally understood to be taking an unjustified risk; the public may well feel that drowsiness is something that is impossible for the individual driver to assess, and may feel, as a consequence, that conviction for operating a vehicle in such a state is excessively harsh. It is possible, though, that such tests could be used initially to supplement the restrictions, such as the tachograph, currently imposed on the drivers of heavy vehicles.

As has occurred in other fields in which new medical knowledge has allowed for an increase in the subtlety of legal response, so too we anticipate that the burgeoning of information concerning states of alertness and sleep disorders will lead to a more coherent legal response in cases involving criminal responsibility in sleep-related offences. The old metaphors of control and voluntariness do not survive the evolving appreciation of neuro-physiological substrates of behaviour. From the ethical point of view too, greater awareness of sleep issues will similarly lead to tensions and dilemmas. Some aspects of these dilemmas will be no different from the usual problem which faces any doctor who believes that a patient poses a danger to others – should this information be communicated to those who are at risk even if this means breaching the confidence of the patient? Even if there is no question of breaching confidence, communicating the danger of somnambulistic violence to a couple may be potentially damaging to their relationship. This might be an issue where, say, a husband could prove a danger to a newly-born child sleeping in close proximity to the parents' bed. The obligation to warn in such a case is a moral one; the obligation of a doctor to notify driving licence authorities of a patient's condition may be a legal one (as it is in Ontario, for example) or may again be a matter for the medical conscience. The consequences of mandatory notification, of course, are potentially severe, as the effect of such provisions may be to discourage patients with a sleep problem from seeking help. This could have the effect of increasing, rather than diminishing, the risk to others.

In this book we set out to address these issues of sleep disorder in a way that will assist both the lawyer and the doctor in their involvement in what has rapidly become a complex field of knowledge. In our opening chapter, 'An overview of sleep physiology and sleep disorders', Sloan and Shapiro provide an account of sleep and of the disorders of sleep. Abnormal sleep behaviours which come before a criminal court require explanation, and modern sleep medicine can in many cases not only provide an explanation of the aetiology of such conditions but may also provide a prognosis which is essential for the legal disposition of the case. Somnambulism, and other sleep-related phenomena, are not bizarre and inexplicable behaviours to be treated by courts with scepticism; they are capable of scientific understanding and, in many cases, are perfectly susceptible to treatment.

Fundamental issues of responsibility are discussed by McCall Smith and Shapiro in 'Sleep disorders and the criminal law'. Over the past four decades, the criminal courts have developed the defence of automatism to deal with behaviour that lacks the voluntariness traditionally required for criminal conviction. This chapter traces this development and analyses the way in which the courts in a number of jurisdictions have dealt with cases of somnambulism. There is also a discussion of the approach of the criminal law to the rather more common situation where drivers have fallen asleep at the wheel. Common to both of these aspects of the legal problem is the issue of consciousness and the role it plays in the legal attribution of responsibility. Just what is involved in saying that a person was, at a particular time, unconscious? Does this involve the absence of all awareness of what is happening, or may a person be unconscious even if, like the somnambulist, there is some reaction to external stimuli?

The theme of violent conduct is further explored in 'Dangerous behaviours by night', by Broughton and Shimizu. Here the authors give an account of the conditions in which sleep-related violence may occur and discuss the issue of how a medical diagnosis may be made in such cases. It is one thing to observe and document such conduct in the sleep laboratory; it is another matter to reach the conclusion, after the event, that a violent episode was likely to have been committed during sleep. Yet this is exactly what is required of the expert witness who believes that the circumstances of the case point to such an explanation. It is interesting to observe that, at least in some of the more recent cases, courts appear to have been ready to listen to evidence of sleep disorder in cases where otherwise inexplicable acts of violence have been involved. Following on from this analysis of dangerous behaviours is an interesting study by Federoff and others of a sleep-related criminological problem, this time involving the sleeping victims of sexual attack.

From the specifically criminal focus of these earlier chapters, we proceed to the broader legal implications of sleep disorders and drowsiness. In 'Civil liability issues arising out of sleep deprivation and sleep disorders', Shuman examines the legal implications of sleep disorders for those who have either been harmed by a sleepy defendant or who have been responsible for causing sleepiness in employees or for failing to warn patients of drowsiness following upon the prescription of drugs. These issues are of growing importance as awareness grows of the role of sleep in industrial and other accidents. At the same time, however, the expansion of legal liability is a matter of concern for the courts, and new grounds of liability will be subject to close scrutiny.

Pack, Pakola and Findley, in 'Regulations for driving for patients with sleep disorders', examine the extent to which sleep disorders affect driving ability and the likelihood of road accidents. The question of the point at which sleep-related conditions should preclude a patient from driving is a delicate one, and their survey of the response in a number of jurisdictions (including the United States, the United Kingdom, Australia and Canada) reveals a variety of regulatory frameworks. Again, the issue of mandatory reporting raises its head, and a balancing of public safety against individual freedom comes into play, just as it does in the issue of the criminal liability of the sleep-disordered defendant.

The final two chapters deal with alertness and drowsiness and the factors that determine these states. Mitler and Poceta, in 'Chronobiologic and medical aspects of alertness', consider the impact of chronobiology on our understanding of wakefulness and examine certain tests which may be of assistance in providing an objective measure of levels of this state. This theme is also examined by Fleming in 'Pharmacological aspects of drowsiness', in which the impact of drugs, both recreational and therapeutic, on wakefulness is discussed at length. This is an issue of very considerable practical importance for the courts, and it is hoped that this chapter will prove useful in those cases where criminal or civil liability may depend on the impact in which prescribed or other drugs have induced a drowsy state.

The overall effect of the studies presented in this volume is to underline the significant effect that sleep disorders have on a wide range of human behaviour and to underline the importance of this effect for the law. While the over-medicalisation of human behaviour is rightly treated with suspicion by those lawyers who feel that psychiatry has already undermined the central tenets of individual responsibility which underpin the law, it is nonetheless true that the law must take into account insights that flow from greater medical understanding. Sleep research has thrown an important light on certain forms of human behaviour which in the past might have been written off as either substandard or simply perverse. The impact of these insights on the law is likely to grow.

1

An Overview of Sleep Physiology and Sleep Disorders

E.P. Sloan and C.M. Shapiro
University of Toronto

INTRODUCTION

Sleep tends to be considered as a time of quiescence and tranquillity, a time when the body and mind relax to recuperate from the day's activity, a time when relatively little happens. These assumptions are partially incorrect since sleep is, in fact, an active process. It is when sleep is disturbed or when events take place as a direct consequence of sleep deprivation that we realize how vital sleep is to the normal functioning of the individual.

What is sleep?

Sleep consists of two distinct physiological states: rapid eye movement (REM) sleep and non-REM sleep. Non-REM sleep is divided into four stages: stage 1 (light sleep), stage 2 (consolidated sleep), and stages 3 and 4 (deep or slow wave sleep). A certain proportion of the night is spent in each stage of sleep, occurring in discrete episodes (Figure 1).

The process of falling asleep can be subdivided into a number of stages, with characteristic physiological events taking place with this transition. However, stage 1 is considered to be the transitional stage between wakefulness and sleep. The electroencephalograph (EEG) becomes slower and rolling eye movements appear in the record. Shortly after, stage 2 or consolidated sleep is reached, with the appearance of sleep spindles and high voltage potentials known as *K* complexes. As sleep deepens to stages 3 and 4, the EEG is

Forensic Aspects of Sleep. Edited by C.M. Shapiro and A. McCall Smith.
© 1997 John Wiley & Sons Ltd.

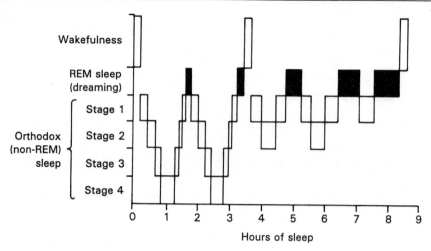

Figure 1. Cycles of REM and non-REM sleep across the night in a healthy person. Each cycle lasts approximately 90 minutes. Most slow wave sleep occurs in the early part of the night while most REM sleep occurs in the latter part of the night

dominated by high voltage slow wave activity (Figure 2). Throughout each of the above stages, muscle tone is maintained and eye movements are relatively rare. Approximately 90 minutes after sleep onset, REM sleep is reached, during which most dreaming activity takes place. REM sleep is a time of activation and increased autonomic nervous system variability, during which the EEG is similar to that of wakefulness, i.e. low voltage, high frequency activity. Muscle atonia and bursts of eye movements are fundamental aspects of REM sleep, which is mediated by a highly specialized neuronal system. Heart rate may increase during REM sleep and breathing may become more rapid and irregular. Penile erections invariably occur during REM sleep in men, irrespective of dream content. Recording of penile tumescence during sleep can be used to differentiate between organic and psychological impotence.

Throughout the night there is a cycling between non-REM and REM sleep. There are also brief episodes of wakefulness, which are usually too short to be remembered in the morning. The greatest proportion of slow wave (deep) sleep normally occurs in the first third of the night and most REM sleep occurs in the last third. The amount of time spent in each stage of sleep varies according to age (Figure 3). A young healthy adult, for example, spends approximately 5% of the night in stage 1, 45% in stage 2, 6% in stage 3, 14% in stage 4, 28% in REM sleep, and approximately 2% awake during the night.[1] An older person, however, will spend approximately 16% of the time awake and will have a significant decrease in deep and REM sleep and an increase in the lighter stages of sleep. Normal values for sleep times for different ages are given in Table 1. Levels of alertness are assessed by the Maintenance of

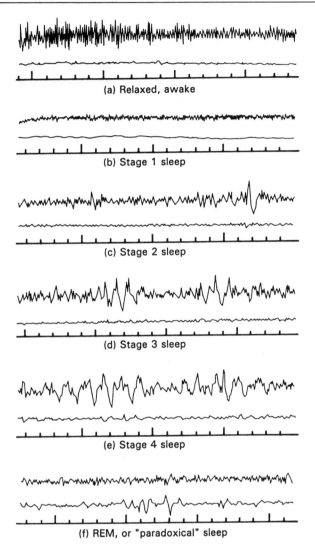

Figure 2. Changes in the electroencephalogram (EEG) across the stages of sleep. Note how the activity becomes slower in deep sleep (stages 3 and 4)

Wakefulness Test (MWT), which requires a person to lie in a darkened room for 30 minutes at two-hourly intervals and to try to remain awake.

The function of sleep

Many active physiological processes occur during sleep, indicating that sleep is not a time of quiescence. Energy expenditure is reduced by 5–25% relative

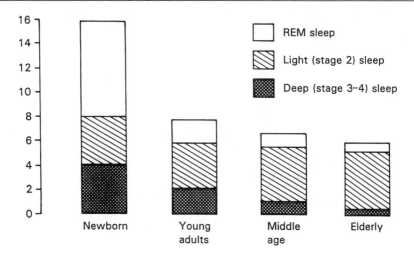

Figure 3. The number of hours of sleep spent in each stage of sleep at different stages across the life span

to wakefulness and oxygen consumption decreases. One study on oxygen consumption during sleep[2] suggests that at the onset of sleep, and particularly in slow wave sleep, there is a steady fall in body temperature. Normal physiological control seems to be suspended in REM sleep. Examples of this include the observation that humans cannot sweat and be in REM sleep.[2] The response to oxygen and CO_2 is dampened in REM sleep.[3] Men have erections[4,5] and women have increased vaginal blood flow during REM sleep – processes which play no apparent physiological role.

Such observations, with other evidence, have led Trinder *et al.*[6] to postulate a 'misregulation' of physiological processes in sleep, whereas others have incorporated these and other observations into an energy conservation hypothesis.[7] Trinder *et al.* have extended the notion of physiological instability at the point of sleep onset to suggest that the evolution of physiological control mechanisms have been largely for the benefit of waking function, and, for example, the dramatic fall in respiration during the initial stages of sleep sets the stage for sleep apnea (see below), which occurs more commonly in men.

This misregulation has clinical consequences. Examples include the triggering of nocturnal asthma,[8] the occurrence of painful nocturnal erections[9] and possibly the impact on the circadian distribution of cardiovascular related death.[10,11]

The physical and psychological effects of sleep deprivation suggest that sleep serves a specific function. A number of diverse theories concerning this function have been put forth, from an evolutionary theory concerning the

Table 1. The percentage of sleep in each stage according to age group*

Stage	3–5	6–9	10–12	13–15	16–19	20–29	30–39	40–49	50–59	60–69	70–79
						Age					
W†	0.88	0.27	1.55	1.10	1.87	1.26	1.47	6.29	4.33	7.73	16.0
	1.66	0.70	1.32	1.01	1.28	0.53	1.84	5.63	4.95	8.93	11.7
1	1.94	2.30	3.65	4.25	4.02	4.44	5.71	7.56	7.56	9.73	9.47
	2.30	2.30	2.28	3.01	3.74	4.18	4.17	5.64	4.85	7.69	6.59
2	48.12	47.95	46.16	44.00	49.05	45.54	56.89	54.75	64.71	56.79	55.49
	41.95	47.88	49.36	48.66	49.43	52.37	53.77	54.01	57.80	54.78	54.78
3	2.59	3.60	5.24	5.53	5.76	6.21	5.67	5.37	3.23	2.06	1.36
	3.40	3.13	2.95	5.20	5.65	5.27	6.42	7.51	6.49	4.50	6.30
4	16.21	18.55	17.01	18.42	17.28	14.55	6.79	3.18	1.69	0.60	0.00
	18.91	16.68	16.66	16.49	17.78	12.42	7.58	4.54	4.41	2.67	3.74
REM	30.26	27.33	26.39	26.70	22.02	28.00	23.47	22.85	21.48	23.09	17.68
	31.75	29.31	27.43	25.63	22.12	25.23	26.22	26.67	21.77	21.43	19.46

* The upper figures are for males and the lower for females.
† Brief periods of wakefulness.

need to sleep at a time when danger from predators is likely to be highest, to the energy conservation theory and homeostasis theory.

The restorative theory suggests that sleep is a time of restoration and growth for the body and for the brain. Evidence for this theory comes from a number of sources, such as the effects of exercise[12] and pregnancy on sleep,[13] as well as from observations of growth hormone release in slow wave sleep.[14] Furthermore, energy utilization and cell division observations[15] support this hypothesis. A variety of studies have shown clear qualitative as well as quantitative changes in sleep when there is (teleologically) greater need for restoration. Sleep deprivation results in an increase in the quantity and quality of sleep, and particularly of slow wave sleep, as well as an increase in levels of circulatory growth hormone. It has been shown that after a substantial amount of exercise there is a decrease in the time it takes to fall asleep; the amount of slow wave sleep and total sleep time increase and there is a reduction in REM sleep.[12] These changes, however, may be specific to athletes who are physically fit since exercise does not increase slow wave sleep in normally sedentary subjects.[16,17] The increased metabolic activity during wakefulness may underlie the increased need for sleep, especially deep sleep. Growth hormone release takes place mainly at night and particularly during slow wave sleep.[14,18] Pregnancy, a time of increased metabolic activity, is associated with an increase in slow wave sleep, suggesting that slow wave sleep increases at a time of growth. There is an increasingly recognized link between immune processes and sleep.

Another compelling theory of sleep regulation is that of Borbely,[19,20] who proposes that sleep serves a homeostatic function (process S), whereby slow

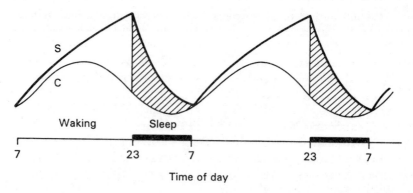

Figure 4. The increase in the propensity for slow wave sleep (S) across the day. The circadian process (C) is also shown

wave (deep) sleep in particular fulfils a sleep need and is therefore higher during the first part of the night, decreasing as the night progresses. Evidence for this theory comes from a variety of studies, including those on the effect of sleep deprivation. There is a rise in slow wave propensity during wakefulness throughout the day (Figure 4). Webb and Agnew[21] have shown that slow wave sleep increases as a function of prior waking. Sleep deprivation causes a prominent rise in slow wave activity during recovery sleep.[22] The increase may be due to an increase in brain metabolism during prior wakefulness.[23] The rebound of slow wave sleep after sleep deprivation takes precedence over the rebound of REM activity. This suggests that REM sleep expression is hampered by an elevated slow wave sleep pressure. REM sleep and total sleep appear to be regulated by a circadian (approximately 24 hour) process – process C – which is independent of prior wakefulness but interacts with the homeostatic process S to determine the prior timing of sleep and wakefulness. Process C is also involved in the regulation of plasma levels of certain hormones, such as melatonin and cortisol, and core body temperature regulation.

SLEEP DISORDERS

Healthy sleep is that quality and quantity of sleep required to maintain optimal alertness during desired waking hours. According to the National Commission on Sleep Disorders Research in the USA,[24] approximately 40 million adults in the USA suffer from a specific sleep disturbance such as sleep apnea, narcolepsy or severe insomnia. A further 20–30 million people have intermittent sleep problems. Sleep disorders affect people of all ages. Sudden Infant Death Syndrome (SIDS), from which many infants die each year, is linked to sleep, although the exact etiology is not yet understood.

Older children may suffer from sleep apnea, sleep terrors, nightmares and behavioural problems, such as separation anxiety, which can create difficulties around bedtime. Disorders such as Kleine–Levin syndrome and narcolepsy may manifest in adolescence. A wide range of sleep disorders are seen in adulthood – sleep apnea, parasomnias, movement disorders and sleep disorders associated with psychiatric illness. During old age many of these problems are exacerbated, while others, such as 'sundowning' and the sleep problems associated with dementia, develop.

The International Classification of Sleep Disorders (ICSD)[25] divides sleep disorders into four main categories: the dyssomnias, the parasomnias, sleep disorders associated with medical or psychiatric illness, and proposed sleep disorders.

The dyssomnias are disorders that produce insomnia or excessive daytime sleepiness and include 'intrinsic sleep disorders' (those which either originate or develop within the body or arise from causes within the body, e.g. narcolepsy, sleep apnea, restless legs syndrome); 'extrinsic sleep disorders' (those which originate or develop from causes outside of the body, e.g. environmental noise), and 'circadian rhythm sleep disorders' (caused by disruption to the biological clock, e.g. disorders resulting from jet lag, shift work and shifts in sleep phase).

The parasomnias are disorders of arousal and partial arousal, e.g. sleepwalking, of the sleep stage transition, e.g. rhythmic movement disorder, and disorders associated with REM sleep, e.g. nightmares. The parasomnias are often a manifestation of central nervous system activation, with autonomic nervous system change and skeletal muscle activity being the predominant features. These disorders are of particular legal relevance and are discussed in detail in Chapter 2.

Medical and psychiatric sleep disorders include those associated with the variety of psychiatric diagnoses, such as anxiety, depression, alcoholism, panic disorder, and disorders associated with medical illnesses, such as cerebral degenerative diseases, epilepsy, cardiac ischemia and chronic obstructive pulmonary disease.

The ICSD[25] category of 'proposed sleep disorders' includes those sleep disorders that are newly described and for which further information is needed to establish whether they constitute sleep disorders, rather than being at the extreme end of the normal range. Further information is needed before the nature of these disorders is established. Disorders in this group include short sleeper and long sleeper, sleep-related laryngospasm and the sleep choking syndrome. It is, of course, possible that other, as yet not formally recognized, disorders may be appreciated in time. We are struck, for example, by those patients with no slow wave sleep and those with bizarre EEG features after taking a variety of specific drugs. The latter may have particular medico-legal consequences.

INSOMNIA

All sleep disorders can cause insomnia and/or excessive daytime sleepiness, either directly or indirectly.

Insomnia refers to the perception of inadequate or non-restorative sleep. It may take the form of difficulty initiating sleep and maintaining sleep during the night, or awakening early in the morning and being unable to get back to sleep. Daytime tiredness may be the presenting feature. Virtually everyone experiences an occasional night of poor sleep but when insomnia becomes persistent it must be treated because it can have profound long-term effects. People who suffer from transient insomnia which is left untreated often suffer from persistent or recurrent insomnia at a later date. Ford and Kamerow, in a landmark study, found that patients with a serious sleep problem were significantly more likely to develop a psychiatric disorder than those patients in whom there was no sleep disorder.[26] These findings highlight the importance of early treatment of insomnia, since in some cases it may lead to psychiatric illness.

There are many different causes of insomnia: social, medical, psychological, biological, environmental. Psychiatric problems, such as depression and anxiety, account for the largest proportion of referrals.

The prevalence of insomnia changes across the life cycle (Figure 5), with prevalence being highest in the elderly population. Furthermore, females suffer more from insomnia than males at all ages, the prevalence rates in adults being 40% and 30%, respectively.

During childhood, insomnia may result from colic or illness, from anxiety at being separated from the parent, or as a result of the mother's depression or discord within the family. Sleep terrors and nightmares are common during childhood and the latter may result in anxiety about going to bed. Sleep apnea, due to enlarged tonsils or adenoids, may also contribute to disturbed sleep.

During adolescence, there is often a tendency to stay up late, particularly at weekends, in spite of the fact that at this age there is a need for increased sleep. Social and academic pressures, often combined with a part-time job, create considerable stress. There is evidence that a shift in circadian rhythmicity may be a 'normal' feature of adolescence, so that the biological need for sleep is out of synchronization with the socially acceptable time for going to bed, such that the adolescent does not need to retire until late at night. However, he or she must get up at a regular time in the morning to attend school, with the result that a 'sleep debt' builds up over time.

There are many causes for insomnia in adulthood. The effect of sleep apnea on sleep continuity has been discussed above. Sleep problems are a feature of many psychiatric disorders. Depression, for example, is accompanied by a specific pattern of sleep: early morning awakening, and a shortened latency to the onset of the first REM period; the distribution of slow wave sleep and

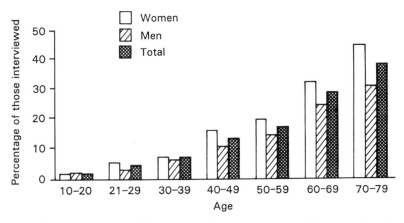

Figure 5. The consumption of sleeping medication across the life span, reflecting an increase in sleeping problems as age increases

REM sleep across the night are altered. One fifth of depressed people suffer from excessive daytime sleepiness and fatigue. Appropriate treatment of the depressive illness is often effective in dealing with the insomnia, although in some cases specific treatment of the insomnia may be required. Furthermore, certain drugs, such as fluoxetine (Prozac), which is prescribed for depression, may actually exacerbate sleep problems, and this drug-induced insomnia may need to be specifically treated. The latter point is true of many prescription and non-prescription drugs. Certain psychotropic, cardiovascular, anticholinergic and decongestant drugs, diuretics and histamine blockers have a disruptive effect on sleep. Alcohol taken before bedtime has a profound effect in that it increases snoring and worsens apnea. It decreases the latency to sleep onset, and sleep efficiency is increased in the early half of the night, but this is followed by increased sleep fragmentation and arousals in the second half of the night, as well as an increase in REM sleep and thus in dreaming activity. Long-term use of alcohol results in increased sleep fragmentation and arousals during the night. When a person who is alcohol dependent abstains from alcohol, it may take as long as two years for the sleep architecture to normalize.

Nicotine and caffeine also have marked effects on sleep in that they are both powerful stimulants and reduce sleep efficiency. Smokers, for example, sleep on average half an hour less than non-smokers each night. Other 'social' drugs, such as cocaine, marijuana and heroin, disrupt sleep significantly even though, in some cases, they may initially make the consumer sleepy.

Psychological factors play an important role in a form of insomnia known as psychophysiological insomnia, in which the patient has developed an expectation of not sleeping. The process of preparing for bed and the bedroom environment act in a paradoxical way as arousing stimuli and often evoke anxiety about not sleeping, which then keeps the person awake. Consequently, a vicious cycle of insomnia and anxiety develops. This form of insomnia is treated by psychological techniques, such as encouraging the patient to relax before bedtime, establishing an association between the bedroom and sleeping, a technique known as 'sleep restriction' but more correctly termed 'bed restriction', and changing the patient's attitudes towards not sleeping. The latter is important since some insomniacs become so anxious about the effects that insomnia may have on their health and ability to perform, that the anxiety actually interferes with their ability to sleep.

Many medical conditions cause insomnia, as do the medications that are used to treat these conditions. Patients with cardiovascular and respiratory disease commonly complain of insomnia and sleep disruption. Many patients with asthma suffer from nocturnal attacks,[27] so that the total amount of sleep time is reduced. The respiratory stimulants, such as theophylline, which are prescribed for asthma also tend to disrupt sleep.

A high percentage of the population complains of insomnia at some time or other, and for a proportion of these people, insomnia is a serious and debilitating condition.

SLEEP APNEA

Sleep apnea refers to the cessation of respiration when a person is asleep. The result of the apnea is that the sleeping person cannot breath and arouses in order to resume breathing. This may happen literally hundreds of times during the night, with the result that the quality of sleep is severely compromised, leading to excessive daytime sleepiness, a common presenting complaint.

Sleep apnea can be due to an obstruction in the airway, in which case it is referred to as obstructive sleep apnea (OSA), or it can result from a failure of the neural mechanisms that control respiration. The latter type is referred to as central sleep apnea (CSA). CSA is less common than OSA and the exact prevalence is unclear since many patients may be asymptomatic. It appears to be more prevalent in males than in females, although, as with OSA, the prevalence is similar after menopause.

OSA has significant effects on the quality of life, health and emotional status of the sufferer. The disruption to sleep throughout the night leaves the sufferer excessively tired during the day. Problems develop in relationships, emotional well-being is at risk, and performance at work is often affected. In children with OSA, decreased learning ability and an increase in behaviour problems are usually a result of the excessive daytime sleepiness.

There are risks to physical health as well. OSA is associated with hypertension, coronary heart disease, stroke, myocardial infarction, cognitive impairment and memory loss, psychiatric illness and impotence. High blood pressure has been found in 50% of patients with OSA and it is thought that a significant proportion of deaths attributed to cardiovascular disease may be the result of OSA. According to the National Commission on Sleep Disorders Research in the USA,[24] individuals with untreated OSA are estimated to be seven times more likely to have automobile accidents than the rest of the population.

OSA occurs in all age groups, races and socioeconomic classes. It is more common in men than in women at the pre-menopausal age, with a ratio of 8:1.[25] There is evidence, however, to indicate that certain groups of pre-menopausal women, such as those who are obese, may be more at risk for OSA than was previously thought to be the case.[28] There are a number of risk factors for OSA. These include overweight, a large neck size, age (OSA is most common in the fifth to the seventh decades of life), craniofacial abnormalities and substance (alcohol, drug, tobacco) use. Sleep deprivation may also be an important risk factor. Enlarged tonsils and adenoids are important risk factors in children. As mentioned already, male gender is a risk factor in the pre-menopausal age group. This suggests that progesterone may play a protective role in younger women.

Treatment of OSA

The first approach to treatment is usually behavioural in nature, with the patient being advised to lose weight and not to sleep in the supine position as apneas are more common in this position. In cases where medical illness underlies the apnea, appropriate treatment of the illness may alleviate the sleep apnea. Removal of enlarged tonsils or adenoids is effective in children. The most common and successful treatment is continuous positive airway pressure (CPAP),[29] which involves the patient wearing a mask which is attached to a pump-like device and blows air into the respiratory tract to maintain patency throughout the night (Figure 6). The effect of CPAP is usually immediate and patients find it to be extremely beneficial, although some find the device cumbersome and disturbing. In a minority of cases, surgery is used as an intervention for OSA, to remove excess tissue or to correct jaw misalignments. The efficacy of such treatments remains to be determined. Dental appliances have a potential role in some patients.

NARCOLEPSY

Narcolepsy is a debilitating neurological condition of unknown etiology but is thought to involve dysfunction of the brainstem sleep–wake mechanism. It

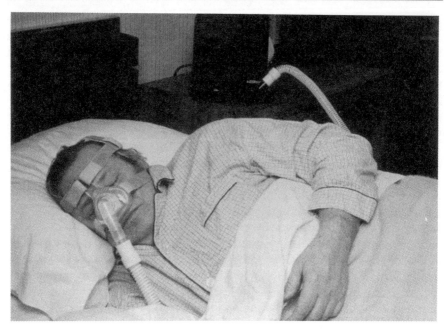

Figure 6. A sleep apnea patient using a CPAP machine

is an inherited condition which affects 0.05–0.6% of the population.[30,31] This places it as a condition more frequent than multiple sclerosis although it is far less recognized. The typical age of onset is between 15 and 30 years. Narcolepsy is characterized by four major symptoms: excessive daytime sleepiness, hypnagogic hallucinations at sleep onset, cataplexy or muscle weakness in association with the expression of strong emotion such as laughter or anger, and paralysis during arousal from sleep. All of these features can be understood as part of a malfunctioning of the mechanism which controls REM sleep. This mechanism has the role of ensuring muscle atonia at a time when the brain is active. Sleep paralysis is, for example, the awakening of the individual without the 'switch' for restoring muscle tone being activated. This occasionally occurs in normal individuals.

Narcolepsy has a profound effect on the lives of patients in whom it has not been treated. Excessive daytime sleepiness and the tendency to fall asleep uncontrollably may render them unable to carry on working, and may put patients or others in danger. Patients can become socially isolated. Since the initial manifestation of the disorder usually takes place during adolescence, students may be considered lazy and inattentive by their teachers, and academic achievement tends to deteriorate. Occasionally, narcolepsy is misdiagnosed as schizophrenia.

One of the distinctive features of narcolepsy seen in the sleep clinic is a shortened REM latency during nocturnal sleep and on multiple sleep latency testing (MSLT) repeated entry into REM sleep. The daytime cataplexy which patients may experience is thought to be due to the intrusion of REM sleep into wakefulness.

It is invariably the case that narcolepsy is not diagnosed correctly for many years. Treatment consists of management of the symptoms, since there is no cure for the disorder as yet. The excessive daytime sleepiness is treated with stimulants, and the cataplexy and REM sleep related symptoms are treated with REM suppressing agents, particularly certain antidepressant medications. Patients are counselled about sleep hygiene strategies, such as taking brief naps during the day and limiting environmental factors that may cause stress and thereby exacerbate the symptoms, which may be helpful.

There are concerns about the long-term use of such stimulant and antidepressant medication because of tolerance, dependence and side effects, but careful and regular monitoring of the effectiveness of these drugs is not only good clinical practice but also shows long-term benefits in this patient population.

MOVEMENT DISORDERS

Periodic limb movements (PLM) during sleep, or nocturnal myoclonus, is characterized by repetitive and frequent limb movements during sleep. All of the limbs may be involved but the most typical movement is extension of the big toe, with flexion of the ankle, knee and hip. The contractions occur at intervals of 10 to 120 seconds. The patient is often unaware that he or she is doing this but the movements have a disruptive effect on sleep since they often result in a brief arousal, reducing the restorative effect of sleep and causing excessive daytime sleepiness. PLM are noted in approximately 11% of pregnant women, and prevalence increases with age in both sexes. They also occur in association with certain medical illnesses, such as rheumatoid arthritis (30% of patients) and disorders requiring hemodialysis (15–20% of patients). In addition, certain drugs, such as the MAOIs and SSRIs, and withdrawal of others, such as benzodiazapines, can induce PLM. Confusingly, PLM may occur in patients who are being treated with CPAP for sleep apnea, a reason that may contribute to the failure of CPAP to relieve daytime sleepiness. It is for reasons like this that treatment in a sleep clinic usually is not a 'one-off' event.

CHRONIC FATIGUE SYNDROME AND FIBROMYALGIA

Chronic fatigue syndrome (CFS) is an incapacitating exhaustion or fatigue of at least six months' duration, leading to at least a 50% reduction in activity level, in the absence of medical and psychiatric causes. Patients with CFS complain of a number of symptoms, such as sore throat, generalized muscle weakness, muscle discomfort, sleep disturbance and neuropsychological complaints, such as forgetfulness and inability to concentrate. They also have a number of physical signs: low grade fever, non-exudative pharyngitis and palpable or tender anterior or posterior cervical or axillary lymph nodes. Patients often experience disability and are unable to work at some point in the illness. Onset of the disease may be sudden, following an acute viral illness, or gradual. In the latter case it tends to be associated with psychiatric or medical illness. The duration of CFS is typically two to three years, although in some cases it may last for five to six years. CFS affects 20–25% of the adult population and has a female:male ratio of 2:1.[32] It typically presents in the 25–40 year age group.

Fibromyalgia is a chronic musculoskeletal condition characterized by widespread muscle pain and stiffness. Like CFS, fibromyalgia affects more women than men and the typical age at which people are affected is 40–50 years old. It is estimated that between 10 and 15% of the general population are affected. The most common symptom of fibromyalgia is generalized pain, which tends to worsen after physical exercise. Fatigue is problematic, with the majority of patients complaining of difficulty initiating sleep, and restless and non-restorative sleep. Other common symptoms are morning stiffness, peripheral joint pain and swelling, bladder frequency, symptoms of irritable bowel syndrome and memory problems. Depression does not appear to be more prevalent in fibromyalgia, although the severity of pain is correlated with psychological disturbance.

Clinical examination may be unremarkable and the diagnosis tends to be made by excluding systemic disease. However, virtually all patients with fibromyalgia will experience tenderness at certain anatomical sites when palpated. There are 18 tender points and for a diagnosis of fibromyalgia to be made pain must be experienced at 11 of these sites upon palpation.

There is no cure for fibromyalgia or CFS but the most effective means of managing the symptoms are educating patients about the condition and encouraging them to increase exercise. Tricyclic antidepressant medication appears to be beneficial in reducing musculoskeletal pain and counteracting sleep disturbance. Management of substandard sleep can help a number of patients, and recent studies from Denmark have suggested a role for a specific new (SSRI) antidepressant.

THE PARASOMNIAS

Parasomnias are physical events that occur intermittently or episodically during the night. They are disorders of arousal, partial arousal and sleep stage transition, with autonomic nervous system activation and skeletal muscle activity being the predominant features. Patients with parasomnias often have a family history for the disorder.

The ICSD[25] classifies the parasomnias into four categories: arousal disorders, sleep–wake transition disorders, parasomnias usually associated with REM, and other parasomnias.

Arousal disorders

The arousal disorders include confusional arousals, sleepwalking and sleep terrors, caused by impaired arousal from sleep. They typically occur out of slow wave sleep, usually when the patient is coming out of stage 4 sleep.[33] These parasomnias are most common in children, with prevalence decreasing with advancing age.

Sleepwalking usually occurs during the first third of the night, during deep sleep. According to Guilleminault,[34] it occurs in 1–15% of the population, and is more common in boys than in girls. Bixler *et al.*[35] report an incidence of 2.5% in adults while Cirignotta *et al.*[36] report that 1.4% of adults who had sleepwalked in childhood continued to do so in adulthood.

Sleepwalking involves recurrent episodes of arising and walking about, which end with the patient awakening spontaneously or going back to bed. During these episodes the patient is completely unresponsive to communication and is difficult to awaken. Attempts to restrict movement may cause aggressive reaction.

Sleepwalking may be accompanied by eating, or other purposeful behaviour, such as a child getting into the parents' bed. The fact that sleepwalkers are seemingly unaware of their surroundings and unresponsive to others can result in them harming themselves, for example by falling down the stairs or walking into a glass door. There is usually amnesia for the event upon awakening.

The tendency to sleepwalk increases after sleep deprivation, when there is likely to be a rebound of slow wave sleep, after the use of CNS depressant medication and after alcohol consumption. Treatment strategies should be introduced when the problem causes stress to the patient or family and rarely need to be used with children, who tend to outgrow the condition. Precipitating factors, such as sleep deprivation, should be avoided and precautions should be taken to ensure that sleepwalkers will not harm themselves during an episode. Benzodiazapine and tricyclic medication may be helpful since these drugs tend to reduce the amount of slow wave sleep. Psychotherapy is effective in some cases.

Sleep terrors are episodes of extreme autonomic nervous system activation that occur out of slow wave sleep, although in young children they are also seen during light sleep. The patient sits up with a start, gives a piercing cry and appears to be highly distressed. Autonomic arousal is evident, with tachycardia, tachypnea, increased muscle tone and mydriasis (pupil constriction) accompanying the episode. Sleep terrors tend not to be associated with dreaming or mental activity, which differentiates them from nightmares, after which the patient can recall a terrifying dream. Patients often recall experiencing shortness of breath or heart palpitations before the event. As is the case with sleepwalking, the patient usually cannot be aroused from a sleep terror episode and the episode must be left to run its course.

Drug treatment is usually unnecessary in children since they grow out of the disorder as they get older but it is important for the parent to ensure that the environment in which the child will be sleepwalking is safe. Adult patients with sleep terrors may find benzodiazapine or tricyclic medication beneficial, and in some cases, psychotherapy and stress reductions are warranted.

Sleep–wake transition disorders

Disorders in this group occur at the transition from wakefulness to sleep and vice versa, and occasionally at the transition between stages within sleep. They are noted in otherwise healthy people and are not considered pathological although there is the possibility of injury, embarrassment or disruption of the bed partner's sleep.

Parasomnias usually associated with REM sleep

The most common disorder in this category is nightmares – frightening dreams which cause the patient to awaken, with little of the confusion or disorientation typical of night terrors. Nightmares are estimated to occur in 10–50% of children between the ages of three and six. Approximately 50% of adults have a nightmare occasionally. In some instances, nightmares can be linked to stressful life events or to a psychiatric diagnosis.[37]

REM sleep behaviour disorder (RBD) is characterized by an absence of the inhibition of motor neurons that is normally seen during REM sleep and enhancement of phasic motor drive so that it may seem that the patient is acting out the dream. Upon awakening, the patient can recall the dream, which usually involves fighting or self-defence. Injury often results from one of these episodes as the patient may collide with the wall or with furniture. RBD is more common in males than in females and it is most prevalent after 60 years of age. It may occur in an acute form as a result of toxic metabolic processes, such as drug withdrawal, and in a chronic form, which is either idiopathic or associated with neurological disorders. It has been reported to occur after psychological trauma[38] and as a result of stress,[39] although such cases are rare. For patients in the idiopathic category, RBD is not associated with psychopathology or detectable neurological disorder, although there may be a genetic component to this type of RBD.[40]

The exact pathophysiology of RBD in humans is not well understood. In experimental cats, loss of REM atonia has been found to be necessary for the expression of behaviour during REM sleep. Bilateral pontine tegmental lesions lead to a persistent absence of REM atonia associated with prominent motor activity during REM sleep.[41–43] Other areas within the central nervous system that may exert control over muscle tone during REM sleep are the medulla[44] and the hypothalamus.[45] It is possible that the changes that damage these areas are responsible for RBD in humans also. However, the fact that a large proportion of patients have the idiopathic form of RBD[46] suggests that in many cases there may not be a neuropathological cause for the condition.

The sleep architecture of people with RBD is normal, although there may be excessive slow wave activity and there is often a characteristic persistence of muscle tone during REM sleep, with the onset of REM sleep being marked by an increase of chin electromyogram (EMG) activity, rather than a decrease, which is usually noted.[39,40] There may be excessive limb movement during REM sleep, or muscle twitching, gross body movements or complex and violent behaviours. It is not uncommon to get a report from a mild-mannered 70-year-old man that both he and his wife are distraught because they are being awakened to find him apparently trying to strangle her, believing her to be an intruder.

Treatment often is not called for, other than stressing the need for the patient to take precautionary measures to avoid injury to self or to others. In those cases where pharmacological treatment is warranted, clonazepam[47] and desipramine[48,49] seem to be the most efficacious in minimizing the violent behaviour and vivid dream recall.

Other parasomnias

This category of parasomnias consists of disorders that cannot be classified in the other sections, such as sleep bruxism, sleep enuresis and primary snoring. Some rare conditions, such as sleep-related abnormal swallowing syndrome and sudden unexplained nocturnal death syndrome, are included in this category.

Sleep bruxism, episodic grinding or gnashing of the teeth, resulting from contraction of the masseter and other muscles, is a common condition, occurring in approximately 5–20% of the population. People tend to be unaware that they have bruxism, although for bed partners the condition can be very disturbing. Bruxism can occur in all stages of sleep. With respect to etiology, it is associated with anatomical malformations of the jaw, which can be corrected; it is more common in mentally retarded people and in comatose patients, suggesting some CNS involvement. It may be inherited in some people. Psychological factors are implicated also since stress can aggravate bruxism. Treatment usually takes the form of a dental appliance which is worn at night. In certain cases correction of anatomical defects is warranted. Stress management and relaxation training may be beneficial for some people.

Sleep enuresis, defined as involuntary micturition during sleep, tends to be more common during childhood and more common in males. During childhood, enuresis is idiopathic. It is probably due to incomplete toilet training or to a small functional bladder or an insensitive bladder. In adults enuresis is linked to organic factors, such as urogenital pathology, urinary infection, neurological disease, or metabolic or endocrine dysfunction, or to other sleep disorders, such as sleep apnea. Enuresis occurs in all stages of sleep and is not always accompanied by arousal. It is an embarrassing condition and can result in social distress. Management involves diagnosis and treatment of underlying conditions, where applicable. Behavioural management, such as reducing fluid intake in the evening and bladder control training, is often effective in cases of idiopathic enuresis. Pharmacological treatment may be required in certain cases where the condition is particularly problematic or distressing. Imipramine is a suitable choice because of its anti-cholinergic effect, which promotes urine retention.

Primary snoring, a condition that is significantly more common in men than in women, is included in the category of 'other parasomnias' since it is related to cardiovascular disease,[51] and is often a precursor of obstructive sleep apnea.[52] It can cause severe social problems since bed partners are invariably disturbed by the noise. There are a number of treatment approaches. Weight loss and altering position if snoring occurs when supine, avoidance of alcohol, and hypnotics and other sedative drugs are effective behavioural measures that can be taken. Surgical interventions in the form of uvulopalatopharyngoplasty (UPPP) and, more recently, laser assisted surgery (LAS) may be helpful. More complex surgical procedures are available where snoring is associated with facial malformations. If snoring is associated with obstructive sleep apnea, it is best managed with CPAP.

EFFECT OF SHIFT WORK ON SLEEP AND PERFORMANCE

A significant proportion of the work force is involved in shift work. Some people adapt readily to the demands that shift work places on their routine while others find the disruption more than they are able to deal with. In recent years a number of serious industrial accidents have been related to sleepiness during, or as a result of, night shifts. The proportion of automobile accidents increases at night, despite the fact that there are fewer drivers on the road at this time. A Danish study, in which the EEG and electro-oculogram (EOG) were recorded, found that machine operators had a significant increase in sleepiness during night shifts, and one fifth of the workers had one or more unintentional naps during the night.[53]

One of the reasons why shift workers have difficulty in adapting to shift work is that the circadian system does not adapt immediately to the change, so there is a mismatch between the internal body clock and lifestyle. Shifts in temperature, melatonin and other rhythms take place gradually, with the result that the shift worker is working at a time when the body is preparing to sleep, and is trying to sleep when the body is preparing to be active. During this time both performance at work and daytime sleep are affected detrimentally. It is the case for many workers that shifts change quite rapidly so that the circadian system is starting to adapt when the shift is changed and a re-alignment is required. Shift workers often suffer from problems such as gastrointestinal and cardiovascular problems, general ill health and fatigue.

There are some techniques that can be implemented to reduce the impact of shift work. Shift rotation should be from morning, to evening, to night, rather than from evening, to morning, to night, and days off should be taken after night shift to allow for the sleep debt to be dealt with before other shifts are started. In some circumstances rapid rotation of shifts, for example every one to two days, may prove beneficial in avoiding temporal disorientation, although performance during the night shift may be reduced. Shift workers should avoid caffeine, alcohol and tobacco as much as possible, but particularly during the latter half of the night shift, as they will affect sleep the next day. Strategic napping during the night may be also helpful.

There is increasing recognition of the medico-legal implications of shift work. Companies are beginning to recognize a responsibility for evaluating workers. One example of this is the provision of a book by Canada Post for the education of shift workers.[54]

CONCLUSION

Sleep disorders affect people of all ages and are more prevalent than previously recognized. According to the report of the National Commission on Sleep Disorders Research,[24] 40 million adults in the USA suffer from a specific sleep disorder, while millions more are sleep deprived as a result of shift work or lifestyle choices or patterns. The consequences of sleep disorders can be far reaching, ranging from discomfort and embarrassment to cardiovascular disease, industrial and automobile accidents, and death. Similar figures could be expected for other industrialized countries.

REFERENCES

1. Williams R.L., Karacan I., Hursch C.J. *Electroencephalography of Human Sleep: Clinical Applications.* New York, Wiley, 1974.

2. Shapiro C.M., Goll G.C., Cohen G.R., *et al.* Heat production during sleep. *J. Appl Physiol*, 1984, **56**:671–677.
3. Douglas N.J., White D.P., Weil J.V., *et al.* Hypoxic ventilatory response decreases during sleep in normal males. *Am Rev Respir Dis*, 1982, **125**:286–289.
4. Fisher C., Gross J., Zuch J. Cycle of penile erections synchronous with dreaming (REM) sleep: preliminary report. *Arch Gen Psychiatry*, 1965, **12**:29–45.
5. Karacan I. Clinical value of nocturnal erection in the prognosis and diagnosis of impotence. *Med Aspects Hum Sex*, 1970, **4**:27–34.
6. Trinder J., Whitworth F., Kay A., Wilkin P. Respiratory instability during sleep onset. *J Appl Physiol*, 1992, **73**(6):2462–2469.
7. Berger R.J. Bioenergetic functions of sleep and activity rhythms and their possible relevance to aging. *Fe Proc*, 1975, **34**:97–102.
8. Shapiro C.M., Caterrall R., Montgomery I., *et al.* Do asthmatics suffer broncho-constriction during rapid eye movement sleep? *Br Med J*, 1986, **292**:1161–1164.
9. Matthews B.J. and Crutchfield M.B. Painful nocturnal erections associated with rapid eye movement sleep. *Sleep*, 1987, **10**:184–187.
10. Muller J., Stone P.H., Turi Z.G., *et al.* Circadian variation in the frequency of onset of acute myocardial infarction. *N Engl J Med*, 1985, **313**:1315–1322.
11. Muller J., Tofler G.H., Stone P.H. Circadian variation and triggers of onset of acute cardiovascular disease. *Circulation*, 1989, **79**:557–565.
12. Shapiro C.M. Energy expenditure and restorative sleep. *Biol Psychol*, 1982, **15**:229–239.
13. Driver H.S. and Shapiro C.M. A longitudinal study of sleep stages in young women during pregnancy and post-partum. *Sleep*, 1992, **15**:449–453.
14. Born J., Muth S., Fehm H.L. The significance of sleep onset and slow wave sleep for nocturnal release of growth hormone and cortisol. *Psychoneuroendocrinology*, 1988, **13**:233–243.
15. Adam K., Oswald I. Protein synthesis, bodily renewal and the sleep–wake cycle. *Clin Sci*, 1983, **65**(6):561–567.
16. Griffin S.J. and Trinder J. Physical fitness, exercise and human sleep. *Psychophysiology*, 1978, **15**:47–50.
17. Montgomery I., Trinder J., Paxton S., Fraser G., Meaney M., Koerbin G. Aerobic fitness and exercise: effects on the sleep of younger and older adults. *Aust. J. Psychol*, 1987, **39**:259–272.
18. Mendelson W.E.B. *Human Sleep: Research and Clinical Care.* New York, Plenum, 1987, pp 129–179.
19. Borbely A.A. Effects of light and circadian rhythm on the occurrence of REM sleep in the rat. *Sleep*, 1980, **2**:289–298.
20. Borbely A.A. Sleep regulation: circadian rhythm and homeostasis. In: G.D. Pfaff (Ed) *Sleep. Clinical and Experimental Aspects*, Vol 1. New York, Springer-Verlag, 1982, pp 83–103.
21. Webb W.E. and Agnew H.U.L. Stage 4 sleep. Influence of time course variables. *Science*, 1971, **174**:1354–1356.
22. Borbely A.A., Baumann F., Brandeis D., *et al.* Sleep deprivation: effect on sleep stages and EEG power density in males. *Electroencephalogr Clin Neurophysiol*, 1981, **51**:438–493.
23. Horne J.A. Human slow wave sleep and the cerebral cortex. *J Sleep Res*, 1992, **1**:122–124.
24. The National Commission on Sleep Disorders Research in the USA. Wake Up America: A National Sleep Alert, Vol. 1. US Government Printing Office, Washington, DC, 1993.

25. American Sleep Disorders Association. *International Classification of Sleep Disorders: Diagnostic and Coding Manual*. Allen Press, Kansas, 1990.
26. Ford D.E. and Kamerow D.B. Epidemiologic study of sleep disturbances and psychiatric disorders. *JAMA*, 1989, **262**:1479–1484.
27. Turner-Warwick M. Epidemiology of nocturnal asthma. *Am J Med*, 1988, 85(1B):6–8.
28. Sloan E.P. and Shapiro C.M. Obstructive sleep apnea in a consecutive series of obese women. *Int J Eating Disorders*, 1995, **17**:167–173.
29. Sullivan C.E., Issa F.G., Bertfian-Jones M., *et al.* Home treatment of obstructive sleep apnea with continuous positive airway pressure applied through a nose mask. *Bull Eur Physiopathol Respir*, 1984, **20**:49–54.
30. Dement W.C., Zarcone V., Varner V. *et al.* The prevalence of narcolepsy. *Sleep Res*, 1972, **1**:148.
31. Dement W.C., Carskadon M.A., Ley R. The prevalence of narcolepsy. *Sleep Res*, 1973, **2**:147.
32. Wooten V. Medical causes of insomnia. In: M.H. Kryger, T. Roth, W. Dement (Eds) *Principles and Practice of Sleep Medicine*, 2nd edn. W.B. Saunders, Philadelphia, 1994.
33. Gastaut H. and Broughton R.J. A clinical and polysomnographic study of episodic phenomena during sleep. *Biol Psychiatry*, 1965, **7**:197–221.
34. Guilleminault C. Disorders of arousal in children: somnambulism and night terrors. In: C. Guilleminault (Ed) *Sleep and its Disorders in Children*, New York, Raven Press, 1987, pp 243–252.
35. Bixler E.O., Kales A., Soldatos C.R. *et al.* Prevalence of sleep disorders in the Los Angeles metropolitan area. *Am J Psychiatry*, 1979, **136**:1257–1262.
36. Cirignotta F., Zucconi M., Mondini S. *et al.* Enuresis, sleepwalking and night-mares. An epidemiological survey in the Republic of San Marino. In: C. Guilleminault and E. Lugaresi (Eds) *Sleep–Wake Disorders. Natural History, Epidemiology and Long Term Evolution*. New York, Raven Press, 1983, pp 237–241.
37. Hartmann E. Nightmares and other dreams. In: M.H. Kryger, T. Roth, W.C. Dement (Eds) *Principles and Practice of Sleep Medicine*, 2nd edn. W.B. Saunders, Philadelphia, 1994.
38. Hefez A., Metez L., Lavie P. Long term effects of extreme situational stress on sleep and dreaming. *Am J Psychiatry*, 1987, **144**:344–347.
39. Sugita Y., Taniguchi M., Terashiam K. A young case of idiopathic REM sleep behavior (RBD) specifically induced by socially stressful conditions. *Sleep Res*, 1991, **20A**:394.
40. Schenck C.H., Bundlie S.R., Smith S.A. *et al.* REM behavior disorder in a 10 year old girl and aperiodic REM and NREM sleep movements in an 8 year old brother. *Sleep Res*, 1986, **15**:162.
41. Hendricks J.C., Morrison A.R., Mann G.L. Different behaviors during paradoxical sleep without atonia depend on pontine lesion site. *Brain Res*, 1982, **239**:81–105.
42. Jouvet M., Sastre J.P., Sakai K. *Psychophysiological Aspects of Sleep*. Park Ridge, NJ, Noyes Medical Publishers, 1981.
43. Freidman L. and Jones B.E. Study of sleep–wakefulness states by computer graph-ics and cluster analysis before and after lesions of the pontine tegmentum in the cat. *Electroencephalogr Clin Neurophysiol*, 1984, **57**:43–56.
44. Lai Y.Y. and Siegel J.M. Medullary regions mediating atonia. *J Neurosci*, 1988, **8**:4790–4796.
45. Morrison A.R. Is the pons the site of rapid eye movement sleep generation in normal individuals? *Sleep Res*, 1991, **20A**:57.

46. Schenck C.H., Hurwitz T.D., Mahowald M.W. REM sleep behavior disorder. *Am J Psychiatry*, 1988, **145**:652.
47. Schenck C.H., Mahowald M.W. A polysomnographic, neurologic, psychiatric and clinical outcome report on 70 consecutive cases with the REM sleep behavior disorder (RBD): sustained clonazepam efficacy in 89.5% of 57 treated patients. *Cleve Clin J Med*, 1990, **57**:s 10–24.
48. Masumoto M., Mutoh F., Naoe Y. *et al*. The effects of imipramine on REM sleep behavior disorder in three cases. *Sleep Res*, 1991, **20A**:351.
49. Cowen P.J., Geary D.P., Schacter M. *et al*. Desimipramine treatment in normal subjects. *Arch Gen Psychiatry*, 1986, **43**:61–67.
50. Giaros A.G., Incidence of diurnal and nocturnal bruxism. *J Prosthet Dent*, 1981, **45**:545–549.
51. Hoffstein V., Mateika J.H. and Mateika S. Snoring and sleep architecture. *Am Rev Respir Dis*, 1991, **143**:92–96.
52. Partinen M. and Guilleminault C. Daytime sleepiness and vascular morbidity at seven-year follow-up in obstructive sleep apnea patients, *Chest*, 1990, **97**:37–32.
53. Gillberg M., Keckland G., Akerstedt T. Relations between performance and subjective ratings of sleepiness during a night awake. *Sleep*, 1994, **17**:236–241.
54. Shapiro C.M., Heslegrave R. *Making the Shift Work*. Toronto, Joli Joco Publications, 1996.

2

Sleep Disorders and the Criminal Law

A. McCall Smith* and C.M. Shapiro‡

*University of Edinburgh and ‡University of Toronto

The implications that sleep disorders have for the law fall into two main categories. Most notably, there is the question of the criminal liability of those who either engage in harmful activity while actually asleep – the somnambulists – or whose conduct is in some way affected by a sleep disorder. This category includes those situations in which an accused person successfully raises a defence of automatism – a complete defence to a criminal charge – as well as those in which although the conduct of the accused has been affected by a sleep disorder, consciousness has not been entirely compromised and no defence is allowed. The other area of legal concern is that of civil liability for damage resulting from sleepiness. Claims may arise in this context either against the person who causes the damage or against another person who has been responsible in some other way for the acts of the person who causes the damage. These civil issues are addressed separately; in this chapter we are simply concerned with the issue of criminal liability. The essential question here is how the criminal law should deal with those who commit a harmful act while acting somnambulistically. How are we to distinguish between the 'true somnambulist' and the person who has acted in a state of dissociation? How can the criminal courts protect society from dangerous conduct while at the same time avoiding the conviction of those who cannot be said to have full control over their actions?

Forensic Aspects of Sleep. Edited by C.M. Shapiro and A. McCall Smith.
© 1997 John Wiley & Sons Ltd.

THE MORAL BASIS OF CRIMINAL LIABILITY

The basic approach of Anglo-American criminal law to the issue of criminal responsibility is founded on the twin requirement of an *actus reus* (an unlawful or wrongful act) accompanied by *mens rea* (a guilty mind). Unless both of these elements are present in a particular case, there can be no criminal liability. Thus, if there is a defence turning upon the mental element – such as mistake or insanity, both of which are matters affecting *mens rea* – there will be no conviction, even if an unlawful act (*actus reus*) was committed by the accused. Similarly, if for whatever reason there is no *actus reus*, there will be no conviction, even if the mental element can be established.

The courts have always stressed that before there can be an *actus reus*, there must be a *voluntary act* on the part of the accused person, who must have *done something* in the sense of either having acted or having culpably omitted to perform an action. This requirement is often expressed in terms of volition and the will: a voluntary act is a *willed* movement in a sense in which a reflex act (or any other automatic act) is not.[1] This has led courts to observe that there can be no criminal liability where a person acts under overwhelming physical force or where the conduct in question is a reflex action.[2] In such cases there is no legally relevant action, no voluntary act. More recent jurisprudence has sought to escape from the notions of willed action espoused in earlier court decisions and has concentrated on the role of consciousness in the notion of the voluntary act. The legal philosopher H.L.A. Hart, for example, defines voluntary action as action which the actor 'takes himself to be doing', thus placing the emphasis on awareness or consciousness of the act.[3] There has also been analysis in terms of control; a voluntary act is one over which the actor has control; it is not voluntary if he cannot stop himself from performing it. Reflex action, for example, may be action which the actor takes himself to be doing, but which is beyond his control. The control-based approach, although useful, can lead to difficulties in the analysis of actions performed by persons suffering from powerful compulsions or addictions, and for this reason the criterion of consciousness is preferable.

The minimum requirement of a voluntary act for the imposition of criminal liability is not an arbitrary matter; as with other aspects of the *actus reus / mens rea* concept it springs from a fundamental moral conviction that we should be accountable only for those acts which are properly referable to an individual actor who, firstly, is capable of bearing moral responsibility, and who, secondly, has made a deliberate choice to act in the way in which he acts. This moral standpoint excludes, in general, liability for the acts of others (collective and vicarious liability), just as it excludes the imposition of liability on those below the age of responsibility or the mentally disordered.

Capacity for liability is seminal here. Moral responsibility requires the responsible subject, one who not only understands the nature of his acts but who is also capable of assessing them in moral terms. A child, for example, may have an understanding of the nature of acts, but may not be capable of moral assessment. This may also be expressed as ignorance; the child is ignorant of the full implications of his action, just as may be the mentally disordered person. The essential point here is the absence in the actor's mind of a specific element which is considered critical for accountability, whether it is ignorance or awareness.

A person whose consciousness is impaired may be considered non-accountable on grounds of incapacity. The impairment of consciousness will prevent a full understanding of any acts performed in that state, and the actor therefore has essentially the same excuse as is available to the person suffering from a mental disorder. In both cases the act is not referable to the actor's real self; it is an act which results from an intervening factor beyond his control. In a very real sense, then, the person who performs acts in a state of impaired consciousness might say: 'these acts are not acts *of mine*; my conscious self would not have endorsed them'.

Although this may at first sight seem to accord with everyday notions of moral responsibility, there are certain troubling aspects of actions performed in conditions of impaired consciousness. Although the actor might not have been fully conscious of what he did, and although his normal inhibitions may not have been present at the time, the action can still be said to spring from some mental event or cause. But where do we locate such a mental event, and even if we succeed in locating it, how does the actor stand in relation to it? The fact that the actor did what he did in a state of impaired consciousness does not necessarily mean that he did not *want* – in some sense – to do what he did.[4] If this want or desire existed in the mind of the actor, then why should he not be held responsible for it? The mere asking of this question will strike some as absurd, or possibly even morally insensitive, and yet it is necessary to pose this in order to understand the real basis of the moral exculpation in such cases and to test the legal response against a moral standard.

Assistance in this enquiry comes from a surprising quarter – the law relating to intoxication. Many legal systems in the Anglo-American mould – the majority, in fact – deny a defence to a person who commits a crime in a state of intoxication.[5] Thus, even if the accused establishes that he was intoxicated to the extent of not being aware of what he was doing or to the extent of not being able to form an intent to act, this will generally have no effect on his criminal liability. In certain cases – those where the crime is one of specific intent (theft, for example) – intoxication may be a defence, but in crimes of basic intent (such as assault), where all that is required is the intent to commit the act itself rather than to focus on any consequence or ulterior motive, intoxication is irrelevant. In cases of murder, intoxication may operate to reduce murder to manslaughter; in this context it has a mitigating effect rather than a totally exculpatory effect.

Holding the intoxicated offender responsible for his actions appears to offend the basic *mens rea* requirement that there should be no liability in the absence of an intention to perform the prohibited act. If a person is so intoxicated as to be incapable of forming such an intention, it is difficult to see how he can be guilty of a criminal offence. This logic has been accepted in certain systems – by the High Court in Australia[6] and, more recently, by the Supreme Court in Canada[7] – but the majority of systems simply fail to accord to intoxication an excusing role. The grounds for this refusal are a combination of policy considerations and considerations of principle. The policy considerations are that if such a defence were to be accepted, there would be widespread public dissatisfaction, particularly on the part of the victims of intoxicated offenders, who typically do not regard intoxication as an excuse. The principled case in favour of liability rests on the assertion that culpability resides in becoming intoxicated in the first place, or depends on the argument that actions performed by an intoxicated person are in a significant sense desired by that person and therefore referable to him. A controversial example of this latter rationale is to be found in the recent decision of the House of Lords in the case of *R. v. Kingston*.[8] In this case a man who had committed an unlawful sexual act on a boy after having been drugged against his will had his conviction of sexual assault upheld on the grounds that even if the drugging had compromised his inhibitions, the act in question was still one which he wanted to perform and for which he should be held accountable.

The significance of the intoxication analogy for our present subject is this: the mere fact that consciousness is impaired in some way will not of itself be enough to relieve an actor of responsibility. There will be cases of action in which although the actor could not control himself or was not fully aware of what was happening, he may still be held responsible on the grounds that his acts reveal culpable internal motives. This, however, comes perilously close to responsibility for character, rather than for acts, and there are strong objections to this form of responsibility.

The most acceptable moral response to those acts performed by a person in a state of impaired consciousness is to treat them as lacking an essential element in responsible action, namely the opportunity for choice. A somnambulist, a person in a state of hypoglycaemic automatism, or a person whose consciousness is impaired through dissociation does not *choose* to act in the same way as one whose mental state is not so impaired. Absence of real choice should be fatal to any attribution of responsibility, and should therefore be a complete excuse. People should be punished for making a choice that is referable to an autonomous self; a choice that is referable to a compromised self is simply not a choice that any theory of moral accountability should recognise.[9]

Generally speaking, the law accepts this moral view and places the threshold of liability at a voluntary act or an act under the control of the actor. Both voluntariness and control amount to the same thing in effect – an act beyond the actor's control is involuntary, and vice versa. Within this broad category of involuntary acts there is a category of unconscious acts, which are sometimes portrayed in the courts as the clearest case of involuntary action. If a person is unconscious at the time of acting, then anything which is done in such a state is not a matter for which he will be responsible. The difficulty with this approach, however, is that the criminal law does not make clear what it means by consciousness and this leaves the status of certain acts uncertain. In particular, if the actor is to some degree aware of his surroundings, or capable of acting in response to stimuli (as is the case with a somnambulist), then is there unconsciousness in the sense intended by the law? In the same vein, the metaphor of control proves to be inadequate when applied to certain cases of action performed in an abnormal mental state. This was shown in one of the driving cases, discussed below, in which a driver, in a state of hypoglycaemia, was held to be in control of his car although his consciousness at the time was certainly substantially impaired.

A powerful argument against the either/or approach that the law applies to consciousness or control is that such a distinction is too arbitrary to perform the subtle task of determining responsibility. An insistence that only those who are completely unconscious, or who totally lack control over their actions, will be held non-responsible has the effect of denying a defence to all but a very small number of those whose mental state is compromised in some way. To identify the criteria of complete unconsciousness or loss of control in this way also fails to reflect the reality of the automatism defence as it is currently applied. As the law stands, a defence of automatism is, in fact, allowed to those who are not completely unconscious or who are still, in a sense, controlling their actions. This would certainly be true of the victim of concussion. Such a person may have resort to a defence of automatism and may be described, according to the existing legal criteria, as acting in a way that is not under his control, and yet the reality is that he is, strictly speaking, not unconscious and he may, further, be said to have some control over his acts. What is required of us is a rethinking of the basis upon which responsibility is attributed in these circumstances and a redefinition of the legal defences that are applied in puzzling, borderline cases such as somnambulism. To do this, we should first address the issue of consciousness and then see how somnambulistic and similar states fit a more appropriate concept of consciousness.

Is the somnambulist unconscious?

Consciousness is the totality of a person's thought, feelings and perception. It incorporates being aware of one's own existence and one's own mental states, and implies that one is able to take cognisance of sensations. In psychiatry, it is the part of the psyche which is the object of immediate attention or awareness, and is set up in contradistinction to the subconscious or unconscious. Consciousness is not a single entity – it is composed of certain elements, each of which plays an important role in producing the final phenomenon. These elements are: (i) vigilance, a biological concept, related to reticular formation functioning, and which results in varying degrees of reactivity ranging from coma at one extreme to optimal responsiveness at the other; (ii) a behavioural component, which is possibly related to hippocampus functioning and which involves reactions to the environment; and (iii) a psychic awareness (a cortical phenomenon) of facts and the content of mental phenomena. While it may be possible to say that a person is either conscious or unconscious, it is also true that there are different levels of consciousness. These are often differentiated clinically in terms of alert wakefulness, lethargy, obtundation, stupor and coma. The uncontroversial cases of consciousness and unconsciousness are to be found at either end of this spectrum; in between there are states in which varying degrees of vigilance, reactivity and awareness are to be found.

It is often assumed that a neurophysiological description of consciousness can be given. While the brain wave activity associated with alertness can easily be characterised, the fundamental mechanisms of neurophysiological events that provide the essence of consciousness are currently only speculative theories. Perhaps the best of the current theories is that of Gerald Edelman, who has propounded a biological theory.[10] Edelman suggests that there are two components of consciousness: *primary consciousness*, comprising perceptual experiences and simple sensations, and *higher order consciousness*, which includes the ability to use language, as well as self-consciousness or awareness.

To describe the functioning of primary consciousness, Edelman proposes a brain map in which a sheet of neurons in the brain furnishes a representation of sensory stimuli present in the environment. Different brain maps are used at different times, and while some are active, others fade out of use. This implies that there is an active process of selection going on, with communication occurring backwards and forwards between various maps of cells as external stimuli are perceived and handled.

Higher order consciousness requires a form of memory which allows us to engage in a continuous process of sorting and resorting sensations based on previous archived sensations. This involves processes of (i) categorisation, (ii) learning (in which the brain gives priority to some sensory experiences over others), (iii) distinguishing between what is intrinsic to the individual and what is extrinsic, (iv) putting a sequence of events into a logical order, (v) interaction between the three features of primary consciousness and the process of time sequencing and conceptualisation, and, finally, (vi) there must be a complex system of interconnections between this special memory system and the neuronal maps that allow for the initial perceptual conceptualisations of sensations.

This provides a plausible theoretical construct of how consciousness might work. What it also demonstrates is that without the multiple processes involved in consciousness, full consciousness cannot exist. It is not necessarily the case that the elimination of, say, two of the nine components (three for primary consciousness and six for higher order consciousness) will result in less conscious awareness than if one of them were to be eliminated. Nor does it mean that the partial loss of one of these components will render a person incapable of full consciousness. Yet any defect in these components will represent a detraction from the complex process of consciousness and may justify the use of the term 'impaired consciousness'.

It is the strongest of moral intuitions that responsibility is dependent on consciousness. The complete absence of consciousness demands exculpation, in that the self which is to be blamed was simply not present at the time of acting. Impaired consciousness is another matter; if one of the components of consciousness is not present, the issue of responsibility surely rests on the moral weight to be attributed to that particular feature. A person who suffers from a distortion of consciousness, resulting in the misperception of certain features of the external world, may still be quite accountable from the moral point of view, whereas one whose impairment prevents the exercise of judgement may not be held responsible. It all depends, then, on the degree of impairment and the identification of what is affected.

Any human action (other than sub-cortical reactions or movements of the body) will require the presence of at least some degree of consciousness. If primary consciousness is absent, then there can be no movement, and the issue of responsibility hardly arises. The somnambulist satisfies the test of primary consciousness, as the three necessary components are present. Most of the components of higher order consciousness, however, are faulty in the somnambulistic state, even if the third feature, the ability to distinguish between what is extrinsic or intrinsic to the individual, is functioning. A person in a dissociative state will also satisfy a number of the criteria but will fail on others; the ordering of experiences in terms of past and future self is defective in such a person, as will be the process of retrieval of memory and the relating of current stimuli or retrieved archival memories. Similarly, a person suffering from confused awakening (sleep drunkenness) will be aware of surroundings and will be capable of performing what may appear to be controlled acts, and yet will not enjoy the proper functioning of those components that make up higher order consciousness.

If we associate moral responsibility with the ability to make judgements, this capacity clearly does not function properly in the somnambulistic state in that there is a significant detraction from the components of higher order consciousness. But how are we to measure the degree of impairment that will justify exculpation on these grounds? The difficulties inherent in this are illustrated in the law's experience of the problem.

THE RESPONSE OF THE CRIMINAL LAW

The rise of the defence of automatism

The criminal law's response to acts performed in a state of impaired consciousness is to be found in two distinct defences, the defence of insanity and the defence of automatism. The defence of insanity is the more well-established of the two defences, and was definitively stated for English law and related systems (including many jurisdictions in the United States) in the nineteenth-century case of Daniel McNaghten.[11] The McNaghten Rules, which form the basis of many statements of the law, both codified and uncodified, provide that an accused will be acquitted on the grounds of insanity if he can establish that, as a result of a 'disease of the mind', he did not know the 'nature and quality' of his acts or, if he did know their nature and quality, he did not know them to be wrong. This is a cognitive test, and would clearly be capable of covering those cases where mental disorder results in a significant impairment of consciousness. The insanity defence, however, is limited in its application by the requirement that there be a disease of the mind (a legal term which has caused considerable difficulty for the courts and for forensic psychiatrists). Consciousness-impairing conditions that cannot be said to result from an identifiable disease of the mind will not fall into this category.[12]

The limited nature of the protection offered by the defence of insanity became apparent in the course of this century, and legal systems looked for ways in which the harsh consequences of punishing mentally abnormal offenders could be avoided. The defence of diminished responsibility provided one route to this, allowing for the reduction of charges of murder to manslaughter in those cases where the exacting requirements of the defence of insanity cannot be met. Thus, homicides committed in a state of depression may be treated sympathetically through the acceptance of a plea of diminished responsibility even if they would not qualify for a complete defence of insanity.

The second major development arose in response to those cases where an accused person acted in a state of impaired consciousness, either brought about by factors other than mental disorder or, even if attributable to mental disorder, incapable of fulfilling the rigid and exacting requirements of the McNaghten Rules. This was the defence of automatism, which in English law first appeared in cases such as *R. v. Charlson*[13] and *R. v. Kemp*[14] in the mid-

1950s and which was further developed and explained in a series of cases over the following decades. In *Kemp* the accused suffered from arteriosclerosis, a condition which, by impeding the blood supply to the brain, would be capable of affecting consciousness. It was argued that this was a physical disease and that there was therefore no scope for the defence of insanity, but this argument was rejected by the court. The notion of automatic conduct, springing from a disease of the mind and justifying an insanity verdict, was thus endorsed. Some four years later, in *Bratty v. Attorney General for Northern Ireland*[15] the law on automatism was further clarified, and a distinction was made between two forms of automatism – insane automatism and non-insane automatism. If a defence was to be one of insane automatism, the verdict of insanity was appropriate, in the same way as in any other insanity case. If non-insane automatism was established, the appropriate response would be complete acquittal. This distinction between the two forms of the defence has survived, and is currently embodied in the law on this subject in many jurisdictions.

In *Bratty*, the appellant had been charged with the murder of a woman, whom he had strangled. His explanation for the act was that a 'blackness' had come upon him after his sexual overtures to the victim had been rejected. It was apparent that the accused was of low intellect, and there was some suggestion that he suffered from epilepsy, yet the court took the view that the overall evidence as to abnormality was weak. On appeal to the House of Lords, the court accepted that there could be a complete defence of automatism where a person's acts are the result of a condition other than a disease of the mind (somnambulism and concussion were cited as examples of such situations). In other cases, those of 'insane automatism', the insanity verdict is required. At the time, this inevitably led to the detention of the accused in a secure psychiatric hospital.

Lord Denning's speech in *Bratty* is of particular importance as it is here that enduring criteria for distinguishing between the two forms of automatism defence were first clearly identified. In Lord Denning's view, the test of whether the condition productive of automatism is a disease of the mind or not is that of whether it is a 'mental disorder which has manifested itself in violence and is prone to recur'. This criterion has been criticised on the grounds that it stresses the social danger of the condition as the basis for its qualification as a disease of the mind, a test which would be too broad and which would embrace conditions such as diabetes, epilepsy and somnambulism. Yet in spite of this objection, the criterion proved an enduring one, even if recent cases have abandoned the manifestation of violence and likelihood of recurrence aspects of the test and have stressed instead the question of whether the cause of the automatism is an external or internal cause.

The internal/external cause distinction was first explored in English law in the case of *R. v. Quick*.[16] In this case a diabetic psychiatric nurse assaulted a patient when he was in a state of hypoglycaemia. The accused argued that he was unaware of his actions at the time, but that this unawareness was not a result of a disease of the mind (had it been a result of such a disease the automatism would have been treated as insane and Quick would have been subjected to hospital detention). The court recognised the absurdity of treating a diabetic as insane and in order to avoid this result developed the distinction between a malfunctioning of the mind caused by disease and a malfunctioning of the mind 'of purely transitory effect caused by the application to the body of some external factor such as violence, drugs, including anaesthetics, alcohol and hypnotic influences'. In this case, the use of insulin by the accused caused the malfunctioning, and the insulin was an external factor. The automatism therefore could have been considered to be non-insane automatism, and it was held that this should have been put to the jury to consider.

The decision in *Quick* succeeded in moving the law away from the emphasis on the criteria of past violence and the likelihood of recurrence. In later cases, both in England and in other Commonwealth countries, the courts explored the scope of the internal/external distinction and considered its application in a number of specific conditions. In *R. v. Sullivan*[17] the automatic conduct had been caused by an epileptic seizure, to which the accused was prone. Following upon such a seizure, Sullivan assaulted an elderly man and was charged with causing grievous bodily harm; medical evidence was led to the effect that the assault was likely to have been committed in a post-ictal state of confusion, and, indeed, the nature of the violence was such as to suggest that this was the case. The issue for legal determination then became that of whether automatism caused by epilepsy was a malfunctioning resulting from a disease of the mind or whether it originated in another, external cause. In the end result, the House of Lords, to whom the matter was referred on appeal, decided in favour of a broad concept of disease of the mind which embraced not only transitory phenomena (such as a post-ictal confusional state) but also more permanent mental conditions. No distinction was made between organic causes or functional, provided the malfunctioning proceeded from a disease. Epilepsy, it was ruled, was a recurring pathological disorder of the brain and was therefore an internal rather than an external factor.

The development of Canadian and Australian cases closely followed that of the English cases, with a fundamental distinction being made between external and internal causes of automatism. In Canada, the most influential case to embody this distinction was the case of *Rabey* v. *The Queen*,[18] in which Martin JA pointed out (in the Ontario Court of Appeal judgment):

> In general, the distinction to be drawn is between a malfunctioning of the mind arising from some cause that is primarily internal to the accused, having its source in his psychological or emotional make-up, or in some organic pathology,

as opposed to a malfunctioning of the mind which is the transient effect produced by some specific external factor such as, for example, concussion. Any malfunctioning of the mind, or mental disorder having its sources primarily in some subjective condition or weakness internal to the accused (whether fully understood or not), may be a 'disease of the mind' if it prevents the accused from knowing what he is doing, but transient disturbances of consciousness due to certain specific external factors do not fall within the concept of disease of the mind.

Scots law was different; a decision of the High Court in 1962, *H.M. Advocate v. Cunningham*[19] declined to recognise non-insane automatism as a defence, ruling that the only form of automatism which could result in a complete defence, and therefore acquittal, was insane automatism. This decision was widely regarded as an unfortunate one, and there was substantial criticism of it both amongst commentators and in the courts. This criticism bore fruit: in *H.M. Advocate v. Ross*[20] the High Court accepted that automatism resulting from an external cause would be treated as a complete defence. Subsequent judgments have been at pains to emphasise that this defence can only apply if there is complete loss of control of action – also described in the cases as a requirement of a 'total alienation of reason' – and this must be brought about through no fault of the accused himself.

In contrast to the relatively unified treatment of automatism in the various Commonwealth jurisdictions, the approach to automatism adopted in the United States has varied widely from state to state. In some jurisdictions it has been considered under the rubric of the insanity defence,[21] while in others it has been treated as bearing on *mens rea*, and in particular on the requirement of intention.[22] A further approach, more in line with the defence of sane automatism discussed above, has involved the courts' treating automatism as a factor which negates the voluntary act requirement of the *actus reus*.[23] This latter view of automatism is certainly compatible with the provisions of the American Law Institute's *Model Penal Code*, section 2.01 of which requires the proof by the prosecution of a voluntary act. The Code excludes from the category of voluntary acts those acts which occur during unconsciousness or sleep, as well as reflex or convulsive acts.

SOMNAMBULISM: THE RESPONSE OF THE LAW

By 'somnambulism' is meant here activity which takes place while the actor is asleep. It embraces simple movements, of the sort that might be encountered in a night terror, as well as complex series of movements, such as those found in the case of the 'sleepwalker'. The term does not cover dissociation, nor conduct that is committed in a state of less than full alertness. These forms of conduct are separately considered below.

In a number of legal decisions on the subject of automatism, the courts have referred to somnambulism as a classic illustration of automatic action. These cases, however, have been concerned with automatism resulting from factors other than sleep – legal decisions dealing specifically with the subject of somnambulistic action are fewer and further between. One of the earliest cases in respect of which reasonable documentation exists is the Scottish case of Simon Fraser,[24] which was decided in 1859. The accused in this case was a father who had strangled his infant son in sleep, a crime for which there appeared to be no explanation. Medical evidence suggesting that this was done in sleep was accepted by the prosecution, which abandoned the trial in exchange for an undertaking from the accused that he would in future sleep alone. In the earlier part of the twentieth century several American cases considered the matter, treating somnambulism as a form of insanity.[25] Elsewhere in the common law world, the next case to confront the issue directly is the case of *R. v. Cogden*,[26] an Australian decision of 1950. The accused in this case was acquitted of the murder of her daughter, whom she had attacked while the latter was in bed. The court accepted that the killing was somnambulistic, although the precise grounds of the acquittal are not clear (the case is not reported in the law reports). According to the defence evidence, Mrs Cogden had been suffering from sleep disturbances, involving vivid and alarming dreams. She had consulted her doctor about this – an important fact from the evidential point of view – and on the night in question she claimed to have dreamed that she was being attacked by soldiers and spiders. She awoke to find that she had killed her daughter with an axe.

There continued to be the occasional prosecution for violent offence in which somnambulism could be an explanation, even if there was still no full discussion by a court of the full legal implications of somnambulism and its place within the automatism defence. Legal analysis of these cases is either non-existent or unsatisfactory, owing to the absence of appellate decisions on the matter and of full law reports. Oswald and Evans refer to three cases in which there was a prosecution, but no conviction, owing to jury sympathy or the prosecutor's willingness to drop the case in the light of psychiatric evidence.[27] In the first of these, which occurred in England in 1951, a husband was acquitted of criminal charges relating to an attempted strangulation and axe assault on his wife. There was psychiatric evidence in this case of the frequency of somnambulistic strangling behaviour by husbands on their wives, and the jury may well have been swayed by the wife's evidence in her husband's favour. In 1978 a wife who stabbed her husband 15 times (not to fatal effect) claimed to have been asleep at the time and the charges were dropped. Then, in a Scottish case in 1983, a 14-year-old boy stabbed his 5-year-old cousin with a bread knife after going downstairs at night. He claimed not to have any memory of the incident and it was suggested in psychiatric evidence that the boy, who had been tormented by others during the day, acted to attack his tormentors in a dream sequence. Again the prosecution was abandoned.

Other offenders who are believed to have acted somnambulistically have not been so fortunate. Buchanan, for example, describes a patient who was convicted of indecent exposure in circumstances suggestive of somnambulism. The accused in this case had walked up and down a communal balcony while quite naked, apparently unaware of the presence of his neighbours.[28] Much will depend on the credibility of the evidence and the willingness of a jury to accept that the defendant acted somnambulistically. The defence may have a difficult task in this respect, and may fail to satisfy sceptical jurors, as happened in the prosecution in Pennsylvania in 1994 of a sleep apnea patient who fatally shot his wife, allegedly in a state of confusional arousal following upon sleep apnea. The facts of this case, comprehensively discussed by Nofzinger and Wettstein,[29] were that the accused claimed that the first thing he remembered after going to bed at the normal time was awakening to the sound of gunshot. Expert evidence was led at the trial to the effect that the accused may well have been suffering from sleep drunkenness at the time, or, alternatively, that he may have experienced a hypnagogic hallucination as a result of fragmentation of sleep produced by sleep apnea. In the face of this, the prosecution stressed the absence of any evidence of somnambulism or any other sleep-related behaviour disorder. They also emphasised the existence of a motive for the killing, the accused's later failure to aid his victim, and the difficulties involved in extracting a firearm from beneath a waterbed while asleep. The jury preferred the prosecution's version of events and the accused was convicted of first-degree homicide.

Somnambulism examined: the case of Parks

Although earlier legal decisions contain incidental judicial remarks on the status of somnambulism and the availability of the automatism defence in sleepwalking cases, the first to examine the issue in satisfactory depth is the landmark Canadian case, *R. v. Parks*,[30] a decision of the Supreme Court of Canada. The facts of this case are remarkable. The accused was a young married man who had found himself in increasing difficulties following upon an embezzlement he had carried out against his former employer. The strain of his unemployment, coupled with the anxiety over impending criminal proceedings, appeared to affect his sleep, with the result that by the time of the incident he was sleeping very little at all. On the evening in question he had fallen asleep on the couch of his living room and in the early hours of the morning had got up from the couch, put on shoes and a jacket, and then driven his car some twenty-three kilometres along a busy road. The journey he made, which involved making six turns and led to his encountering eight sets of traffic lights, would have taken about twenty minutes to make. He arrived at the home of his parents-in-law, parked the car and extracted a tyre lever from the car. He then entered the home, fetched a knife from the kitchen, and went into the bedroom where he attempted to strangle his father-in-law and where he inflicted a series of knife wounds on both the father-in-law and the mother-in-law.

Parks claimed that during the journey in the car and the actual assault he was asleep and that the attacks were therefore somnambulistic acts for which he was not responsible. The medical evidence called for the defence supported this proposition, and as a result of this unanimous medical interpretation of the events, the court accepted that this was, in fact, a case of somnambulistic homicide.[31] The legal question which then had to be addressed was whether in a case of somnambulism the defence of non-insane automatism was available, or whether the defence to which Parks should have had resort was that of insane automatism. The implication of this distinction has been explained above; the former would result in unconditional acquittal, while the latter would lead to a psychiatric disposal.

The factor which would decide the classification of somnambulism in terms of the sane/insane distinction was the question of whether somnambulism could be considered a disease of the mind. In the view of the trial judge, although medical evidence of what would be considered a disease of the mind would not be determinative (the court having the final power to decide that), great weight was to be attached to the uncontradicted defence medical evidence, to the effect that the sleep disorder from which the defendant suffered was not categorised as a mental illness, disorder or disease of the mind. A similar view was taken in the Ontario Court of Appeal, although at this stage there was further analysis of the causation question. It was accepted that there would be a disease of the mind if there was an 'illness, disorder or abnormal condition which caused impairment of the . . . faculties of reason, memory and understanding'. According to the court, however, Parks experienced a disorder of sleep or an abnormal condition – a fact which was accepted by the medical witnesses – but this disorder or abnormal condition *did not cause the impairment of the relevant faculties*. This somewhat fine point was explained by one of the judges in the following terms:

> Accepting the evidence of the doctors . . . it seems that for some reason a sleep-walker can perform very complex and to all outward appearances deliberate acts while the faculties of reason, memory and understanding are not functioning. However, the condition or state of sleepwalking does not itself cause the cessation of these faculties. The sleepwalking occurs notwithstanding the absence of their functioning. Indeed, the cessation of function occurs before the sleepwalking begins, namely, when the person falls asleep. The cessation of function lasts throughout the sleepwalking episode. However, while the lack of function of the faculties of reason, memory and understanding coincides with the sleepwalking episode, it is not caused by it. Therefore, the disorder of sleep or the abnormal

function are not the cause of the impairment. In the absence of what I see to be the essential causal connection between the disorder or abnormal condition on the one hand and the impairment of the human mind and its functioning on the other, I cannot see that the disorder or abnormal condition impaired the respondent's mind or its functioning.[32]

When the case came before the Supreme Court of Canada, the Chief Justice took a similar approach to the causal question, saying that there was no evidence that sleepwalking was the cause of the accused's state of mind, and that therefore there could be no question of insanity. The issue of causation is important here, because of the importance the law attaches to the internal/external distinction.

It is difficult to follow the logic of the Parks decision in this respect. What caused Parks to behave as he did? One answer to this is that the behaviour in question was caused by the fact that he suffered from a sleep disorder. If Parks had not suffered from this disorder, then he would not have engaged in the somnambulistic conduct in question. He did not sleepwalk because he was asleep – the proposition advanced by the trial judge and endorsed in the Supreme Court judgment; sleep is merely the backdrop (in causal terms) to the somnambulistic conduct. The conduct in question – the homicide – was not caused by sleep but by a sleep disorder, a fact which is surely made clear if one asks the question: Why did Parks kill his father-in-law? The answer to this is that he did so because he was a somnambulist, and that, further, he was a somnambulist because he had a sleep disorder. The most significant cause of his conduct, therefore, is his sleep disorder. A sleep disorder is surely an external cause, in the same way in which organic illness producing unconsciousness is an internal cause of that unconsciousness. It may be that the organic condition will not be considered a mental disorder, but it is still internal.

The issue turns to an extent on what is meant by an impairment of the mind or abnormal condition. The court in Parks considered that unconsciousness – the suspension of reason, memory and understanding – was the relevant impairment. If this is so, then one can certainly see why it would be said that this impairment was caused by sleep, a normal condition. But we are really concerned here with abnormal mental *processes* not just with abnormal mental states in a passive sense. If we look at the mental processes of the somnambulist, we see that these are impaired because of the sleep disorder. It is clear that somnambulism proceeds from some mental processes. These mental processes are abnormal, in that in the normal case thought in sleep is not translated into action. It is not therefore unconsciousness with which one should be concerned; the focus should be on unconscious mental processes, and the particular features of these which make the somnambulist's acts of significance do not proceed from sleep but from sleep disorder.

Although the causation argument was important in *Parks*, other considerations were canvassed, and particular attention was paid to policy factors. The court was at pains to stress that a disorder of the mind was a legal concept, influenced by policy considerations, and not purely a medical matter. This is the point which had been made by the Ontario Court of Appeal in *Rabey*,[33] and cited with approval by the Supreme Court in *Parks*:

> I take the true principle to be this: it is for the judge to determine what mental conditions are included within the term 'disease of the mind', and whether there is any evidence that the accused suffered from an abnormal mental condition comprehended by that term. The evidence of medical witnesses with respect to the cause, nature and symptoms of the abnormal mental condition from which the accused is alleged to suffer, and how that condition is viewed and characterised from the medical point of view, is highly relevant to the judicial determination of whether such a condition is capable of constituting a 'disease of the mind'. The opinions of medical witnesses as to whether an abnormal mental state does or does not constitute a disease of the mind are not, however, determinative, since what is a disease of the mind is a legal question.[34]

Whether a condition is a disease of the mind or not depends then – to some degree, at least – on what the consequences will be of the labelling. The main policy factor at work is that of social protection. If a condition is likely to lead to a person's posing a danger to the public, then the court has a legitimate interest in protecting the public by ordering the detention of the accused person. This social protection aspect of the concept of a disease of the mind was identified by Lord Denning in *Bratty* v. *Attorney General for Northern Ireland*,[35] where he identified the criteria of a mental disorder in this context as the fact that the condition had manifested itself in violence and was prone to recur.

The issue of recurrence has been the cause of some debate, and there have been a number of decisions in which the test of likelihood of recurrence has been subjected to criticism. In *Rabey*, for example, the court pointed out that if Lord Denning's proposition were to be tested by stating its converse, its flaws would be revealed:

> It would be quite unreasonable to hold that a serious mental disorder did not constitute a disease of the mind because it was unlikely to recur. To do so would be to exclude from the exemption from responsibility afforded by insanity, persons, who by reason of a severe mental disorder were incapable of appreciating the nature and quality of the act or of knowing that it was wrong, if such mental disorder was unlikely to recur.

A further objection would be a medical one. The possibility of recurrence of a condition is one which medical experts may be unable to predict with any accuracy, and it might be wondered whether the classification of a condition should rest on such an uncertain feature.

To avoid the difficulties of the Denning criteria, the courts in a number of cases resorted to the internal/external dichotomy, trusting this device to do the task of distinguishing those cases in which the accused could safely be acquitted from those where the safety of the public requires his detention and possibly treatment. In many cases the internal/external distinction will perform that task adequately, as it will single out as internally-caused conditions those conditions which do, in fact, pose a threat and exclude those which do not. In some circumstances, though, the application of an internal/external test will produce curious results unless resort is made to strained refinements. This was shown in the *Quick* decision,[36] where the test might have pointed to diabetes being an internal cause of a hypoglycaemic state had the court not identified insulin as being an external cause.

The Supreme Court in *Parks* chose not to rely on the internal/external distinction, which they felt did not lend itself to situations of somnambulism. The court opted instead for a much more flexible approach in which a number of factors play a role, including that of the likelihood of recurrence of a condition. In this case, the medical evidence as to this likelihood was unambiguous, with the principal defence expert in sleep disorders, stating that the recurrence of violence was 'absolutely improbable'. It is significant that, with an eye to future cases in which a different conclusion as to recurrence might be reached, the court said that, with different medical evidence, future courts may choose to classify somnambulism as a disease of the mind. This demonstrates the weight given to the social protection aspect of the matter and the court's clear concern over the need to take into account public anxieties as to the release of dangerous persons. While *Parks* may be clear authority, then, for the proposition that somnambulistic acts may be treated as non-insane automatism and may therefore result in a complete acquittal, the most important factor in practice in every case will be the medical evidence, particularly medical evidence as to the possibility of recurrence. If there was evidence of a regular pattern of violence during sleep – a pattern which was thought to be likely to recur – then it is quite open for a Canadian court, under *Parks*, to label the condition as a mental disorder and to resort to an insane automatism defence.

The authority of the decision in *Parks* was subsequently invoked in *R.* v. *Watkins*,[37] another case in which the defence of non-insane automatism was raised. The accused in this case, an off-duty policeman, had been arrested after driving his car erratically. He was found to have an excessive amount of alcohol in his blood and was charged with the offence of impaired driving. His defence was that at the time of the driving he was asleep.

Although Watkins had not consulted a doctor about somnambulism, there was credible evidence from his former wife to the effect that he had regularly walked in his sleep, sometimes several times a week. On occasions he had performed fairly complex tasks while still asleep, including starting to cook on a barbecue, casting off a boat, and searching the house. This behaviour was more frequent when he was stressed or anxious, but she never approached a doctor on the subject, believing it not to be a major problem.

The medical evidence also pointed in the direction of somnambulism. The medical author of this paper conducted extensive examinations of the accused, including sleep laboratory tests, and concluded that Watkins did in fact suffer from a parasomniac condition and that on a balance of probabilities a parasomniac state was pertaining at the time. This conclusion was based not only on the evidence which pointed to the fact that he was prone to sleepwalk, but the presence on the night in question of certain classic triggering factors, including daytime stress, the excessive consumption of alcohol, and the time of going to sleep. This medical evidence, combined with the evidence of the spouse, was enough to justify the court's conclusion that the accused had not acted voluntarily and that, following *Parks*, in the absence of any evidence to the effect that the condition was a disease of the mind, the appropriate outcome should be an acquittal on the grounds of non-insane automatism.

The contrary view: *R. v. Burgess*

A radically different view of the legal status of the somnambulist was taken by the English Court of Appeal in *R. v. Burgess*,[38] which was decided after the trial stage of *Parks*, but before the decision of the Supreme Court of Canada. *Burgess* did not involve the same sort of sustained and complex conduct as had been present in *Parks*; the accused in this case has visited his neighbour during the evening with a view to watching videos. He had a perfectly good relationship with her, and it was not unusual for them to entertain themselves in this way. On the evening in question they watched the video from the sofa, and she fell asleep, to be woken up after being hit on the head. She found the accused standing above her with the video recorder held high, ready to bring it down on her head. Shortly afterwards, he appeared to come to his senses and showed great concern over what he had done. According to the accused, he had gone to sleep and only regained consciousness at the point at which he was holding her down on the floor. He had no memory of having hit his neighbour. The jury in his trial returned a verdict of not guilty by reason of insanity, and an order was made for the accused's detention in a psychiatric hospital. He appealed against this verdict, arguing that the appropriate defence in these circumstances was non-insane automatism and that he should have been acquitted on these grounds.

The Appeal Court acknowledged, on the basis of the jury verdict, that at the time of the attack the accused did not know what he was doing. The question that had to be resolved on appeal was whether the 'defect of reason' under which he was acting at the time of the attack was one which could be said to result from a disease of the mind. It is apparent from the outset that the Court of Appeal felt that the key to the elucidation of this issue lay in the internal/external distinction. As the Court said, 'One can perhaps narrow the field of inquiry still further by eliminating what are sometimes called the "external factors" such as concussion caused by a blow on the head. There were no such factors here. Whatever the cause may have been, it was an "internal cause" . . .'.[39]

The Court referred, with approval, to what had been said in *Rabey*, a case which it pointed out to have similar facts, even if the medical diagnosis (a dissociative state) in that case had been different:

> Any malfunctioning of the mind, or mental disorder having its source primarily in some subjective condition or weakness internal to the accused (whether fully understood or not), may be a 'disease of the mind' if it prevents the accused from knowing what he is doing, but transient disturbances of consciousness due to certain specific external factors do not fall within the concept of disease of the mind . . . In my view the ordinary stresses and disappointments of life which are the common lot of mankind do not constitute an external cause constituting an explanation for a malfunctioning of the mind which takes it out of the category of a 'disease of the mind'. To hold otherwise would deprive the concept of an external factor of any meaning.[40]

The court similarly found assistance in Lord Denning's criteria of disease of the mind, outlined in *Bratty* v. *Attourney-General for Northern Ireland*,[41] namely that this concept encompasses any mental disorder which has manifested itself in violence and is prone to recur.

Armed with these criteria – the internal status of the condition, the manifestation in violence, and the likelihood of recurrence – the Court reached the conclusion that the medical evidence that had been presented to the trial judge justified a finding that the appellant's conduct resulted from a disease of the mind. In contrast to the attitude of the Ontario Court of Appeal, the Court of Appeal in this case took the view that even if sleep could be said to be a normal condition, sleepwalking – and particularly violence in sleep – could not be regarded as a normal condition. In *Burgess* there was clear medical testimony available to the trial judge to the effect that somnambulism is a pathological condition, properly described as an internal, rather than external, factor. In view of this medical evidence, it is difficult to see how the court could have regarded it as an external factor and therefore justifying a finding of non-insane automatism.

There was a marked difference in the tenor of the medical evidence in *Parks* and *Burgess* which helps to explain the difference in outcome. The medical evidence in *Parks* presented somnambulism as within the range of normality, pointing out that a considerable proportion of people experienced somnambulistic episodes; by contrast, in *Burgess* the medical witnesses spoke of sleep disorder and an abnormality of brain functioning, terminology which naturally points to a conclusion of insane automatism. It is also significant that the medical evidence in *Parks* was not seriously contested at the trial stage, and the defence psychiatrists therefore encountered little challenge in respect of their categorisation of somnambulism. In *Burgess* the prosecution tested the evidence fairly severely, and, indeed, one prosecution witness, an acknowledged and experienced expert in abnormal states of consciousness, Dr Peter Fenwick, suggested in evidence that the accused was not sleep-walking at all, but acting in a state of dissociation.

As a result of these two important cases, both decided at a high level in their respective jurisdictions, the position in other common law jurisdictions would appear to be that somnambulism sits uneasily on the borderline between insane and non-insane automatism. How the matter will be decided in other jurisdictions, where there is no case directly in point, remains to be seen. The deciding issue is likely to be the internal/external distinction, and this, as was shown in the decisions in *Parks* and *Burgess*, is a matter which is going to be heavily influenced by the medical evidence put before the court. It is difficult to see how a sleep disorder can be described as an external factor, as the tendency to sleepwalk or not must be associated with the way in which the individual's brain processes control sleep patterns. This is surely an internal matter, of the same order as a tendency to epilepsy, which the courts have labelled an internal condition in cases such as *Sullivan*.[42]

The alternative explanation: dissociative states and the law

In *Burgess* the explanation of the conduct in question which was advanced by the expert witness for the prosecution suggested that the accused was not sleepwalking at all, but was acting in a dissociative state. Such an explanation certainly deals with the straining of credulity which some of the judges in *Parks* confessed to feeling; long episodes of dissociative conduct – involving apparently purposive behaviour – are probably more common than similar episodes of somnambulistic conduct, and probably also more frequently involve violence. How are these distinguished from somnambulism, and how should the law respond?

Dissociation

Dissociative conduct is conduct in which the normal integrated relationship between memory, identity and consciousness is disturbed. A person acting in a state of dissociation is not unconscious in the normal sense of the term; he is aware of his surroundings and responds to them, but does not relate these surroundings and his reaction to them to his normal self. The 'fracturing of consciousness' may therefore be one way of describing the phenomenon; the consciousness which prevails at the time of the dissociative state is distinct from the consciousness which prevails at other times. At the same time, there could be links; in particular, it could be suggested that the unconscious operates in the dissociative state in the same way as it operates in the normal state. This, of course, is merely another way of saying that the self is still present (in that unconscious motivations clearly constitute part of the normal self). What is different, though, is the role of the morally responsible self, the self which makes deliberate choices of which the actor is aware over time.

The DSM-IV (one of the most widely-used psychiatric diagnostic manuals) identifies five principal dissociative disorders: dissociative amnesia, dissociative fugue, multiple personality disorder, depersonalization disorder; and dissociative disorder not otherwise specified. The disorder which is closest to somnambulism is dissociative fugue, which is characterised by sudden, detached conduct, often involving wandering, in which the person engages in complex conduct in a state of awareness but in which there is amnesia in relation to real identity. There is usually a sudden recovery, after which there may be no memory of what happened in the fugue state. Multiple personality disorder also raises tantalising issues of legal responsibility, but is quite distinct from the somnambulistic state.[43]

It is certainly the case that somnambulism and dissociative fugue share certain superficial features. For example, in both there is an apparent lack of awareness of the surrounding environment, although an individual in either of these states does not usually harm himself by tripping over an object in his path. With reference to our earlier discussion of consciousness, the individual shows some degree of consciousness in not tripping over the object, but some impairment of consciousness is evident by virtue of the fact that the individual might perform this action in a public place in the nude and be oblivious to his state of undress. In both cases, there may be total lack of recall of the events that occurred.

The distinguishing features include, firstly, the more common incidence of personality disorders amongst individuals experiencing the fugue states. In general, individuals engaging in somnambulistic behaviour do not have extensive psychiatric contact. Secondly, individuals evincing fugue states are more likely to have other dissociative features. Standard assessment instruments for dissociative states may include questions about, for example, whether or not individuals have clear memories for important events in their lives; certainty about recollections of events or whether they appeared as dreams; and whether or not they become so involved in a fantasy or daydream that it feels as though it was really happening to them. These individuals might occasionally find that they have writings, drawings or notes among their belongings that they must have done but cannot remember doing, and may feel that they act very differently in one situation compared with another, and that they are two different people. Thirdly, parasomnias emerge in limited circumstances, namely, from sleep, and typically from the first third of the sleeping period. (For further characteristic features of the parasomnias which serve to distinguish them from other conditions, see the following chapter). Finally, fugue states are generally longer in duration than somnambulistic behaviours. A fugue state may go on for hours or even days; somnambulism usually lasts for no more than half an hour.

A good account of dissociative conduct which illustrates the circumstances in which the disorder may occur and the possibilities it creates for conflict with the criminal is that given by Bisson in a case described in 1994.[44] The patient in this case, B, was a young man who had served as a soldier in Northern Ireland and who developed mild symptoms of post-traumatic stress disorder. After his first tour of duty, he experienced a mild dissociative episode, during which his father found him talking about Northern Ireland and yet unable to communicate with him. He completed a second tour of duty, which again involved feelings of fear and stress, and then returned to England, where he was given an unrewarding posting. At this stage he began to experience feelings of heightened irritation, difficulty in concentration, and sensitivity of anything which reminded him of his experience in Northern Ireland.

Four months after his return, B recounted an evening in which he had felt frightened after looking at photographs of family, friends and his Northern Irish tour of duty. He then dressed himself in his combat outfit, fetched his hunting rifle, and drove his car through the security barrier of the barracks in which he was living. He later hijacked another car and drove a distance of some two hundred miles before he was eventually apprehended. He claimed to remember nothing after the point at which he was looking at the photographs.

The medical diagnosis of B was PTSD with mild depressive features. Bisson suggests that the second dissociative episode had several features of a fugue state and 'could be considered as a release from the problems he was experiencing'. Bisson adds:

> The case of B and the other reported cases suggest that criminal acts as a result of dissociative states in PTSD sufferers do occur and clinicians need to be aware of this possibility. Equally as important is the factor that they seem to occur rarely, and certainly do not account for the majority of criminal acts committed by war veterans with or without PTSD. Indeed, it is likely that there is often little relationship between crimes committed by war veterans and their actual war experiences. It is only by rigorous assessment that those who do commit crimes as a result of their experiences will be identified and receive appropriate treatment.

The legal response to dissociative conditions has been sceptical. In a line of earlier Canadian decisions the courts showed themselves to be prepared to accept dissociation as an explanation of bizarre or out-of-character behaviour, and to acquit in such cases on the grounds of sane automatism. This was the result, for example, in *R. v. Gottschalk*,[45] in which a defence of sane automatism was accepted following a psychiatric diagnosis of chronic anxiety and depersonalization. Then, in *R. v. Rabey*,[46] a decision of the Supreme Court of Canada, clear limits were set to this defence. The accused in this case had assaulted a woman with whom he had become infatuated and who had rejected him. The resulting dissociative state, it was held, was a result of a disease of the mind and not the result of an entirely external, psychological blow. A similar view was taken in the English case of *R. v. Hennessy*,[47] which was decided in 1989. In this case, the appellant, a diabetic, sought to establish a defence of non-insane automatism to driving a car after he had been deprived of his licence. He argued that his blood sugar level had been high at the time and that this had been caused, in part, by the effect of stress and anxiety. These, he argued, were external factors. The Court of Appeal, concerned to exclude abnormal mental states caused by stress and anxiety from the ambit of non-insane automatism, ruled:

> In our judgement, stress, anxiety and depression can no doubt be the result of the operation of external factors, but they are not , it seems to us, in themselves separately or together external factors of the kind capable in law of causing or contributing to a state of automatism. They constitute a state of mind which is prone to recur. They lack the feature of novelty or accident . . .

The unwillingness of the courts in *Rabey* and *Hennessy* to allow a defence of non-insane automatism in cases where dissociation has resulted from stressful circumstances has not been reflected in all jurisdictions, and in Australia there have been signs of a more receptive approach after the South Australian decision in *Radford*.[48] In this case the Chief Justice said:

> There is no reason in principle for making a distinction between disturbance of the mental faculties by reason of stress caused by the external factors and disturbance of the mental faculties caused by the effects of physical trauma or somnambulism. The significant distinction is between the reaction of an unsound mind to its own delusions and/or to the external stimuli on the one hand and the reaction of a sound mind to external stimuli, including stress producing factors, on the other hand. I appreciate that if it is true that a state of depersonalisation or dissociation is not itself a disease of the mind, although it may result from mental illness, the result may be that the certain cases of unwilled acts which formerly would have been treated as the result of temporary insanity and would have founded verdicts of not guilty by reason on the ground of insanity, will now result in outright acquittals. I do not see any reason to shrink from that consequence . . . If a person was not morally responsible for the action which is the subject of the charge because that action was an unwilled automatic act, he should not suffer conviction or punishment. If he is not mentally ill and there is therefore no reason to suppose that the act will be repeated, detention for the protection of others is pointless and an embarrassment to the mental health authorities.[49]

The issue came before the High Court of Australia in *The Queen* v. *Falconer*,[50] an appeal brought by a woman who had been convicted of the murder of her husband. The defence had called the evidence of psychiatrists to the effect that at the time of the killing the accused had been in a state of dissociation; this evidence was rejected at the trial and it was the issue of its admissibility upon which the subsequent appeals turned.

The facts in *Falconer* were typical of those cases in which the defence of provocation frequently arises but which, for technical legal reasons, often fail to satisfy the strict requirements of the provocation plea. Mrs Falconer had been separated from her violent and abusive husband. She had recently discovered that he had sexually assaulted two of their daughters; in fact, he was facing criminal charges in connection with these assaults. In the week prior to the shooting, Mrs Falconer had manifested a degree of emotional disturbance and her personality appeared to have changed in some respects. Then, on the day itself, the husband had entered the house, sexually assaulted his wife, and taunted her in relation to the criminal charges and revealed facts which led her to believe that he may have sexually abused a seven-year-old girl who had been in her foster care. In a statement to a psychiatrist, Mrs Falconer described the circumstances surrounding the killing in the following way:

> I don't know how long I stood there in the bedroom. I thought Gordon had gone. I thought, 'I'll get the briefcase to get the papers for the accountant and I'll go and talk to my mother about what he said about Erin' [the foster child]. I went to the wardrobe to get the papers and then I had a feeling that he was reaching for my hair to grab me . . . The next thing that I remember was that I was leaning against the archway of the wardrobe with the gun across my foot and Gordon crouching in the corner.

The High Court ruled that psychiatric evidence as to the state of dissociation in which Mrs Falconer was thought to have been acting at the time of the killing should have been admitted as a potential ground of the defence of sane automatism. A psychological blow, it was accepted, was an external factor, but the crucial issue was the effect which it would have on the individual. This required an assessment of the individual's *response* to the blow; in the case of a person who responded in a pathological way the resulting state of dissociation could be treated as a disease of the mind; in the case of a person whose state of dissociation was a 'normal response', the dissociation would not be a disease of the mind. This distinction was described in the judgment in the following terms:

> The problem of classification in a given case of a transient malfunction of the mind precipitated by psychological trauma lies in the difficulty in choosing between the reciprocal factors – the trauma and the natural susceptibility of the mind to affection by psychological trauma – as the cause of the malfunction. Is

one factor or the other the cause or are both to be treated as causes? To answer this problem, the law must postulate a standard of mental strength which, in the face of a given level of psychological trauma, is capable of protecting the mind from malfunction to the extent prescribed in the respective definitions of insanity. The standard must be the standard of an ordinary person: if the mind's strength is below that standard, the mind is infirm; if it is of or above that standard, the mind is sound or sane. This is an objective standard which corresponds with the objective standard imported for the purpose of the determining provocation . . .[51]

If, then, psychological trauma, is of such a nature that it would cause a 'sound mind' to malfunction *transiently* and to produce the effects required for a defence of insanity (in this case, lack of capacity to understand what one is doing or to know that one ought not to do the act in question), then the malfunction cannot be attributed to a mental disease but to *ordinary human nature*. The court stated a proviso to this, however, which requires that the condition should not be one that is likely to recur. This is the same public safety consideration that has been seen to play a role in virtually all of the discussions of the sane/insane automatism distinction since the qualification was first stated by Lord Denning in *Bratty*.

The importance of the decision in *Falconer* lies in the fact that it now allows in Australian jurisprudence the possibility of a defence of sane automatism for those who act in a state of dissociation, provided that they entered into the dissociative state in circumstances where it would be reasonable for the average person to do so. What the court sought to achieve in this was to allow a defence to those who give way under immense pressure, while denying it to those whose dissociative state is not one with which the court can 'sympathise'. There are very obvious objections which can be taken to this. The purist could argue that the most important consideration is whether the state actually existed and whether it came into existence independently of fault on the part of the individual. If a state of dissociation existed, and was sufficient to mean that the acts committed while in that state were involuntary, then surely the question of whether the ordinary or average person would have got into that state of dissociation is irrelevant to guilt. After all, if there is concussion which is caused by the clearly external factor of a blow to the head, the susceptibility of the individual to concussion would be irrelevant. This does appear to be illogical, but the law does apply similarly illogical rules in the context of other defences. In the defence of provocation, for example, the governing consideration is not whether the individual was in fact provoked to such a point that he lost his self-control, but whether the average person in his circumstances would have been so provoked. In applying this objectively determined limit to such defences, the criminal law is indicating that in spite of the recognition of subjectively-determined excuses, it is still made up of a system of norms which must, for policy reasons, be objectively applied. In determining the limits of excuses, the courts have to take into account the extent to which the public – and the victims and their families – would accept that the accused should have a defence. *Falconer* is a classic case in which the public could be expected to be sympathetic and to accept the acquittal of the accused; the victim was a violent and abusive spouse who was facing charges of incest. It would be quite different, one suspects, if he had been the one to find himself in a dissociative state in which he killed the long-suffering Mrs Falconer. In relation to that particular act – the act of killing – he could have been as morally innocent as she might be felt to be, but that would have been an unacceptable result. The law, therefore, decides matters on principle to an extent, but only to an extent, and the point at which the limits of responsibility are set involves subtle policy questions. This is important to bear in mind when analysing the law's reaction to sleepwalking, where the same policy factors are at play.

FALLING ASLEEP AND LEGAL BLAME: THE DRIVING CASES

Elsewhere in this book there is discussion of the way in which the law regulates the issue and retention of driving licences to those who suffer from sleep disorders or other conditions which are likely to affect the level of awareness. In this section, we look at a number of cases in which the criminal law has addressed the issue of those who have been overcome by drowsiness while driving or who have gone to sleep at the wheel. From the legal point of view this problem is not dissimilar to the problem of automatism, in that in each case the form of conduct in question is involuntary conduct.

The overwhelming majority of cases in the jurisdictions under consideration take a robust line in relation to sleep driving cases and rule out any defence for one who falls asleep at the wheel. In English law, the matter first arose in *Hill v. Baxter*,[52] in which a driver charged with a driving offence was unable to remember anything that happened during part of a journey. He was acquitted on the grounds that he was not conscious at the time of the commission of the offence, and this decision was appealed, successfully, by the prosecution. The Court of Appeal accepted that there may be cases where a person may not be said to be driving at all – as in a case where he has a stroke or an epileptic fit – but in this case the accused appeared to have been controlling the car and directing its movements, which was justification for saying that he was driving.

This reluctance to find that a person was not driving simply because there was some impairment is demonstrated in a number of other cases in which, although there was some degree of automatism – if such a concept is possible – the accused was still able to exercise control over the vehicle. In *Watmore v. Jenkins*,[53] the accused, a diabetic, had taken insulin which did not react appropriately owing to the fact that he had recently suffered from jaundice. The court considered his erratic driving and reached the conclusion that he 'continued to perform the functions of driving after a fashion' and that he could not therefore be held to have had no voluntary control over the vehicle. The defence of automatism was not made out.

R. v. Isitt[54] involved an alleged hysterical fugue, supported by medical evidence. The accused argued that he was suffering from sane automatism as a result of this, but the court held that there must have been a certain amount of 'co-ordination between brain and hand' and that there had also been deliberate action taken to avoid the police. The psychiatric expert witness conceded that the accused's mind must have been 'working to some extent', and this enabled the court to pronounce: 'It is a matter of human experience that the mind does not always operate in top gear. There may be some difficulty in functioning. If the difficulty does not amount in law to either insanity or automatism, is the accused entitled to say "I am not guilty because my mind was not working in top gear"? In our view he is not.' Similarly, in Broome v. Perkins,[55] the accused, a diabetic who suffered a hypoglycaemic attack, drove erratically for five miles. On appeal by the prosecution against his conviction for driving without due care and attention, the Court of Appeal ruled that there was not such a loss of control as to justify a finding of automatism because there was evidence that the car was being controlled, even if imperfectly. The fact that the driver had braked violently when approaching a queue of traffic, for instance, 'must mean that his mind was receiving signals which had caused him to direct his limbs to apply the brakes.' On these grounds, the accused was said to be driving and therefore liable.

A very much fuller analysis of the issue was provided in the judgment of the Court of Appeal in Attorney General's Reference (No. 2 of 1992).[56] A professional heavy goods vehicle driver embarked on a long journey at 11 a.m. and continued to drive until 4 p.m., taking regular breaks along the way. At 6 p.m. he resumed his journey, stopping for a break and a meal at some time between 8.30 p.m. and 9.45 p.m. He then set off again at about 10.30 p.m. and was involved in an accident some twenty-two miles later, when he drove onto the hard shoulder of the motorway and continued in a straight line on this part of the road until he collided with two stationary vehicles, one of which had a yellow flashing light on (two people were killed by the impact). The distance he travelled on the hard shoulder – on which he was on a collision course with the other vehicles – was about seven hundred metres. The accused's driving pattern over the day was within the regulations, a fact which was confirmed by the tachograph readings in the vehicle.

The accused denied being asleep at the time of the accident. He said that he did not see the vehicles in front of him, although he did see a yellow flashing light. The defence led evidence from a psychologist, who expressed the view that the accused was likely to have been 'driving without awareness' (DWA), a state of mind which is trance-like and which can be brought about from driving for long distances. The prosecution's expert, however, disagreed; in his view the events leading to the impact were consistent with the accused having fallen asleep at the wheel. The trial judge ruled that the evidence of the DWA state was sufficient to support a finding of sane automatism, and it is on this basis that the accused was acquitted. The Court of Appeal was then asked to clarify the law as to whether a person who is driving without awareness in this sense can claim the automatism defence.

As in many other automatism cases, the court analysed the matter in terms of control. The expert evidence for the defence did not reveal a total absence of control, as the court pointed out:

> Despite his phrase 'driving without awareness', Professor Brown [the expert witness for the defence] agreed that the driver's body would still be controlling the vehicle, and that there would be subconscious motivation to his steering and that 'although largely unaware of what was happening ahead' and 'largely unaware of steering either', the unawareness was not total. Asked if nothing intrudes into the driver's consciousness when he is in this state, the Professor said: 'I would not go so far as to say nothing, but very little'. There must, as a matter of common sense, be some awareness if, as Professor Brown accepted, the driver will usually be caused to 'snap out' of the conditions by strong stimuli noticed by his eyes.[57]

The fact that there was some degree of control was, in the Court's view, enough to exclude the defence of automatism; as the judge pointed out 'impaired, reduced, or partial control is not enough' for the defence. There must be a 'total destruction of voluntary control'.

Such a total absence of control, one would expect, would be present in the case of a person who goes to sleep at the wheel. Yet even if this is so, the approach of the courts to such situations has not been consistent, and different solutions have suggested themselves at various stages. These have ranged from outright rejection of any defence in such circumstances, to an acceptance of liability only where the driver has manifested negligence, or some other blameworthy state of mind, in continuing to drive when he was aware of the risk of being affected by drowsiness or overcome by sleep.

An example of the strict view is the decision of the Supreme Court of South Australia in *Virgo* v. *Elding*.[58] In this case, the driver said to the police after the incident had taken place: 'I must have fallen asleep, for until I hit the first bump I did not awake, and could not avert the accident'. The magistrate, before whom the driver appeared, charged with driving without due care or attention, ruled that in the absence of any evidence that the driver had received 'some warning that he would fall asleep' he was not prepared to convict. A diametrically opposed view was taken in this case by the Supreme Court, where it was ruled that driving without due care and attention was an objective concept, and how one came to be driving in such a way was immaterial. It was therefore irrelevant how sleep came upon the driver; the fact that he fell asleep meant that he was driving without due care and attention. A similar approach was adopted in the Canadian case of *R. v. Longhurst*.[59] Here the court also inclined to the view that falling asleep at the wheel was in itself indicative of dangerous driving. The following excerpt shows why the judge thought this:

> Longhurst admits that he suddenly fell asleep. There was no medical evidence or in fact any evidence or expert opinion submitted to me that a man will unconsciously go to sleep. It is not like a faint, a heart attack or a fit where a person loses consciousness almost instantaneously. I cannot conceive that a man will go to sleep in an instant. Drowsiness certainly precedes sleep, and Longhurst must have known that he was sleepy . . . It is a long drive . . . these men had been up all night and sleep would have come naturally. A careful driver would have anticipated he was likely to go to sleep and should have taken precautions against doing so. He could have turned off the highway into gateway or a lane and gone to sleep as did his passengers in the rear seat, or he could have stopped the car, got out, walked around and got rid of his drowsiness. There are several things he could have done. He could have stopped at a filling station along the highway and slept there in safety.

More recent cases have tended to the view that the mere fact of having gone to sleep will not in itself indicate culpability. According to these cases, before a driver can be held criminally liable for going to sleep at the wheel, he must have manifested some degree of fault in having failed to anticipate the fact that he was in danger of going to sleep. In Australia the approach favoured in *Virgo v. Elding* was rejected in *Kroon*,[60] a decision of the Court of Appeal for South Australia. In this case a truck driver suddenly moved his truck into the wrong lane of a road and collided head-on with an oncoming vehicle. The three occupants of this vehicle were killed, and the truck driver was consequently convicted of causing death by dangerous driving. The only explanation which the court could find for the accused's presence on the wrong side of the road was that he had gone to sleep at the wheel. The Court of Appeal took the opportunity in this case to overrule *Virgo* on the grounds that a sleeping person simply cannot be said to be driving during the time in which he is asleep, and that therefore he cannot be convicted of driving without due care and attention. At the same time, sleep will not necessarily amount to a defence in such cases, on the grounds that there may be some earlier fault in continuing to drive in circumstances where there is a risk of going to sleep. As the court observed:

> Every act of falling asleep at the wheel is preceded by a period during which the driver is driving while awake and therefore, assuming the absence of involuntariness arising from other causes, responsible for his actions. If a driver who knows or ought to know that there is a significant risk of falling asleep at the wheel, continues to drive the vehicle, he is plainly driving without due care

and attention and may be driving in a manner dangerous to the public. If the driver does fall asleep and death or bodily injury results, the driving prior to the falling asleep is sufficiently contemporaneous with the death or bodily injury to be regarded as the cause of the death or bodily injury.[61]

The court went on to point out that the question of how sleep came upon the accused, far from being irrelevant as suggested in *Virgo*, is in fact central to the question of guilt. The judge took the view that it would only be rarely that a person will be overcome by sleep without warning, and that in most cases there will be drowsiness before consciousness is lost. There will also be cases in which the driver should know, even if he does not feel drowsy, that there is a danger present by virtue of the length of time during which he has driven, the conditions in the vehicle, and the state of his health. In all such cases, it will be clear that there will be fault, but there may still be an issue of how great the degree of fault is, and whether it is sufficient to justify conviction for a serious (indictable) crime. This will be determined, the court suggested, by the degree of departure from the standard of conduct expected of the reasonable person in the circumstances.

The issue reached the High Court of Australia in *Jiminez*,[62] an appeal against a conviction for causing death by dangerous driving. The driver in this case told the police that he thought he had gone to sleep at the wheel, and the question arose as to whether the trial judge should have instructed the jury to apply a strictly objective standard of what was culpable behaviour in respect of failure to appreciate the risk of going to sleep, or whether he should have allowed for error on the driver's part in assessing the risk. The court accepted that a driver who was asleep but who had manifested no fault in deciding to drive should not be held liable. In the present case, the driver had slept before setting off on the journey and he had not been driving for an excessive period by the time the accident occurred. It was therefore possible that he had made an honest and reasonable mistake as to his fitness to drive, and this was a matter which should have been put to the jury. As a result of this decision, then, it would appear that in Australian criminal law, at least in some cases, a mistake by the accused as to his fitness will be sufficient to justify an acquittal.

In many of the cases it is stressed that feelings of sleepiness should be a warning upon which the driver is required to act if he wishes to avoid being held liable for being overcome by sleep. In the Canadian case of *R. v. May*,[63] however, the court took a more lenient view of the feelings of sleepiness, and held that even if a driver felt sleepy, this did not necessarily mean that he thought he would go to sleep. A person who felt sleepy, then, but who had always been able to stay awake in the face of such feelings of sleepiness, could quite reasonably believe that he was not at risk of falling asleep at the wheel. As the judge in *May* said:

The more boring or monotonous a job, the more likely again that person is to fall asleep. Disturbances of sleep can build up a sleep deficit. A person may not be aware that he is suffering sleep disturbances, and so may not realise that he is at risk of falling asleep. It is a universal experience that we all feel sleepy at times, and we ride out these periods of sleepiness without falling asleep. Therefore, it follows that simply feeling sleepy would not be a warning that we are actually going to fall asleep.[64]

It is unlikely that this view will attract much judicial support. A court is far more likely to concur with the sentiment expressed by the judge in *Hill* v. *Baxter*, where he said:

That drivers do fall asleep is not an uncommon cause of serious road accidents, and it would be impossible as well as disastrous to hold that falling asleep at the wheel was any defence to a charge of dangerous driving. If a driver finds that he is getting sleepy he must stop.

CONCLUSION

Our analysis of the criminal cases dealing with automatism and sleep reveals that the primary issue to be determined is whether the actions performed by the accused were in fact out of his control (see Figure 1). This issue has to be settled at the outset, as it is only after it is resolved that the question of the classification of the automatism as sane or insane automatism can take place. States of mind which do not satisfy this test – on the grounds that the accused had at least some control over what he was doing, or on the grounds that there was at least some awareness of what was happening – are unlikely to satisfy the requirements of the defence and may therefore give rise to find-ings of liability. Yet, as we argued above, the criteria of both control and consciousness are too blunt, and states of mind are better viewed as being somewhere along a line ranging from complete unconsciousness at the one extreme, to full awareness at the other. At least some of the states which would currently satisfy the requirements of the defence of automatism could not be placed at the complete unconsciousness end of the spectrum. A person in a state of hypoglycaemia will observe things and will have some aware-ness of the world around him, and is therefore perhaps in some respect con-scious, even if it is not a consciousness that should justify findings of responsibility. Similarly, a person in a state of dissociation or suffering from confused awakening may behave in a way which is, for that person, quite abnormal and for which he does not deserve to be held liable.

The defence of automatism, in so far as it is linked to this stark dichotomy between consciousness and unconsciousness, or between control and absence of control, is too unsubtle an instrument to do anything but the

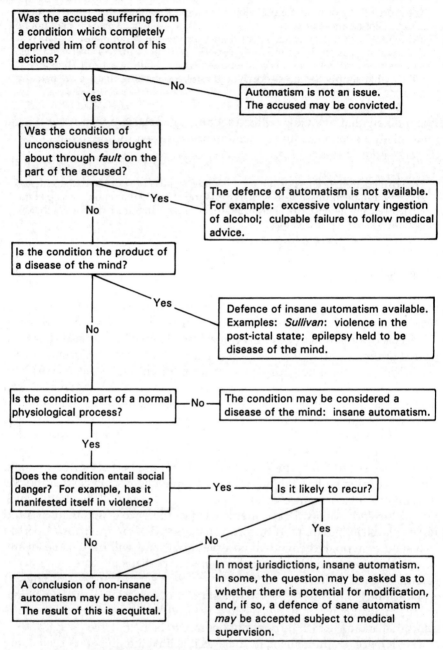

Figure 1. Algorithm of criminal liability for somnambulistic activity

roughest of justice. The various states which we have described which lie somewhere between full awareness and true unconsciousness are not states in which the actor would be held accountable for his actions. While people in such states may not be said to be insane for legal purposes, they are still clearly not fully responsible, and it is to be hoped that the defence of automatism will in future be developed in such a way as to embrace the meritorious cases in this category. Moral intuitions can serve as a very sound guide to the assessment of criminal guilt, and the development of the automatism defence in such a way as to allow for the medical disposition of this category of abnormal offenders should satisfy the strong moral intuition to exculpate (even if under supervisory conditions) those whose behaviour springs not so much from a malignant temperament but from a pathological condition.

The difficulty, of course, is that the criminal law has traditionally thought in all-or-nothing guilty or not guilty terms, and has always relied on a relatively small number of recognised defences to excuse those who do not merit punishment. These defences have been interpreted narrowly, with the result that relatively few defendants who have committed an apparent criminal act will escape conviction on grounds of lack of responsibility. The reasons for holding the line on responsibility are, of course, cogent ones; the criminal justice system would be the subject of derision if it were to make too many allowances for individual circumstances and to compromise too much on the issue of personal responsibility. Virtually everybody can find at least some form of excuse for antisocial conduct, be it in the experiences of childhood, adverse influences, or whatever. For this reason, the criminal law relegates a great deal of explanatory, and even excusing factors, to a role in mitigation of punishment rather than determination of responsibility.

Yet in the case of those who commit offences as a result of a sleep disorder, whether they engage in classic somnambulism, act in a state of confusion, or act dissociatively as a result of sleep deprivation and other factors, it would seem that there are good grounds for the law to take into account the medical explanation of their conduct. The criminal law is currently ill-equipped to deal with this category of persons. The defence of sane automatism will deal with some cases, and achieves a satisfactory result in that it leads to the acquittal of those who cannot be said to be morally responsible for their actions. Yet in some cases this outcome may not be satisfactory from the point of view of social protection. A somnambulist who commits violent acts in his sleep may present a degree of social danger, which needs to be recognised. Insane automatism would allow the courts to respond to this danger, but the suitability of their response depends on the means of disposition they have at their disposal. A flexible system, which does not automatically require detention in a secure hospital, is undoubtedly most desirable. Psychiatric supervision may be far more effective if provided in the patient's normal setting than in an institution in which the patient is an involuntary inmate. It would also be desirable to change nomenclature. 'Not guilty on medical grounds' would be a far more accurate and less damning verdict than 'not guilty on the grounds of insanity' or, worse still, 'guilty but insane'.

'In-between states', such as those of sleep drunkenness or dissociation – states in which consciousness is impaired to a significant extent but in which the demanding criteria of unconsciousness or complete lack of control are not met – give rise to particular difficulties. Such states do not fit easily into existing legally-recognised categories of either automatism or insanity, and persons acting while in such a state of mind stand to be treated by the law as if they were quite normal and disposed of accordingly. The defence of automatism could well be expanded to embrace at least some of these states (as happened in the *Falconer* case), although such an expansion would have to be undertaken cautiously.

NOTES AND REFERENCES

1. Classic statements of this principle include those of O.W. Holmes, *The Common Law*, edited by M. De Wolfe (Belknap Press of Harvard University Press, Cambridge, Mass, 1963) p. 45: 'A spasm is not an act', and J. Austin, *Lectures on Jurisprudence*, 5th edn., edited by R. Campbell, (J. Murray, London, 1885), XVIII–XIX, Vol. 1, p. 411: 'A voluntary movement of my body, or a movement which follows a volition, is an act'.
2. The point is discussed in *Hill* v. *Baxter* [1958] 1 QB 283, and in *Ryan* v. *The Queen* (1967) 121 CLR 205.
3. H.L.A. Hart, *Punishment and Responsibility* (Clarendon Press, Oxford, 1968).
4. For the view that automatic conduct is not inconsistent with consciousness and mental control, see A. Corrado, 'Automatism and the theory of action' (1990) 39 Emory Law Journal 1191.
5. Common law systems differ in the degree to which they refuse to recognise intoxication as a defence. For English law, see *DPP* v. *Majewski* [1977] AC 443; the American position varies from state to state – the Model Penal Code of the American Law Institute allows intoxication some role in crimes requiring intention, but not in those requiring no more than recklessness: MPC, 2.08 (1), (2). In some states, intoxication is never a defence: see, for example, Texas Penal Code, 2, 8.04.
6. *R.* v. *O'Connor* (1980) 54 Aus LJR 349.
7. *R.* v. *Daviault* (1955) 33 CR (4th) 165.
8. [1994] 3 ALL ER 353.
9. One of the best known modern statements of the centrality of choice in this context is to be found in H.L.A. Hart's *Punishment and Responsibility* (Clarendon Press, Oxford, 1968), p. 28; see also, M.S. Moore, 'Choice, character and excuse' in E.F. Paul, F.D. Miller and J. Paul (eds), *Crime, Culpability and Remedy* (Blackwell, Oxford, 1990), p. 29.
10. G.M. Edelman, *The Remembered Present: A Biological Theory of Consciousness* (Basic Books, New York, 1989).
11. For an account of the McNaghten case and its impact on the criminal law, see N. Walker, *Crime and Insanity in England* (Edinburgh University Press, Edinburgh, 1968), p. 84.

12. For discussion of the scope and rationale of the insanity defence, see J. Radden, *Madness and Reason* (Allen & Unwin, London, 1985); H. Fingarette, *The Meaning of Criminal Insanity* (University of California Press, Berkeley, Ca, 1972); F. McAuley, *Insanity, Psychiatry and Criminal Responsibility* (Round Hall Press, Dublin, 1993).
13. [1955] 1 WLR 317.
14. [1957] 1 QB 399.
15. [1963] AC 411.
16. [1973] QB 910.
17. [1984] AC 156; [1983] 3 WLR 123.
18. [1980] 2 SCR 513; 114 DLR (3d) 193.
19. 1963 JC 80.
20. 1991 SCCR 823.
21. For example, *Cooley* v. *Commonwealth* 479 SW 2d 89 (Ky, 1970); *People* v. *Higgins* 5 NY 2d 607, 159 NE 2d 179 (1959).
22. *State* v. *Welsh* 8 Wash. App. 719, 508 P. 2d 1041 (1973).
23. *Jones* v. *State* 648 P. 2d 1251 (Okla, 1982).
24. 1859 3 Irv. 467.
25. *Tibbs* v. *Commonwealth* 128 SW 871 (1910); *Bradley* v. *State* 277 SW 147.
26. Unreported. For facts and comment, see N. Morris, 'Somnambulistic homicide: ghosts, spiders and North Koreans' (1951) Res Judicata 29.
27. I. Oswald and J. Evans, 'On serious violence during sleep-walking' (1985) 147 Br J Psychiatry 688.
28. A. Buchanan, 'Sleepwalking and indecent exposure' (1991) 31 Med Sci Law 38.
29. E.A. Nofzinger and R.M. Wettstein, 'Homicidal behavior and sleep apnea: a case report and medicolegal discussion', (1995) 18 Sleep 776.
30. *Trial:* Supreme Court of Ontario, 5 January 1990; *Court of Appeal:* (1990) 56 CCC (3d) 449; *Supreme Court of Canada:* (1992) 75 CCC (3d) 287.
31. The assertion that a somnambulist could drive in traffic for a considerable distance has strained legal credulity. However, on somnambulistic driving, see: C.S. Schenck and M.W. Mahowald, 'A polysonmographically documented case of adult somnambulism with long-distance automobile driving and frequent nocturnal violence: parasomnia with continuing danger as a noninsane automatism? (1995) 18 Sleep 765.
32. (1990) 56 CCC (3d) 449 at p. 466.
33. See note 18.
34. (1977) 37 CCC (2d) 461 at p. 473.
35. See note 15.
36. See note 16.
37. Unreported; Ontario Court of Justice (Provincial Division), 30 October 1992.
38. [1991] 2 All ER 769.
39. At p. 773.
40. (1978) 37 CCC (2d) 461 at p. 478.
41. See note 15.
42. See note 17.
43. S.L. Hallech, 'Dissociation phenomena and the question of responsibility' 1990 (38) Int J Clinical and Experimental Hypnosis, 298; M. Steinberg, J. Bancroft and J. Buchanan, 'Multiple personality disorder in criminal law' (1993) 21 Bull Am Acad Psychiatry Law 345.
44. J.I. Bisson, 'Automatism and post-traumatic stress disorder' (1993) 163 Br J Psychiatry 830.
45. (1974) 22 CCC (2d) 415.
46. See note 18.

47. [1989] 1 WLR 287.
48. (1985) 42 SASR 266.
49. At p. 276.
50. [1990] 65 Aus LJR 20. For discussion, see P.A. Fairall, 'Voluntariness, automatism and insanity: reflections on *Falconer*' 1993 Crim L Jnl 81.
51. At p. 30.
52. [1958] 1 QB 277.
53. [1962] 2 All ER 868.
54. (1978) 67 Cr App R 44.
55. (1987) 85 Cr App R 321.
56. [1993] 4 All ER 683.
57. At pp. 686–687.
58. [1939] SASR 294.
59. (1940) 75 CCC 356.
60. (1990) 52 Aus Crim R 15.
61. At p. 18.
62. (1992) 59 Aus Crim R 308.
63. (1990) 19 MVR (2d) 312.
64. At p. 319.

3

Dangerous Behaviours by Night

R.J. Broughton* and T. Shimizu‡
Ottawa General Hospital, and ‡University of Akita

INTRODUCTION

For many years the occurrence of sleep-related, usually nocturnal, injurious behaviour was a minor theme in the literature on sleep and its disorders. However, with the rise of the field of sleep disorders medicine and the increasingly litigious nature of society, the phenomenon has become a high profile one. Indeed, a recent issue of the journal *Sleep*[1] was dedicated to the topic. One of the curious characteristics of this now burgeoning literature is the lack of consideration of sleep-related violent behaviour in the context of the literature on waking violence, whether human[2-5] or animal.[6-9] Whatever the sleep or wake state in which violence arises, experts are challenged with determining whether the behaviours represent:

(i)   innate violence regulated by brain mechanisms such as those governing predatory behaviour,
(ii) defensive violence usually as a reaction against behavioural restraint, or
(iii) learned violence, in individuals who carry over such acquired behaviours from wakefulness into sleep.

The conditions in which sleep-related violent behaviour has been reported to be relatively common contain some degree of impaired 'consciousness'. This is true for the two most frequent causes, i.e. sleepwalking/sleep terrors[10-12] and REM sleep behaviour disorder (RBD).[13] Consciousness may be defined as the brain function[14] of awareness.[15,16] To be legally responsible

Forensic Aspects of Sleep. Edited by C.M. Shapiro and A. McCall Smith.
© 1997 John Wiley & Sons Ltd.

for one's actions, one must be both aware (conscious) of them and able to control them. However, conscious awareness is not an all-or-none phenomenon but rather occurs in gradients. One may be fully aware, partially aware or unaware. Similarly, control of one's behaviour may also range from complete to absent during states of impaired consciousness.

In discussing dangerous sleep-related behaviours, some authors distinguish between aggression and violence, using the word violence to denote any intense potentially damaging behaviours, and aggression to denote the subgroup of such behaviours which are directed towards another individual. This distinction is also emphasized in the literature on violence and epilepsy.[17-20] From a forensic point of view the importance of determining whether dangerous behaviours are directed towards others is crucial for, as we shall see, one of the distinguishing criteria in law between non-insane automatisms not springing from a 'disease of the mind', and insane automatisms so springing, involves consideration of the need to protect the public. To quote Lord Denning in *Bratty* v. *Attorney General for Northern Ireland*, 'It seems to me that any mental disorder which has manifested itself in violence and is prone to recur is a disease of the mind. At any rate it is the sort of disease for which the person should be detained in hospital'.[21] The medico-legal aspects will be discussed following a review of the incidence, phenomenology, etiology, pathophysiology and treatment of sleep-related dangerous behaviours.

INCIDENCE

The overall prevalence of clinical sleep disorders, including those in which sleep-related dangerous behaviour *may* occur, is relatively well known[22-24] and, generally speaking, is in the order of 10% of individuals in each decade of life. However, both the overall prevalence of sleep-related violent or aggressive behaviours, and their incidence in the individual sleep disorders remain largely undocumented. Only two studies have assessed the latter. In a group of 64 consecutive adult patients with sleepwalking or sleep terrors, Moldofsky et al.[25] found that 38 (59%) exhibited harmful behaviour of some type, 26 (41%) showed serious violence, and 9 (14%) had violent aggression towards others. Similarly, in a group of 41 adult patients presenting with some form of 'nocturnal wandering',[26] 29 (71%) had exhibited violent behaviours and 16 (39%) had shown aggression against others.[27] The final diagnosis in the 29 violent patients was somnambulism in 23, sleep-disordered breathing in 3, temporal lobe epilepsy in 2, and RBD in a single patient. It would appear from the literature that sleep-related violent behaviour is considerably less frequent in children than adults.

Males exhibit a much higher incidence of sleep-related violence than females,[25,27] paralleling that which exists for waking violence. Although cultural factors no doubt play a role, there is now evidence indicating that an innate biological basis of gender difference exists across a large number of species, and that high testosterone levels are associated with violent behaviours even in females.[28] The sometimes essentially immediate appearance of aggression during dissociated sleep states with no evidence of motivation, such as can occur in abrupt confusional arousals,[29] or the REM sleep without atonia in RBD[30] also strongly implies, in such cases, a fundamental role for innate brain mechanisms. It should also be recalled that pontine lesioned cats have REM sleep periods without atonia during which they exhibit predatory and territorial defensive behaviours.[31] This strongly suggests the presence of innate mechanisms of aggression in an animal model of human RBD.

PHENOMENOLOGY

The actual violent events are almost always only described by the relatives of the patient or by patients repeating descriptions of others; they are seldom observed or objectively documented by the physician–investigator. Some early reports with detailed behavioural descriptions include those of Sandler,[32] Pai,[33] Oswald[34] and Bonkalo[29]. Injurious behaviours have been extremely diverse, and include self-injury (abrasions, cuts), damage to objects (breakage), injury to others, (clubbing, attempted strangulation) and even indecent exposure[35-37] and homicide.[29, 38-42]

ETIOLOGY

The most common sleep disorders associated with sleep-related injurious behaviours are, as already mentioned, sleepwalking and RBD. Many other conditions, however, have been involved. A reasonably complete list is presented in Table 1.

Parasomnias

Confusional arousals with partial or dissociated sleep states are at times associated with a lashing out or other injury of self or others.[29] These have been described mainly in slow wave sleep (SWS) arousals from the first third of the night; and have at times been invoked in those suffering from sleep apnea.[43]

Sleepwalking is a condition in which sleep-related injurious behaviours have been reported frequently.[35,39,44-46] It has at times led to homicide,[38,47,48,] an extensively studied instance of which is the Ken Parks case.[42]

Table 1. Disorders with demonstrated potential for sleep-related violence

Parasomnias	Disorders of arousal
	Confusional arousals
	Sleepwalking
	Sleep terrors
	REM sleep behaviour disorder
	Paroxysmal nocturnal dystonia
	Sleep-related epileptic seizures
	Frontal
	Infero-mesial
	Nocturnal eating syndrome
	Nocturnal delirium
	'Overlap' parasomnias
	CA/ST/SW
	NREM/REM*
	Non-epileptic/epileptic
Non-parasomniac disorders	Obstructive sleep apnea
	Idiopathic CNS hypersomnia
	Alcohol/hypnotic-related hypersomnias
	Cerebral degenerative disorders
	RLS and periodic movements in sleep
	Intensified sleep starts
	Waking aggression
	Malingering

*CA, confusional arousals; ST, sleep terrors; SW, sleepwalking; NREM, non-REM; REM, REM Sleep

Sleep terrors are much less frequently associated with violent behaviours. However, a few case reports exist[49] of patients in whom sleep terrors lead to somnambulism in a single attack.[50]

REM sleep behaviour disorder is a condition in which the motor atonia and paralysis of REM sleep do not occur, thereby permitting complex, and at times violent, behaviours. It was first described in patients with CNS pathology of various types,[51-56] including alcoholic encephalopathy, and was subsequently studied in detail by the Minnesota group,[30,45,57,58] who found that RBD is often also observed in otherwise normal elderly persons. Injurious behaviour is quite frequent, perhaps due to the disinhibition of innate behaviour patterns and the explosive, often myoclonic, nature of the movements. Homicide has not yet been reported in this condition.

Nocturnal delirium can occur as a distinct parasomnia, especially in demented patients and those with organic CNS lesions.[59,60] The intensified mental confusion and cognitive impairment of such patients often leads to their responding to behavioural resistance with aggression towards family members, nursing home attendants or hospital personnel.

Paroxysmal nocturnal dystonia is a condition of sleep-related dystonic movements of either long or short duration.[61-64] There is evidence, especially for the short lasting forms, that such episodes may represent frontal lobe seizures.[65] Self-injury may occur during the dystonic movements in bed; however, aggression towards others has not to our knowledge been reported and, if it exists, must be extremely rare.

Episodic nocturnal wandering is a category of initial diagnosis introduced by Pedley and Guilleminault[26] to group conditions in which leaving the bed and wandering about take place; some features are suggestive of an epileptic mechanism. Many such cases, however, do not have a convincing epileptic etiology,[66] whereas some do.[67] Violence can occur[27] and the underlying sleep disorder can usually be allocated to a final diagnosis such as sleepwalking.

Sleep-related epileptic seizures can only be diagnosed with certainty when there is documentation of an ictal EEG discharge[68,69] either on the scalp or by special electrodes (e.g. minisphenoidals or stereo-EEG). A positive therapeutic response to 'anti-epileptic' medication is not sufficient by itself for diagnosis, as such substances affect non-epileptic as well as epileptic brain functions. The diagnosis may be made difficult by the existence of epileptic foci deep in the brain without evident scalp discharges, by obscuring of EEG by movement artefacts during seizures, and by other technical problems. However, even in epileptic patients, classical parasomnias such as sleep terrors are much more apt to be a co-existent non-epileptic event.[70] As in epileptic seizures during wakefulness, innate ictal violence is extremely uncommon and aggression usually represents a response to behavioural restrictions during an epileptic seizure associated with impaired consciousness or, even more frequently, during a state of post-ictal confusion.

Non-parasomnia disorders

Violent or aggressive sleep-related behaviours have been described in association with a number of non-parasomniac sleep disorders.

Narcolepsy can lead to amnesic automatic automatisms[71] and narcoleptic drivers have at times had serious and even lethal accidents.[72,73] It should also be noted that the condition is associated with an increased incidence of RBD.[74,75]

Sleep apnea syndrome and upper airway resistance syndrome may be associated with confusional arousals, sleep terrors or sleepwalking. This is particularly the case when deep rebound sleep, with marked increase of slow wave sleep, initially occurs with treatment by nasal CPAP.[76,77]

Organic brain syndromes may play a role in violent behaviours when RBD is associated with brainstem tumour,[51] alcoholism,[52,55] olivopontocerebellar degeneration,[53,56] progressive supranuclear palsy,[54] Shy–Drager syndrome,[78] Parkinson's disease[79] and Machado–Joseph disease.[80] This is also true for nocturnal delirium.

Sleep disorders for which to our knowledge sleep-related violence has *not* yet been reported include the circadian sleep–wake disorders and nocturnal

Table 2. Pathophysiological factors potentially involved in sleep-related violence

---

Immediately prior sleep stage
Circadian time-of-day
Degree of concomitant sleep pressure
   Total and partial sleep deprivation
   Sleep micro-fragmentation
Speed of arousal from prior sleep
Physiological level of arousal during violence
Co-existent microsleeps after arousal
Incomplete or dissociative sleep–wake states
Overlapping sleep–wake states
Cognitive misperceptions, illusions, hallucinations, dreams
Effects of drugs, alcohol and other substances
Sleep-related hypoxemia
Presence of brain lesions
Epileptic (ictal and post-ictal) confusional states
External resistance against behaviours
Psychogenic dissociative states?

---

psychogenic dissociative disorder. Finally, of course, motivated and conscious nocturnal aggression masquerading as a sleep disorder must always be considered.

PATHOPHYSIOLOGY

A large number of physiological mechanisms have been implicated in the sleep disorders potentially associated with dangerous and injurious behaviours. In addition, a number of predisposing, facilitating and triggering factors have been identified. These are summarized in Tables 2 and 3, respectively.

The non-REM (NREM) arousal disorders of confusional arousals, sleep terrors and sleepwalking show evidence both of a partial awakening in which the brain event related potentials maintain some of the features of sleep[11] and of sleep–wake dissociative features.[81] The fundamental reason to consider these conditions to be disorders of arousal is that forced arousal in predisposed individuals with the attacks can induce a full-blown clinical episode, thereby indicating that the arousal process itself is abnormal.[11] Attacks tend to occur under conditions combining high pressure for sleep with causes of sleep fragmentation.[42,82] The relative importance of speed of arousal, degree of arousal and other specifics of the arousal process in facilitating violent or aggressive behaviours is uncertain. To date there is no evidence favouring innate brain mechanisms for violence in such cases. Other features which

Table 3. Predisposing, facilitating and immediate triggering factors

Predisposing factors for parasomnias	Family history
	Gender
	Physical and sexual abuse
	Waking aggression
Facilitating factors for occurrence on a particular night	Increased sleep pressure
	Prior sleep deprivation
	Irregular sleep patterns
	Night shift work
	Increased sleep fragmentation
	Stress
	Pain
	Alcohol and certain drugs
Immediate triggering factors	Exogenous environmental stimuli
	Endogenous stimuli including REM arousal

may be involved include possible misperceptions and resistance to behavioural restraints by an incompletely awakened, confused mind. Recurrent 'microsleeps' after arousal may also play a role.

In RBD, the other main cause of sleep-related injurious behaviour, the situation is different. Rather than representing an incomplete awakening, episodes arise within an REM sleep state lacking its normal atonia and paralysis. The behaviours appear clearly to be innate and are often explicable in the context of reported dreams after awakening occurs. There is no evidence that forced awakenings can precipitate episodes, thereby supporting the existence of a dissociated REM sleep state rather than an abnormal arousal process. Unlike the NREM arousal disorders, genetics do not appear to play a significant role, nor is recovery from sleep deprivation a predisposing factor. Stress has been confirmed as a facilitating factor in both sleepwalking[42] and RBD.[83] In the NREM arousal disorders, a history of having been sexually abused may play a role in the genesis of sleep-related violence.[25] In addition, CNS-active pharmacological agents have been implicated in facilitating violent episodes in both sleepwalking[84–86] and RBD.[87]

In parasomnias of epileptic origin, ictal or post-ictal confusion may play a similar role. As is the case for epileptic seizures in wakefulness, there is little or no evidence for innate ictal aggression, and such behaviours appear almost always to represent resistance to behavioural restraint during periods of mental confusion.

Overlap diagnoses are of increasing interest. In the SWS arousal disorders, it is well documented that intermediate forms exist between confusional arousals, sleep terrors and full-blown sleepwalking.[11,88–90] A fairly common example is the sleep terror that finishes by the person getting out of bed and presenting with somnambulism.[11] Some have even suggested that distinctions

Table 4. Investigation of a person with putative sleep-related violent or aggressive behaviours

(i)   History and physical examination
(ii) Psychological and psychiatric assessments
(iii) Overnight polysomnography
Full scalp EEG
Special electrodes
(iv) Telemetric recording
(v)   Video recording
(vi) Ambulatory monitoring
(vii) Neuroimaging techniques

between these parasomnias should not be recognized. Episodes have been described beginning in stage 2 sleep, especially when they recur on a single night,[12] and can even take place in NREM-to-REM sleep transitions.[11]

The involvement of both NREM and REM sleep mechanisms may occur in a patient who either has more than one type of parasomnia or who exhibits a single parasomnia pattern which arises from both states. A particular example of the latter is a case report of Machado–Joseph disease with nocturnal wanderings arising in both NREM and REM sleep.[80]

Similarly, individual patients may show evidence that both non-epileptic and epileptic mechanisms are involved. Passouant et al.,[91] for instance, described a patient in whom sleep terrors regularly evolved into generalized tonic–clonic epileptic seizures.

Although some patients, therefore, unquestionably present features at the borderlines of the classical parasomnia patterns by showing behavioural characteristics that overlap across diagnoses, combined involvement of NREM and REM sleep, or apparent participation of both non-epileptic and epileptic mechanisms, are relatively infrequent. The diagnostic patterns of the International Classification of Sleep Disorders[92] are much more common and the criteria for the individual specific entities should be retained.

INVESTIGATION

Any patient with a history of sleep-related violent behaviour requires careful investigation to fully document the condition and arrive at a firm final diagnosis. The main investigative approaches are summarized in Table 4.

A detailed history and physical examination are essential. Most information must be obtained from the sleeping partner, the family or other observers, as patients are typically totally unaware and amnesic of their behaviours. Care should be taken to ask about the behavioural details, the role of behavioural resistance, any potential motivation for violence, possible facilitating and triggering factors, time of night, presence or absence of recalled mental activity or dreaming, possible involvement of drugs or alcohol, family history of the sleep disorder, and other salient features.

Psychological and psychiatric assessment are often indicated. Neuropsychological testing of individuals with possible organic brain syndrome or suffering the cognitive deficits frequently present in sleep apnea[93,94] may elucidate causes of impaired consciousness other than those attributable to partial or dissociated sleep states. Personality testing by the Minnesota Multiphasic Personality Inventory (MMPI) or other standardized tests, documentation of depression by the Beck's or other mood inventories, and formal intelligence testing may all be helpful.[42] Detailed psychiatric assessment may reveal an occult motivation for violent behaviour.

Nocturnal polysomnography (PSG) is an essential step, and more than one study may be necessary. In patients with infrequent parasomnias or with disorders such as sleepwalking and sleep terrors known to reduce in frequency during laboratory testing, it may not be possible to document an event. However, even if one is not recorded, the PSG may show features supportive of the provisional clinical diagnosis. The PSGs of persons with sleepwalking may show frequent SWS-to-wake transitions,[95] bursts of hypersynchronous slow waves,[96] frequent micro-arousals[97] or complex behaviours in bed without actual walking.[10,98] Sleep terror patients may also exhibit frequent SWS-to-wake arousals and autonomic instability independent of episodes.[82] RBD patients often have REM periods without atonia associated with complex gestures in bed without a full-blown episode or before these clinically appear.[99] And, of course, patients with sleep-related epileptic seizures may show inter-ictal EEG discharges, although these are frequently absent in patients with frontal lobe seizures of mesial origin.[65,100]

Full scalp EEG during sleep studies is recommended for all patients with suspicion of sleep-related epileptic seizures. In a patient with suspected infero-mesial temporal lobe seizures, minisphenoidal electrodes may be helpful. However, due to possible injury to soft tissues, pharyngeal electrodes should never be used.[101]

Telemetry is very useful for permitting free movement of the subject unencumbered by wires or cables led to a plug-in box. It has been used in the investigation of somnambulism since the 1960s.[10]

Videotape recording, either alone or in association with telemetry, is of great help in documenting objectively the behavioural features for later review and analysis. The videotelemetry systems developed for 'intensive monitoring' of patients with epilepsy, which permit split screen (EEG/video) recording, are the best. However, even amateur home videos done by family members can be of great value.

Ambulatory monitoring using portable recording devices is another helpful technique.[102] It is particularly useful for parasomnia patients after a traditional PSG has ruled out concomitant sleep disorders (e.g. sleep apnea, periodic limb movement disorder) without recording a parasomnic event and for patients with infrequent parasomnias. The technique has been in continuous use in our centre for two decades. Guilleminault et al.[27] reported it to be particularly useful to determine the final diagnosis in patients presenting with nocturnal wandering.

Neuroimaging techniques such as computerized tomography (CT scans), magnetic resonance imaging (MRI) and positron emission tomography (PET scanning) may be helpful in localizing structural or functional abnormalities. Particularly well documented is the usefulness of MRI in the localization of lesions in patients with RBD.[103-105]

MANAGEMENT

There is no specific management for sleep-related violence or aggression. Studies have documented that the associated sleep disorder is often present for many months or years before such damaging behaviours appear. This indicates the need for early diagnosis and treatment of the underlying disorder. In many instances facilitating or precipitating factors of the sleep disorder can be identified, and avoiding or minimizing such factors may be of great help. These may include various specific stresses, sleep deprivation, intake of alcohol and other CNS active substances, or other such factors. Procedures to avoid injury of self or others may be useful, especially in patients with a recurrent predictable pattern of violence. These might include hiding sharp objects, locking doors and similar strategies. Finally, in many and perhaps most patients, violence or aggression appears only when their behaviours are being restricted; such restrictions should therefore be totally avoided or at least minimized.

MEDICO-LEGAL CONSIDERATIONS

Medico-legal issues

English law assumes that everyone who has reached the age of discretion is sane and accountable for his or her actions – the legal doctrine of *mens rea*. The individual is not guilty unless the mind is guilty. Three main considerations can negate the guilty mind. Firstly, the mind may be innocent as in certain instances of lowered intelligence. Secondly, there may be a 'disease of the mind' as legally defined by the McNaghten Rules that: 'at the time of committing the act the party accused was labouring under such a defect of reason, from disease of the mind, as not to know the nature and quality of the act he was doing, or, if he did know it, that he did not know he was doing what was wrong'.[106] Thirdly, the mind may be absent so that any action carried out is automatic. This would include any action without knowledge of the action. Most cases with sleep-related violence or aggression invoke the legal concept of automatism, which has been extensively reviewed by others.[106–108]

The law, unlike medicine, recognizes two types of automatism, sane and insane varieties. Sane automatism is present when there is no legal 'disease of the mind'. The causes are often external to the person, such as a blow to the head or substance intake. Insane automatism is legally present when the actions arise from a pre-existing 'disease of the mind'. The causes are then internal to the person and include mental disease as medically defined. A second legal consideration or policy component for insane automatism is the presence of a 'continuing danger' to society. In practical terms, this involves assessment of the probability of repetition of violent behaviours towards others. Non-guilt can therefore ensue from either sane or insane automatisms. The main practical issue after trial is that in the former instance the person is allowed his or her freedom, usually under a physician's care, whereas in the latter the person is placed in an institution for the criminally insane.

The issue of the probability of recurrence of sleep-related violence or aggression is correspondingly of major importance. Unfortunately, no hard statistics exist. There is general agreement that, although recurrence can take place, it is rare. Schenck and Mahowald[46] found only 12 such cases in all reported patients in the literature with violent behaviour associated with RBD. In the Guilleminault et al.[27] follow-up study of 41 patients with sleep-related violence none had recurrent violent behaviour after a minimum of seven months. It must be stressed, however, both that no studies of sleep-related violence have used a prospective follow-up approach, and that the incidence of repetition in appropriately treated cases is unknown.

A few authors have suggested that violence during sleepwalking should be considered as an insane versus sane automatism. Fenwick[106] supports this on the basis that the cause is internal and involves a genetic transmission, whereas only the triggering factors (stress, drugs, alcohol) are external. He compares sleepwalking with epilepsy: 'a sleepwalker may arise from his bed, murder, plead automatism, and be set free, while an epileptic who arises from his bed in a postictal confusional state, murders, and pleads automatism, must be sent to a psychiatric hospital and probably be detained there for many years'. We disagree with this position for several reasons. There is no evidence in the literature that sleepwalkers have a higher incidence than the general population of medically defined mental illness, neuropsychological deficits or brain pathology, all of which are elevated in epilepsy. Moreover, sleepwalking does not express an abnormal brain state as does epilepsy, but rather a simple and relatively minor dysfunction of a normal state, as it consists of deepened sleep associated with difficulty of full awakening upon arousal from sleep. As emphasized in the *Parks* case, sleepwalking in otherwise normal subjects is a dysfunction of a normal state and there is no evidence for any underlying 'disease of the mind'.[42] In most instances, therefore, categorizing sleepwalking as an insane automatism with the resultant custodial requirements makes no medical, legal or humanitarian sense. However, as indicated by the statements of the Supreme Court of Canada, in some instances (e.g. in individuals in whom a definite 'disease of the mind' co-exists, or when recurrence of violence is probable), a different judgement might be appropriate.

Another highly questionable conclusion is that of Roper,[109] who believes that a sleepwalker might form an intent to commit a crime in wakefulness and that this 'could lead to it being carried out during sleepwalking under certain circumstances'. Roper based his argument on a single case of sleepwalking with bulimia, in which the patient raided the refrigerator during somnambulistic episodes. This patient also had a snake phobia. When a toy snake was placed on the kitchen table in the evening, the refrigerator was unopened during sleepwalking episodes, whereas when the snake was removed, refrigerator raiding returned.

Roper's deduction appears ill founded. The snake-related aversion to opening the refrigerator could equally have occurred during the somnambulistic episodes rather than from seeing the snake prior to retiring. It is well known that sleepwalkers are at least partially aware of their environment, as they generally do not trip over furniture, can show quite highly coordinated activities involving objects and can react to others trying either to awaken them or to alter their behaviours. There is currently no evidence to support the contention that sleepwalkers can either form an intent for violent behaviour in wakefulness and carry it out during sleepwalking or can form such an intent during sleepwalking itself.

Assessing the role of a sleep disorder in nocturnal violence

Guidelines are needed for determining the putative role of a sleep disorder in a specific violent act. Mahowald *et al.*[110] have proposed such guidelines which, in our current knowledge, are reasonable. However, these guidelines require application to a variety of instances and diagnoses to determine their overall validity. They may be summarized as:

(i)   There should be reason on history or investigations to suspect a bona fide sleep disorder.

(ii) The violent action is typically brief (minutes).

(iii) The behaviour is typically abrupt, immediate, impulsive, senseless and without motivation.

(iv) The victim is usually someone who merely happened to be present.

(v)   After the action, perplexity and horror are typically present.
(vi)   Partial or complete amnesia exists for the events.
(vii) In the case of sleepwalking, sleep terrors and confusional arousals, the episodes:
     (a) usually occur in the first third of the night
     (b) may be precipitated by efforts to awaken the subject
     (c) may be facilitated by alcohol, sedative/hypnotics or prior sleep deprivation.

Guidelines for expert witnesses and giving expert testimony

The provision of guidelines for expertise testimony in medico-legal matters has been the focus of a number of recent articles.[111-115] Most of this literature is directly relevant to the field of sleep disorders medicine. The American Sleep Disorders Association has also made progress in this area. Their guidelines include:[116]

An expert witness should have the following qualifications:

(i)   A current, valid, unrestricted medical licence.
(ii)   Relevant medical qualifications, specifically be a holder of a diploma of the American Board of Sleep Medicine.
(iii)   Familiarity with the clinical practice of sleep disorders medicine and involvement in clinical practice at the time of the events.

Expert testimony should follow a number of guidelines:

(i)   Testimony should be impartial – for which the ultimate test is a willingness to prepare testimony that could be presented unchanged for use by either the plaintiff or the defendant.
(ii)   Fees should relate to time and effort and not be contingent on the outcome of the claim.
(iii)   The expert witness should be willing to submit testimony for peer review.
(iv)   The expert witness should make records from his or her previous expert witness testimonies available to the attorneys and expert witnesses of both parties.
(v)   The expert witness must not become a partisan or advocate in the legal proceedings.

In closing, it should be appreciated that forensic medicine and the law are in the early stages of applying legal principles to specific medical sleep disorders, and that much progress and change can be anticipated in the near future. Those in the field must both acquire new knowledge concerning a number of aspects of sleep relevant to such cases, and assume a very large educational responsibility. The latter includes an increasing effort by sleep disorders physicians to educate medical and legal colleagues, and also the public, about sleep disorders and the issues involved in sleep-related violence and aggression. Perhaps public education is the most crucial area, as the juries in forensic medicine trials are made up of lay individuals who often assume a level of expertise concerning sleep that is quite inappropriate: after all, they experience sleep every day.

REFERENCES

1. Forensic medicine and sleep. *Sleep*, 1995, **9**:721–786.
2. Mark, V.H. and Ervin, F.R. *Violence and the Brain*. New York: Harper and Row, 1970.
3. Fromm, E. *The Anatomy of Human Destructiveness*. New York: Holt, Rinehart and Winston, 1973.
4. Montagu, A. *The Nature of Human Aggression*. New York: Oxford University Press, 1976.
5. Whalen, R.E., ed. *The Neuropsychology of Aggression*. New York: Plenum Press, 1974.
6. Lorenz, K. *On Aggression*. New York: Harcourt, Brace & World, 1966.
7. Clemente, C. and Lindsley, D.B., eds. *Aggression and Defence: Neural Mechanisms and Social Patterns*. Los Angeles: University of California Press, 1967.
8. Delgado, J.M.R. Offensive–defensive behavior in tree monkeys and chimpanzees induced by radio stimulation of the brain. In: S. Garattini and E.B. Sigg, eds. *Aggressive Behavior*. New York: Wiley, 1969, pp. 109–119.
9. Eleftheriou, B.E. and Scott, J.P., eds. *The Physiology of Aggression and Defeat*. New York: Plenum Press, 1971.
10. Gastaut, H. and Broughton, R. A clinical and polygraphic study of episodic phenomena during sleep. In: J. Wortis, ed. *Recent Advances in Biological Psychiatry*, Vol. VII. New York: Plenum Press, 1965, pp. 197–221.
11. Broughton, R.J. Sleep disorders: Disorders of arousal? *Science*, 1968, 159:1070–1078.
12. Fisher, C., Kahn, E., Edwards, A. and Davis, D.M. A psychophysiological study of nightmares and night terrors. I physiological aspects of the stage 4 night terrors. *J. Nerv. Ment. Dis.*, 1973, **157**:75–98.
13. Schenck, C.H., Bundlie, S.R., Patterson, A.L. and Mahowald, M.W. Rapid eye movement sleep disorder: a treatable parasomnia affecting older adults. *JAMA*, 1987, **257**:1786–1789.
14. James, W. Does consciousness exist? *J. Philos. Psychol. Sci. Meth.* 1904, **1**:477–491.
15. Nagel, T. What is it like to be a bat? *Philos. Rev.*, 1974, **83**:435–450.
16. Broughton, R. Human consciousness and sleep/wake rhythms: a review and some neuropsychological considerations. *J. Clin. Neuropsychol.* 1982, 4:193–218.
17. Delgado-Escueta, A.V., Mattson, R.M., King, L., Goldensohn, E.S., Spiegel, H., Madsen, J., Crandall, P., Dreifuss, F. and Porter, R.J. The nature of aggression during epileptic seizures. *N. Engl. J. Med.*, 1981, **305**:711–716.
18. Treiman, D.M. Epilepsy and violence: medical and legal issues. *Epilepsia*, 1986, **27** (suppl. 2):S77–S104.

19. Treiman, D.M. Psychobiology of ictal aggression. In: D. Smith, D. Treima and M. Trimble, eds. *Advances in Neurology*, Vol. 55. New York: Raven Press, 1991, pp. 341–356.
20. Fenwick, P. Aggression and epilepsy. In: *Epilepsy and Behavior*. Wiley-Liss, 1991, pp. 85–96.
21. [1963] AC 411.
22. Bixler, E.O., Kales, A., Soldatos, C.R., *et al.* Prevalence of sleep disorders in the Los Angeles metropolitan area. *Am. J. Psychiatry*, 1979, **136**:1257–1262.
23. Klackenberg, G. Incidence of parasomnia in children in a general population. In: C. Guilleminault, ed. *Sleep and its Disorders in Children*. New York: Raven Press, 1987, pp. 243–252.
24. Partinen, M. Epidemiology of sleep disorders. In: M. Kryger, T. Roth and W.C. Dement, eds. *Principles and Practice of Sleep Disorders Medicine*, 2nd edn. Philadelphia: WB Saunders, 1994, pp. 437–452.
25. Moldofsky, H., Gilbert, R., Lue, F.A. and MacLean, A.W. Sleep-related violence. *Sleep*, 1995, **18**:731–739.
26. Pedley, T.A. and Guilleminault, C. Episodic nocturnal wanderings responsive to anticonvulsant drug therapy. *Ann. Neurol.*, 1977, **2**:30–35.
27. Guilleminault, C., Moscovitch, A. and Leger, D. Nocturnal wandering and violence. *Sleep*, 1995, **18**:740–748.
28. Albert, D.J., Jonik R.H., Walsch, M.L. and Petrovic, D.M. Testosterone supports hormone-dependent aggression in female cats. *Physiol Behav.*, 1989, **46**:185–189.
29. Bonkalo, A. Impulsive acts and confusional states during incomplete arousal from sleep: criminological and forensic implications. *Psychiatr. Q.* 1974, **48**:400–409.
30. Schenck, C.H. Milner, D.M., Hurwitz, T.D., Bundie, S.R. and Mahowald, M.W. A polysomnographic and clinical report on sleep-related injury in 100 adult patients. *Am. J. Psychiatry* 1989, **146**:1166–1173.
31. Jouvet, M. and Delorme, J.F. Locus coeruleus et sommeil paradoxal. *C.R. Séances Soc. Biol.* 1965, **159**:895–899.
32. Sandler, S.A. Somnambulism in armed forces. *Ment. Hygiene*, 1945, **29**:236–247.
33. Pai, M.N. Sleep-walking and sleep activities. *J. Ment. Sci.* 1946, **92**:756–765.
34. Oswald, I. *Sleeping and Waking*. Amsterdam: Elsevier, 1962.
35. Oswald, I. and Evans, J. On serious violence during sleep-walking. *Br. J. Psychiatry*, 1985, **147**:688–691.
36. Tarsh, M.J. On serious violence during sleep-walking. *Br. J. Psychiatry*, 1986, **148**:476.
37. Schenck, C.H. and Mahowald, M.W. Sleepwalking and indecent exposure. *Med. Sci. Law*, 1992, **32**:86–87.
38. Podolsky, E. Somnambulistic homicide. *Med. Sci. Law*, 1960, **1**:260–265.
39. Howard, C. and D'Orban, P.T. Violence in sleep: medico-legal issues and two case reports. *Psychol. Med.*, 1986, **17**:915–925.
40. Bartholomew, A.A. On serious violence during sleep-walking. *Br. J. Psychiatry*, 1986, **148**:476.
41. Fenwick, P. Murdering while asleep. *Br. Med. J.*, 1986, **293**:574–575.
42. Broughton, R., Billings, R., Cartwright, R., Doucette, D., Edmeads, J., Edward, M., Ervin, F., Orchard, B., Hill, R. and Turrel, G. Homicidal somnambulism: a case report. *Sleep*, 1994, **17**:253–264.
43. Nofzinger, E.A. The Butler sleep apnea homicide. A medicolegal case report. *Sleep Res.*, 1995, **24**:312.
44. Broughton, R. and Warnes, H. Violence and sleep: eleven cases. *Sleep Res.*, 1989, **18**:205.

45. Schenck, C.H., Milner, D.M., Hurwitz, T.D., Bundie, S.R. and Mahowald, M.W. Dissociative disorders presenting as somnambulism: polysomnographic, video and clinical documentation (8 cases). *Dissociation*, 1989, **2**:194–204.
46. Schenck, C.H. and Mahowald, M.W. A polysomnographically documented case of adult somnambulism with long-distance automobile driving and frequent nocturnal violences: parasomnia with continuing danger as a noninsane automatism? *Sleep*, 1995, **18**:765–772.
47. Yellowless, D. Homicide by a somnambulist. *J. Ment. Dis.*, 1878, **24**:451–458.
48. Walker, N. *Crime and Insanity in England.* Edinburgh: University of Edinburgh Press, 1968.
49. Brooks, A. *Law, Psychiatry and the Mental Health System.* Boston: Little, Brown, 1974, pp. 233–238.
50. Hartmann, E. Two case reports: night terrors with sleepwalking – a potentially lethal disorder. *J. Nerv. Ment. Dis.*, 1983, **171**:503–505.
51. Barros Ferreira, D.M., Chodkiewizc, J., Lairy, G.C. and Salzarulo, P. Disorganized relations of tonic and phasic events of REM sleep in a case of brain stem tumor. *Electroenceph. Clin. Neurphysiol.* 1975, **38**:203–207.
52. Tachibana, M., Tanaka, K., Hishikawa, Y. and Kaneko, Z. A sleep study of acute psychotic states due to alcohol and meprobamate addiction. In: E. Weizman, ed. *Advances in Sleep Research*, Vol. 2. New York: Spectrum, 1975, pp. 177–205.
53. Shimizu, T., Sugita, Y., Teshima, Y. and Hishikawa, Y. Sleep study in patient's with OPCA and related diseases. In: W.P. Koella, ed. *Sleep 1980.* Basel: Karger, 1981, pp. 435–437.
54. Shimizu, T., Inami, U.Y., Sugita, Y., Iijima, S., Teshima, Y., Matsuo, R., Yasoshima, A., Okawa, M., Tashiro, T. and Hishikawa, Y. REM without muscle atonia (stage 1-REM) and its relation to delirious behavior during sleep in patients with degenerative diseases involving the brain stem. *Jpn J. Psychiatry Neurol.*, 1990, **44**:681–692.
55. Hishikawa, Y., Sugita, Y, Teshima, Y., IIjima, S., Tanaka, M. and Tachibana, M. Sleep disorders in alcoholic patients with delirium tremens and transient hallucinations – reevaluation of the REM rebound and intrusion theory. In: I. Karacan, ed. *Psychophysiological Aspects of Sleep.* Park Ridge: Noyes, 1981, pp. 109–122.
56. Quera-Salva, M.A. and Guilleminault, C. Olivopontocerebellar degeneration, abnormal sleep, and REM sleep without atonia. *Neurology*, 1986, **36**:576–577.
57. Schenck, C.H., Hurwitz, T.D. and Mahowald, M.W. REM sleep behavior disorder: an update on a series of 96 patients and review of the world literature. *J. Sleep Res.*, 1993, **2**:224–231.
58. Schenck, C.H. and Mahowald, M.W. A polysomnographic, neurologic, psychiatric and clinical outcome report on 70 consecutive cases with REM sleep behavior disorder (RBD); sustained clonazepam efficacy in 89.5% of 57 treated patients. *Cleve. Clin. J. Med.*, 1990, 57(suppl):S9–23.
59. Lipowski, Z.J. Delirium (acute confusional states). *JAMA*, 1987, **258**:1789–1792.
60. Fukutani, Y., Katsukawa, K., Matsubara, R., Kobayahi, K., Nakamura, I. and Yamaguchi, N. Delirium associated with Joseph disease. *J. Neurol. Neurosurg. Psychiatry*, 1993, **56**:1207–1212.
61. Lugaresi, E. and Crignotta, F. Hypnogenic paroxysmal dystonia: epileptic seizures or a new syndrome? *Sleep*, 1981, **4**:129–138.
62. Lee, B.I., Lesser, R.P. and Pippenger, C.E. Familial paroxysmal hypnogenic dystonia. *Neurology*, 1985, **35**:1357–1360.

63. Lugaresi, E., Crignotta, F. and Montagna, P. Nocturnal paroxysmal dystonia. *J. Neurol. Neurosurg. Psychiatry*, 1986, **49**:375–380.
64. Montagna, P. Nocturnal paroxysmal dystonia and nocturnal wanderings. *Neurology*, 1992, **42** (suppl. 6): 61–67.
65. Tinuper, P., Cerullo, A., Crignotta, F., Cortelli, P., Lugaresi, E. and Montagna, P. Nocturnal paroxysmal dystonia with short-lasting attacks: three cases with evidence for an epileptic frontal lobe origin of seizure. *Epilepsia*, 1990, **31**:549–556.
66. Maselli, R.A., Rosenberg, R.S. and Spire, J.-P. Episodic nocturnal wanderings in non-epileptic young patients. *Sleep*, 1988, **11**:156–161.
67. Plazzi, G., Tinuper, P., Montagna, P., Provini, F. and Lugaresi, E. Epileptic nocturnal wanderings. *Sleep*, 1995, **18**:749–756.
68. Gastaut, H. and Broughton, R. *Epileptic Seizures: Clinical and Electrographic Features, Diagnosis and Treatment.* Springfield: Chas. C. Thomas, 1972.
69. Broughton, R. Childhood sleepwalking, sleep terrors and enuresis: their differentiation from nocturnal epileptic seizures. In: L. Popoviciu, B. Agian and B. Badiu, eds. *Sleep 1978.* Basel: Karger, 1979, pp. 103–111.
70. Tassinari, C.A., Mancia, D., Dalla Bernardina, B. and Gastaut, H. Pavor nocturnus of non-epileptic nature in epileptic children. *Electroenceph. Clin. Neurophysiol.*, 1972, **33**:603–607.
71. Guilleminault, C., Billiard, M., Montplasir, J. and Dement, W.C. Altered states of consciousness in disorders of daytime sleepiness. *J. Neurol. Sci.*, 1975, **26**:377–393.
72. Broughton, R., Ghanem, Q., Hishikawa, Y., Sugita, Y., Nevsimalova, S. and Roth, B. Life effects of narcolepsy in 180 patients from North America, Asia and Europe compared to matched controls. *Can. J. Neurol. Sci.*, 1981, **8**:299–304.
73. Zorick, F.J., Salis, P.J., Roth, T. and Kramer, M. Narcolepsy and automatic behavior: a case report. *J. Clin. Psychiatry*, 1979, **40**:194–197.
74. Schenck, C.H. and Mahowald, M.W. Motor discontrol in narcolepsy: rapid-eye-movement (REM) sleep without atonia and REM sleep behavior disorders. *Ann. Neurol.*, 1992, **32**:3–10.
75. Mayer, G and Meier-Ewert, K. Motor dyscontrol in sleep of narcoleptic patients (a lifelong development?) *J. Sleep Res.*, 1993, **2**:143–148.
76. Millman, R.P., Kipp. G.J. and Carskadon, M.A. Sleepwalking precipitated by treatment of sleep apnea with nasal CPAP. *Chest*, 1991, **99**:750–751.
77. Pressman, M.R., Meyer, T.J., Kendrick-Mohammed, J., Figueroa, W.G. Greenspon, L.W. and Peterson, D.D. Night terrors in an adult precipitated by sleep apnea. *Sleep*, 1995, **18**:773–775.
78. Wright, B.A., Rosen, J.R., Buysee, D.J., Reynolds, C.F. and Zubenko, G.S. Shy–Drager syndrome presenting as a REM sleep behavior disorder. *J. Geriatr. Psychiatry Neurol.*, 1990, **3**:110–113.
79. Silber, M.H. and Ahiskog, J.E. REM sleep behavior disorder in Parkinsonian syndromes. *Sleep Res.*, 1992, **21**:313.
80. Kushida, C.A., Clerk, A.A., Kirsch, C.M., Hotson, J.R. and Guilleminault, C. Prolonged confusion with nocturnal wandering arising from NREM and REM sleep: a case report. *Sleep*, 1995, **18**:757–766.
81. Broughton, R.J. Confusional sleep disorders: interrelationship with memory consolidation and retrieval in sleep. In: P. MacLean, P.T. Boag and D. Campbell, eds. *A Triune Concept of the Brain* (Hincks Memorial Lectures). Toronto, University of Toronto Press, 1973, pp. 115–127.
82. Broughton, R. Phasic and dynamic aspects of sleep: a symposium review. In: M.G. Terzano, P. Halasz and A.C. Delcerck, eds. *Phasic and Dynamic Aspects of Sleep.* New York: Raven Press, 1991, pp. 185–205.

83. Taniguchi, M., Sugita, Y., Tachibana, N., Jisusaki, Y., Tanaka, C., Honda, H., Saito, M., Uruha S, Inatani, K., Mikami., A., Terashima, K., Tsuisumi, T., Egawa, I. and Teshima, Y. Successful clonazepam treatment for two patients with REM sleep behavior disorder provoked by stressful events. *Seishinka Tiryougak*, 1991, **6**:1277–1284 (in Japanese).

84. Luchins, D.J., Sherwood P.M., Gillin, C., Mendelson, W.B. and Wyatt, R.J. Filicide during psychotrope-induced somnambulism: a case report. *Am. J. Psychiatry.* 1978, **135**:1404–1405.

85. Charney, D.S., Kales, A., Soldatos, C.R. and Nelson, J.G. Somnambulistic-like episodes secondary to combined lithium-neuroleptic treatment. *Br. J. Psychiatry*, 1979, **135**:418–424.

86. Scott, A.I.F. Attempted strangulation during phenothiazine-induced sleepwalking and night terrors. *Br. J. Psychiatry*, 1988, **153**:692–694.

87. Louden, M.B., Morehead, M.A. and Schmidt, H.S. Selegiline (Eldepryl) may activate REM sleep behavior disorder in Parkinsonism. *Sleep Res.*, 1994, **23**:370.

88. Patterson, J.F. Non-rapid-eye-movement parasomnia with behavior disorder. *South. Med. J.*, 1989, **82**:802–803.

89. Hurwitz, T.D., Schenck, C.H. and Mahowald, M.W. Sleepwalking–sleepterrors–REM behavior disorder: overlapping parasomnias. *Sleep Res.*, 1991, **20**:260.

90. Mahowald, M.W. and Schenck, C.H. Dissociated states of wakefulness and sleep. *Neurology*, 1992, **42**:44–52.

91. Passouant, P., Billiard, M. and Paquet, J. Terreurs nocturnes et crises epileptiques chez l'enfant. *Lyon Med.*, 1973, **9**:547–556.

92. Amercian Sleep Disorders Association. *International Classification of Sleep Disorders: Diagnostic and Coding Manual.* Kansas: Allen Press, 1990.

93. Bedard, M.A., Monplaisir, J., Richer, F., Rouleau, I. and Malo, J. Obstructive sleep apnea syndrome: pathogenesis of neuropsychological deficits. *J. Clin. Exp. Neuropsychol.*, 1991, **13**:950–964.

94. Montplaisir, J., Bedard, M.A., Richer, F. and Rouleau, I. Neurobehavioral manifestations in obstructive sleep apnea syndrome before and after treatment with continuous positive airway pressure. *Sleep*, 1992, **15**:S17–S19.

95. Blatt, I., Peled, R., Gadoth, N. and Lavie, P. The value of sleep recording in evaluating somnambulism in young adults. *Electroencephalogr. Clin. Neurophysiol.*, 1991, **78**:407–412.

96. Kales, A., Jacobson, A., Paulson, M.J., Kales, J.D. and Walter, R.D. Somnambulism: psychophysiological correlates. *Arch. Gen. Psychiatry*, 1966, **14**:586–594.

97. Halasz, P., Ujszaszi, J. and Gadoros, J. Are microarousals preceded by electroencephalographic slow wave synchronization precursors of confusional awakenings? *Sleep*, 1985, **8**:231–238.

98. Kales, A., Soldatos, C.R., Caldwell, A.B., *et al.* Somnambulism: clinical characteristics and personality pattern. *Arch. Gen. Psychiatry*, 1980, **37**:1406–1410.

99. Mahowald, M.W. and Schenck, C.H. REM sleep behavior disorder. In: M.H. Kryger, T. Roth and W.C. Dement, eds. *Principles and Practice of Sleep Disorders Medicine.* Philadelphia: WB Saunders, 1989, pp. 389–401.

100. Scheffer, I.E., Bhatia, K., Lopes-Cendes, I., Fish, D.R., Marsden, C.D., Andermann, E., Andermann, F., Desbiens, R., Keene, D., Cendes, F., Constantinou, J., McIntosh, A. and Berkovic, S.F. Autosomal dominant nocturnal frontal epilepsy: a distinctive clinical disorder. *Brain*, 1995, **118**:61–74.

101. Broughton, R.J. Polysomnography: principles and applications in sleep and

arousal disorders. In: E. Niedermeyer and F. Lopes da Silva, eds. *Electroencephalography: Basic Principles, Applications and Related Fields*, 3rd edn. Baltimore: Urban and Schwarzenberg, 1993, pp. 438–809.

102. Broughton, R., Ambulatory monitoring of sleep and its disorders. In: M.H. Kryger, T. Roth and W.C. Dement, eds. *Principles and Practice of Sleep Disorders Medicine*, 2nd edn. Philadelphia: W.B. Saunders, 1994, 978–983.

103. Culebras, A. and Moor, J.T. Magnetic resonance findings in REM sleep behavior disorder. *Neurology*, 1989, **39**:1519–1523.

104. Idezuka, J., Onodera, O., Yuasa, T., Tsuji, S. and Ito, J. MRI findings of olivopon-tocerebellar atrophy and Machado–Joseph disease – diagnostic value of transverse pontine fibers. *Rinsyou Shinkeigaku*, 1993, **33**:289–293. .

105. Kojima, S. Clinical types of spinocerebellar degeneration with MRI imaging. *Rinsyou Shinkeigaku*, 1993, **33**:1294–1296 (in Japanese).

106. Fenwick, P. Automatism, medicine and law. *Psychol. Med. Monogr.*, 1990, **17** (suppl.):1–27.

107. Blair, D. The medicolegal aspects of automatism. *Med. Sci. Law*, 1977, **17**:167–182.

108. Schopp, R.F. *Automatism, Insanity and Psychology of Criminal Responsibility*. Cambridge: Cambridge University Press, 1991.

109. Roper, P. Bulimia while sleep walking: a rebuttal for sane automatism? *Lancet*, 1989, **2**(8666):796.

110. Mahowald, M.W., Bundie, S.R., Hurwitz, T.D. and Schenck, C.H. Sleep violence – forensic implications: polygraphic and video documentation. *J. Forensic Sci.*, 1990, **35**:413–432.

111. Committee on Medical Liability. Guidelines for expert witness testimony. *Pediatrics*, 1989, **83**:312–313.

112. Qualifications and guidelines for an expert witness. *Neurology*, 1989, **39**:9A.

113. American College of Physicians. Guidelines for the physician expert witness. *Ann. Intern. Med.*, 1990, **113**:789.

114. Bone, R. and Rosenow, E. ACCP guidelines for an expert witness. *Chest*, 1990, **98**:1006.

115. Weintraub, M.I. Expert witness testimony: a time for self-regulation? *Neurology*, 1995, **45**:855–858.

116. Mahowald, M.W. and Schenck, C.H. Complex motor behaviour arising during the sleep period: forensic medicine implications. *Sleep*, 1995, **18**:724–726.

4

A Case-Controlled Study of Men who Sexually Assault Sleeping Victims

J.P. Fedoroff*‡, A. Brunet‡, V. Woods§, C. Granger‡,
E. Chow‡, P. Collins*‡ and C.M. Shapiro‡

*The Clarke Institute of Psychiatry, ‡University of Toronto, and §Department of
Corrections, Ontario

INTRODUCTION

Given the sleep patterns and schedules of North American couples, it is likely that the incidence of one partner initiating sex while the other is asleep is not uncommon. However, the incidence of one partner initiating sex with the intent that the other remains asleep is unknown. Paraphiliac sexual disorders and sleep would seem at first glance to be strange bed-fellows since clinical reports of an association are rare[1,2] and the most well known cases of men with sleeping victims reported in the popular literature have involved perpetrators with extreme paraphiliac disorders: criminal sexual sadism and/or necrophilia.[3,4] However, neither the prevalence of sexual assaults on sleeping partners nor the relationship between specific paraphilias and this activity have been established. The purpose of this chapter is to describe a series of men who engaged in sexual activity with sleeping victims.

Forensic Aspects of Sleep. Edited by C.M. Shapiro and A. McCall Smith.
© 1997 John Wiley & Sons Ltd.

METHOD

Samples

All published cases of sexual assault in Ontario from the years 1989–1994, identified through a computer search of the legal database Quicklaw* were manually reviewed for any reference to sleeping victims. All identified cases were retrieved and were entered into the legal sleeping victims (LSV) sample.

A second independent sample was derived from an ethically approved chart review of all of the active treatment cases of a forensic psychiatrist (J.P.F.) in which the patient was: (i) male, (ii) a sex offender and/or paraphiliac and (iii) had committed at least one sexual assault on a sleeping victim. All identified cases were entered into the clinical sleeping victims (CSV) sample.

A third case-control (CC) sample was chosen consisting of patients from the same active treatment list who met the following criteria: (i) male, (ii) a sex offender and/or paraphiliac, (iii) had no known offences against sleeping victims and (iv) had the same primary (presenting) paraphilia or sex offence as the matched case from the CSV group. These cases were entered into the control group.

Statistical analysis

Descriptive group analyses were conducted using means, standard deviations (SD) and percentages. Group comparisons of non-parametric data were made using chi squared analyses. Group comparisons of parametric data were made using analyses of variance (ANOVA), and un-paired, two tailed t-tests, as appropriate. Planned post hoc comparisons were made using Fisher's test.

RESULTS

Samples

Legal sleeping victims (LSV) sample

There were 1100 published cases involving sex offences tried in Ontario from 1989 to 1994. Of these, 26 (2%) met the study criteria for the LSV sample listed above.

---

* QL Systems Ltd, 1 Gore Street, Kingston, Ontario, Canada K7L 2L1.

Clinical sleeping victims (CSV) sample

Of 245 active treatment cases of sex offenders and/or paraphiliacs in the outpatient sex offender/paraphilia clinic at a major Canadian teaching hospital, 25 (10%) met the study criteria for the CSV sample listed above. Table 1 presents the demographic and clinical characteristics of this group in detail.

Case-control (CC) sample

Twenty-five men who met the study criteria for the CC sample listed above were selected from the same treatment group as the CSV sample.

Table 2 summarizes the demographic and victim characteristics of the three groups.

Group demographic comparisons

The LSV group was significantly younger than the other two groups ($F = 7.7$, df(2,73), $p = 0.0009$). There was a trend for members of the LSV group (see Table 2) to be more likely to have assaulted an acquaintance than members of the other two groups (CSV: 7 (28%); LSV: 10 (38%); CC: 3 (12%), $\chi^2 = 4.7$, df = 2, $p = 0.10$). There was a trend for LSV cases to have had fewer reported victims than cases in the CC group ($F = 2.9$, df(2,72), $p = 0.06$). Finally, there was a trend for the two groups with sleeping victims to be more likely to engage in actual intercourse with the victim and to have been intoxicated from drinking alcohol at the time of the offence ($\chi^2 = 11.6$, df = 6, p = 0.07; $\chi^2 = 4.7$, df = 2, $p = 0.10$, respectively). No other significant differences were found between the three groups for the variables listed in Table 2.

Co-morbid axis I psychiatric disorders

Psychiatric diagnoses according to DSM-IV criteria[5] are shown in Table 3 for the CSV and CC groups (diagnoses are not provided for the LSV group since they were not examined by a psychiatrist and/or insufficient information was available).

There were, of course, no differences between the two groups in terms of presenting paraphiliac disorder since they were matched on this variable. There was also no significant difference between the two groups in terms of total number of paraphiliac disorders (1.72 ± 0.79 versus 1.44 ± 0.77, respectively; $t = 1.27$, df = 48, $p = $ NS).

However, when the two groups were compared in terms of other diagnosed paraphiliac disorders for which treatment was not initially requested, significantly more of the CSV group had co-morbid sexual sadism compared to the CC group (44% versus 16% respectively; $\chi^2 = 4.67$, df = 1, $p < 0.05$).

Table 1. Demographic and clinical characteristics of the CSV sample

Case ID	Age	Group referral source*	Marital status	Paraphilia[†]	Non-sexual psychiatric diagnoses[‡]	Total number of victims	Number of sleeping victims
A	52	MD	M	Paedophilia	Dysthymia	1	1
B	67	MD	D	Fetishism	Social phobia Substance abuse	1	1
C	36	L	M	Paedophilia NOS	None	1	1
D	41	MD	M	None	Social phobia Dysthymia	1	1
E	35	MD	D	Paedophilia	ASPD Substance abuse	5	1
F	51	L	M	Paedophilia	ETOH abuse	1	1
G	20	L	S	Sadism	ASPD ETOH abuse	1	1
H	30	MD	M	TVF	Social phobia	1	1
I	35	L	M	None	Social phobia	1	1
J	27	MD	S	NOS Sadism	ETOH abuse Parasomnia	1	1
K	46	L	D	Paedophilia	None	1	1
L	25	MD	M	Voyeurism NOS	Substance abuse Parasomnia Dysthymia	1	1
M	29	L	M	Paedophilia TVF Voyeurism Frotteurism	Substance abuse	3	3
N	37	L	M	None	Social phobia	1	1
O	44	L	D	Paedophilia	Social phobia	3	3
P	43	L	D	Paedophilia Sadism	Social phobia Substance abuse	12	10
Q	33	MD	D	Paedophilia Necrophilia Voyeurism	Substance abuse	3	3
R	22	MD	S	TVF S/M	Schizophrenia Substance abuse	1	1
S	44	L	M	Paedophilia Exhibitionism	Social phobia Substance abuse Delusional disorder (by history)	2	1
T	42	L	D	Paedophilia	Social phobia	1	1

Table 1 (*continued*)

Case ID	Age	Group referral source*	Marital status	Paraphilia[†]	Non-sexual psychiatric diagnoses[‡]	Number of sleeping victims	Number of sleeping victims
U	44	MD	D	Paedophilia	Social phobia	3	2
V	30	MD	D	Voyeurism Exhibitionism Frotteurism	Major depression Substance abuse	3	3
W	28	L	S	Paedophilia Sadism Zoophilia	Substance abuse	3	3
X	32	L	M	Voyeurism Exhibitionism	Substance abuse	>100	30
Y	50	L	S	Paedophilia Sadism	Substance abuse	1	1

* MD, medical referral; L, legal referral.
[†] NOS, not otherwise specified; TVF, transvestic fetishism; S/M, sadomasochism.
[‡] ETOH abuse, alcohol dependence; ASPD, antisocial personality disorder.

Table 2. Demographic and victim characteristics of the three groups

	Sleeping victim samples		No sleeping victim sample
	Clinical (*n* = 25)	Legal (*n* = 28)	Control (*n* = 25)
Mean age (SD)	37 (12)	28 (6)	37 (11)
Marital status			
Single (%)	9 (36)	16 (62)	10 (40)
Married (%)	9 (36)	8 (31)	10 (40)
Divorced/separated (%)	7 (28)	2 (8)	5 (20)
Years of education (SD)	12 (2)	12 (2)	12 (2)
Unemployed (%)	28	10	32
Number of victims (SD)	2 (1)	1 (0.6)	4 (8)
Victim ages (SD)	14.4 (8)	14.7 (8)	14.5 (11)
Sex of Victim(s)			
Male (%)	4 (16)	1 (4)	4 (16)
Female (%)	20 (80)	24 (92)	18 (72)
Both (%)	1 (4)	1 (4)	3 (12)
History of drug abuse (%)	15 (60)		13 (52)
Personal history of sex abuse (%)	8 (32)		7 (36)
Heterosexual orientation (%)	22 (88)		21 (84)
Victim(s) known to offender (%)	20 (80)	22 (85)	18 (72)
Intercourse occurred (%)	8 (32)	11 (42)	6 (24)
Victim drugged (%)	3 (12)	3 (12)	0 (0)

Table 3. Psychiatric diagnoses for the CSV and CC groups

DSM-IV psychiatric diagnoses	CSV, n (%)	CC, n (%)
A. Presenting paraphilia* (%)		
Paedophilia	16 (64)	16 (64)
Sadism/masochism	4 (16)	3 (12)
Voyeurism	1 (4)	1 (4)
Exhibitionism	1 (4)	1 (4)
Transvestism	2 (8)	2 (8)
Fetishism	1 (4)	1 (4)
NOS	0 (0)	1 (4)
B. Primary sexual dysfunction(s) (%)		
Erectile dysfunction	1 (4)	1 (4)
Premature ejaculation	6 (24)	4 (16)
Inhibited orgasm	4 (16)	5 (20)
Inhibited sexual desire	6 (24)	1 (4)
No sex dysfunction	8 (32)	14 (56)
C. Co-morbid axis I disorders (%)		
Mood disorders	6 (24)	8 (32)
Anxiety disorders	13 (52)	4 (16)
Other	1 (4)	1 (4)

* Other paraphiliac disorders were also diagnosed but were not the reason for referral. See text for details.

There were no significant differences between the two groups in terms of other paraphiliac disorders, including paedophilia (64% versus 72%, respectively), voyeurism (16% versus 16%, respectively), exhibitionism (12% versus 8%, respectively), transvestic fetishism (12% versus 12%, respectively), fetishes (28% versus 24% respectively) or sexual paraphilias not otherwise specified (20% versus 4%, respectively).

There was a trend for CSV cases to have significantly more sexual dysfunctions (sex problems expressed by physical difficulties having sex) but sex dysfunctions were also frequent in the CC group (CSV: 68% versus CC: 44%; $\chi^2 = 2.9$, df = 1, $p = 0.09$). However, there were no significant differences in terms of specific sexual dysfunction. Frequencies of specific sexual dysfunctions in the two groups are shown in Table 3, part B.

A summary of co-morbid axis I disorders is shown in Table 3, part C. Anxiety disorders were significantly more frequent in the CSV group compared to the CC group (52% versus 16%, respectively; $\chi^2 = 7.2$, df = 1, $p = 0.008$).

Because the CSV group had a higher frequency of both sadomasochistic disorders and anxiety disorders, a comparison was made in the CSV group to determine if the two types of disorder were more likely to occur together. In the CSV group 7 (28%) had sexual sadism only, 9 (36%) had anxiety disorders only, 4 (16%) had both sexual sadism and an anxiety disorder, and 5 (20%) had neither ($\chi^2 = 1.9$, df = 1, $p = $ NS).

DISCUSSION

Limitations of this study

Before discussing the findings, several important limitations are acknowledged. Firstly, this is a retrospective survey and therefore subject to the usual limitations of such a study. In particular, the LSV group was not personally examined by any of the authors of this paper and it is likely that many details were omitted from the legal descriptions of the cases. For this reason, this group was excluded from all analyses involving co-morbid psychiatric disorders. Similarly, the CSV and CC groups were both obtained from a single, highly specialized outpatient forensic clinic, limiting the generalizability of findings to other populations.

Secondly, the chart reviewers were not blind concerning the study groups to which individuals were assigned. While this could result in some bias, chart reviewers had no specific hypotheses during the data collection phase of this study making systematic bias less likely.

Thirdly, although each member of the CSV and CC groups was assessed in an identical fashion, using a standardized interview schedule (available on request from J.P.F.), a more commonly accepted interview schedule such as the SCID[6] was not used in this study. This is unfortunate as it would have facilitated generalizability of the findings. On the other hand, the SCID does not have diagnostic questions for sexual disorders. In addition, since the interview questions and diagnostic criteria were essentially identical for the CSV and CC groups, differences between the two groups are likely to be valid.

Finally, only males were included in this study.

Given these limitations, there were several interesting findings, which are discussed in the following sections.

Prevalence of the sleeping victim syndrome

Of published legal cases involving sexual offences in Ontario, there were 26 (2%) involving sleeping victims. In comparison, 25 out of 245 (10%) outpatients in a specialized forensic clinic are known to have engaged in sex with sleeping victims. The higher frequency of cases in the clinic sample is easily explained by the fact that much more information was available about them and by the fact that they were significantly older and therefore had had more time in which to commit offences of all types. Further surveys are needed in which the time of onset of interest in sex with sleeping victims and time of onset of the activity are identified. A survey of other population samples, including non-clinical and other forensic samples, should also be conducted. In any case, the frequency of this behaviour is much higher than expected given the scant attention that this syndrome has received in the literature.

Phenomenology and classification of the sleeping victim syndrome

The DSM-IV lists *lack of consent* as one of the pathognomonic features of para-philiac disorders[7] but does not define the term or allow for the fact that *consent* has many variations. The known paraphilias lend themselves to a sub-classification on the basis of degree of consent involved. For example, in some paraphiliac activities the victims are not given the opportunity to consent (e.g. voyeurism, exhibitionism, frotteurism). In others, the victim is legally unable to give consent (e.g. paedophilia, zoophilia) or is unable to withdraw consent (e.g. criminal sexual sadism). In the most extreme cases, consent is not possible because the object of sexual attention is inanimate (e.g. fetishes, necrophilia). Criminal trials of sex offenders often hinge on what type of consent was or was not obtained.[8] Lack of consent is clearly an issue in all cases of sex with sleeping victims. Motivations for engaging in sex with sleeping partners varied according to the degree of consent obtained, as illustrated by the following case examples.

Primary motivation type I: Fulfilment of sadistic or paraphiliac fantasies

The men with sleeping victims who also had a diagnosis of sexual sadism all described arousal from the idea of being with partners who could not resist (because they were unconscious) Cases P and Q illustrate this point:

> P, a 43-year-old divorced factory worker, presented with a long history of 'sneak-ing into the bedrooms of female house guests'. He was extremely aroused by thoughts and fantasies of a partner whom he could control completely. Although he denied specific arousal from the fact that his victims were sleeping, he admit-ted that if his victims awoke and began to actively participate (an event which he insisted was not uncommon) he would lose interest. Although he denied being aroused by physically hurting his sexual partners, he enjoyed tying them up and coercing them into his preferred sexual activities. He came to the attention of the police after spending eight years training a female relative to be the perfect sex slave by repeatedly assaulting her while she slept. This 'training' began when she was three. On examination he was also found to have alcohol dependence, major depression and antisocial personality disorder.

> Q, a 33-year-old divorced mining contractor, presented with a history of sexually molesting a nine-year-old female relative. He had administered sleeping pills to her on numerous occasions in order to fulfil his fantasies of having sex with a life-less partner. He approached other young girls while they were sleeping and would fondle them until they awoke, whereupon he would stop. He also had a history of sexual contact with a dog. He confessed his necrophiliac fantasies after being captured by a police SWAT team following a threatened suicide attempt

with an assault rifle in a motel. He also met DSM-IV criteria for antisocial personality disorder and major depression, and had a history of alcohol abuse. As with the previous case, although Q assaulted sleeping victims, his arousal resulted from having a helpless victim on whom he could enact his sadistic fantasies, rather than from having a sleeping victim *per se*.

Primary motivation type II: Bypassing rejection and/or observation of paraphiliac activities

In others, the sexual anxiety appeared to be related to the knowledge that their primary sexual interests were paraphiliac and therefore unlikely to be acceptable to their partner. Sex with a sleeping partner allowed these men to engage in paraphiliac activities without being observed:

B, a 67-year-old retired divorced accountant, presented with a lifelong foot fetish. He was married for several years to a woman who was unable to tolerate his interest in her feet. He began to surreptitiously indulge in his paraphilia when she was asleep, fondling and kissing her feet while masturbating. He was also attracted to boys' feet. Although he stated in theory he preferred his partners to be awake, all of his paraphiliac activities occurred with sleeping partners. In addition to social phobia, he had an extensive polysubstance abuse history.

X, a 32-year-old former police officer, had a history of voyeurism and exhibitionism since his early adolescence. He preferred to spy on teenaged females who were partially clothed or engaging in sexual activity. He would fantasize about having a relationship with them while masturbating but insisted that he would not have been interested in actually having sex with anyone who became aware they had been spied upon. A night-shift security job at a female young offenders facility provided him with ample opportunity to observe semi-naked young women while they were sleeping. Although he would lift up the covers of victims whom he thought were sleeping, he was never discovered to have molested them in any other way. He insisted he would have had no interest in sexual activity with any of his victims had they woken. He denied a specific interest in sleeping partners. He was able to indulge in his voyeuristic activities for several months until he was caught.

Primary motivation type III: Sexual opportunism

A third subgroup of men in the CSV group appeared to be acting in an opportunistic manner, to avoid going through the usual stages of courtship with their inherent risks of rejection:

R, a 22-year-old paranoid schizophrenic well controlled on neuroleptic medication, had a history of transvestic fetishism (cross-dressing in women's underwear for sexual arousal). One evening after consuming alcohol and hashish, he attempted to have sex with his similarly aged sister while she was asleep. When she awoke he stopped. There was no history of other sexually assaultive behaviour.

Primary motivation type iv: Sex while sleeping

The fourth and final subgroup of men with sleeping victims involves those with a parasomniac sleeping disorder in which sexual activity occurred while the men themselves were asleep:

J, a 27-year-old single factory worker, was self-referred to his family physician because of a problem of 'having sex with my girl-friend while I am asleep'. There were no criminal charges. He felt that this activity occurred more often after consuming alcohol. He was aroused by sadistic fantasies and troilistic activities (threesomes). He underwent an overnight study which revealed a redistribution of slow wave sleep across the night instead of its usual occurrence primarily during the first half of the sleep period. He had frequent spontaneous movement arousals (15 per hour) during slow wave sleep, accompanied by bradycardia (50–66 beats per minute). These results were interpreted as consistent with a parasomniac sleep disorder. He was treated with clonazepam (0.5 mg daily) which decreased but did not completely eliminate his sleep–sex activity. Fluoxetine (20 mg) was added, and completely eliminated the nocturnal sex incidents after two weeks. This remission continued after he discontinued clonazepam (because of tiredness). J denied any interest in or recollection of sex with sleeping partners.

L, a 25-year-old married restauranteur, presented on referral from a physician who had originally assessed him for sexually assaulting his wife almost nightly. On examination, Mr L readily admitted engaging in attempted cunnilingus and sexual intercourse with his sleeping wife. However, he claimed that he was aware of these activities only because his wife told him. He claimed to have no recollection of the events. He admitted arousal from having sex with his wife when she was 'tied up'. He also admitted to past voyeuristic activities. He and his wife also engaged in mutually consenting swinging. He had a past history of polysubstance abuse which was in remission at the time of assessment. His sleep history was significant for snoring, and a personal (as well as) family history of sleepwalking. His wife also described episodes in which he screamed or talked in his sleep. He had day-time sleepiness which he self-treated by consuming up to 30 cups of coffee a day, and by taking power naps, on average once a week. He was referred for assessment in a sleep clinic. Results of an overnight sleep study showed evidence of several abrupt and spontaneous arousals from slow wave sleep (Figure 1), associated with increased heart rate, and compatible with a diagnosis of parasomnia. In addition, episodes of apnoea and hypopnoea and snoring were noted associated with significant arterial oxygen desaturation and compatible with a diagnosis of sleep apnoea syndrome. He and his wife consented to undergo a second study in their home in which a sleep EEG recording of Mr L was made while they were videotaped. Although apnea–hypopnoea and snoring associated with significant arterial oxygen desaturation were again noted, there was no sexual activity recorded. Nevertheless, after treatment with continuous positive airway pressure (CPAP) Mr L's sexual activities with his wife while she was sleeping stopped completely. Two months after beginning CPAP

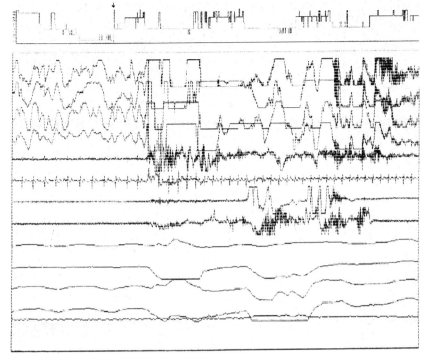

Figure 1. The results of an overnight sleep study, showing evidence of several abrupt and spontaneous arousals from slow wave sleep

(in which there were no night-time sexual assaults) Mr L discontinued CPAP because of discomfort. Night-time sexual assaults resumed within two weeks and ceased again when CPAP was reinstituted.

Although nocturnal penile tumescence (NPT) is a well-described phenomenon, it is believed to be associated with non-erotic dreams occurring during REM sleep.[9] There have also been case reports of sexual activity in the context of delirium resulting from sleep disturbance[10] but, to our knowledge, the syndrome of men engaging in sexual activity with other people while asleep has not previously been described. Unlike NPT, it occurs during stage 4 sleep. The two men in this sample with parasomniac sexual activity described disorientation when awakened during the activity. However, both also had symptoms of sexual sadism (arousal from the idea of non-consensual sex), making it possible that the parasomniac activity represented some disinhibition of underlying wishes analogous to the sleep eating syndrome, in which individuals with food cravings have eaten more while asleep than they would ordinarily.[11] Although it was not possible to definitively prove that sexual activity was occurring during slow wave sleep in either case, this has been achieved in another case not included in this sample.

Axis I psychiatric co-morbidity in men with sleeping victims

There were two major findings concerning co-morbidity of men who had sex with sleeping victims. The first is a statistically significant higher frequency of sexual sadism. This finding was particularly notable since the control group was matched for primary or presenting paraphiliac disorder. Presumably the higher frequency of sadism in the sleeping victim group would be even more pronounced if compared to a randomly chosen group of paraphiliac men in which no attempt was made to match for presenting para-philiac disorders. Further studies to determine the prevalence of sex with sleeping partners in criminal and non-criminal sadists are planned.

The second major finding was a higher frequency of anxiety disorders in the CSV group. In addition to meeting the usual DSM-IV criteria for social phobia, these men appeared to be inordinately anxious concerning sexual relations with a partner. In some cases, this anxiety was related to the idea of simply having conventional (non-paraphiliac) sex. This raises the question of whether undue anxiety about having sex is equivalent to the DSM-IV criteria for social phobia. In any case, the failure to find a significant association between sexual sadism and anxiety disorders in this sample suggests that these are independent risk factors for engaging in sex with sleeping people.

CONCLUSIONS

Sexual activity involving sleeping victims occurs in between 1 and 10% of forensic sex cases. It appears to be associated with sexual sadism, anxiety dis-orders, embarrassment about or fear of detection of sexual activity, opportun-ism, and/or parasomniac sleep. Until more is known about this phenomenon, clinicians should specifically inquire about sleep sex activity in all forensic sex evaluations, especially in men with anxiety disorder or sexual sadism.

To our knowledge, sexual activity during parasomniac sex has never pre-viously been described. As knowledge of the parasomniac sleep sex syn-drome described in this chapter becomes more well known, the likelihood of its use in legal defences will increase. This syndrome appears to be extremely rare. Diagnosis depends on a full psychiatric examination as well as a full sleep study, preferably one in which simultaneous EEG and video recordings are made in which demonstrated parasomnic EEG changes are shown to be associated with sexual activity. CPAP may be an effective treatment for this condition if sleep apnoea syndrome is also present. Fluoxetine may also be an effective treatment option, although further study will be needed to verify this.

ABSTRACT

One of the pathognomonic characteristics of paraphiliac disorders is that the sexual activities do not involve a consenting partner. In order to give consent, a partner must be aware of the activity and its consequences, be free to accept or refuse the activity, and be old enough to give consent. By these criteria, men who have sex with sleeping partners should have a high frequency of paraphiliac disorders. However, the clinical literature about this activity is sparse and there are no systematic descriptions of this population. The purpose of this study was to examine the characteristics of men who have engaged in sex with sleeping partners.

Two samples of men with sleeping victims were studied. The first sample was derived from a computer search of published Canadian legal cases through the computer citation service Quicklaw. The second sample was obtained from a chart review of the current active cases of a forensic psychiatrist specializing in the assessment and treatment of paraphiliac disorders. A case-control sample with no known sleeping victims and matched for presenting paraphiliac disorder or criminal offence was also studied.

Statistical analyses were carried out using contingency tables and chi squared analysis for non-parametric data and un-paired, two tailed t-tests and ANOVAs, as appropriate, for parametric data.

Twenty-six men were identified in the first (legal) sample. The other two samples (clinical and control) consisted of 25 men each. The legal sample were significantly younger than the other two groups ($p < 0.001$) and were more likely to have assaulted acquaintances than the other two groups ($p < 0.05$). The clinical sample had significantly more co-morbid sexual sadism and anxiety disorders than the case-control sample ($p < 0.05$ and $p < 0.05$, respectively) (there was insufficient reliable data on the co-morbid sexual interests in the legal sample to analyse). A new syndrome consisting of men who appear to engage in sexual behaviour while they themselves are sleeping is described. However, no man with a singular preference for sleeping victims, not explicable by another psychiatric disorder, was found.

There are more men who have sex with sleeping victims than the current clinical literature would suggest. There also appears to be more than one motive for this behaviour. A tentative classification system for this syndrome is described.

REFERENCES

1. Fedoroff, J.P. Sexual disorders in Huntington's disease. *Journal of Neuropsychiatry* 6(2), 1994, 147–153.
2. Money, J. *Venuses Penuses: Sexology, Sexosophy and Exigency Theory.* Buffalo, NY: Prometheus Books, 1986.
3. Masters, B. *Killing for Company.* Sevenoaks: Coronet Books, 1986.

4. Masters, B. *The Shrine of Jeffrey Dahmer*. Sevenoaks: Coronet Books, 1993.
5. American Psychiatric Association *Diagnostic and Statistical Manual of Mental Disorders*, 4th edn (DSM-IV). Washington, DC, American Psychiatric Association, 1994.
6. Spitzer, R.L., Williams, J.B.W. and Gibbon, M. *Structured Clinical Interview for DSM-III-R (SCID)*. New York: New York State Psychiatric Institute, Biometrics Research, 1987.
7. Fedoroff, J.P. The differential diagnosis for paraphiliac disorder in women. Manuscript in preparation.
8. Rodrigues, G.P. (general ed.) *Crankshaw's Criminal Code of Canada, R.S.C. 1985*. Toronto: Carswell, 1993.
9. Fisher, C., Gross, J. and Zuch, J. Cycle of penile erection synchronous with dreaming (REM) sleep: preliminary report. *Archives of General Psychiatry* **12**, 1965, 29–40.
10. Fukatani, Y., Katsukaura, K., Matschara, R., Kobayashi, K., Nakamura, I. and Yamaguchi, N. Delirium associated with Joseph disease. *Journal of Neurology, Neurosurgery, and Psychiatry* **56**, 1993, 1207–1212.
11. Schenck, C.H., Hurwitz, T.D., Bundlie, S.R. and Mahowald, M.W. Sleep-related eating disorders: polysomnographic correlates of a heterogeneous syndrome distinct from daytime eating disorders. *Sleep* **14**(5), 1991, 419–431.

5

Civil Liability Issues Arising out of Sleep Deprivation and Sleep Disorders

D.W. Shuman
Southern Methodist University School of Law

Although courts have long recognized civil liability claims and defenses for injury caused by loss of consciousness or diminished alertness, sleep related civil liability issues have recently increased in frequency and complexity. In part, as reflected in this book, these issues have increased in frequency and complexity as a consequence of expanding scientific knowledge about sleep deprivation and sleep disorders and their consequences for accidents and injuries. And, in part, as reflected in our daily lives, these issues have increased in frequency and complexity because we live in an increasingly competitive society in which both businesses and individuals are required to work harder and faster to survive economically (often referred to as the Toronto Syndrome).[1] Against the background of this evolving scientific knowledge and changing society, this chapter describes both traditional and evolving bases for civil liability claims and defenses arising out of sleep deprivation and sleep disorders.

To provide a context for understanding these issues, I describe a four-part categorization for civil liability issues arising out of sleep deprivation and sleep disorders. The first and most traditional category is a civil liability tort claim in the courts for the harm directly caused by the conduct of a person with sleep deprivation or a sleep disorder. A typical case in this category addresses the liability of a driver for falling asleep at the wheel and causing injury to another motorist.

Forensic Aspects of Sleep. Edited by C.M. Shapiro and A. McCall Smith.
© 1997 John Wiley & Sons Ltd.

A second category of liability, which largely arose in the latter part of the 20th century, is a civil liability tort claim in the courts for breach of the duty of a health care provider treating a person with a sleep disorder, or with a therapy that affects attention or drowsiness, allegedly owed to a third person injured by the patient as a consequence of the disorder or its treatment. A typical case in this category addresses a physician's duty/liability to the injured third person for negligently failing to inform the patient about the risks of drowsiness and driving while under the medication prescribed by the physician.

A third category of cases addresses employer liability arising out of sleep deprivation and sleep disorders. Vicarious liability (*respondeat superior*) is a common law tort doctrine that renders employers civilly liable in the courts, without regard to their fault, to third persons for harm negligently caused by their employees acting within the scope of their employment. Workers compensation is a statutory administrative system that renders employers liable, without regard to their fault, for injuries to their employees arising out of their employment. This third category of cases addresses a broadening of employers' liability to third parties for injuries caused by their employees that occur outside of the traditional employment relationship, and a broadening of the employer's liability for worker injuries that occur outside the workplace, claimed to be caused by employment related sleep deprivation or disorders. A typical case seeking to expand employer liability addresses the employer's duty to a person injured by an employee driving home from work after a lengthy period of work without sleep, and/or the employer's liability for harm to the worker in the above scenario.

A fourth category of cases, using the traditional doctrine of contributory negligence, as well as proximate cause, has sought to apply research on sleep deprivation and sleep disorder to address claimants' legal responsibility in civil liability tort claims in the courts for their role in accidents that have caused them injury. A typical case in this category addresses the impact of the claimant's own sleep deprivation and the claimant's legal responsibility for the cause of the accident for which the claimant seeks compensation.

Ordinarily, when judging common law tort liability for negligence, the relevant legal inquiry to assess the behavior of the parties asks whether they acted as society expects a reasonable person to act under the circumstances. The metric used to gauge this is referred to as an objective rather than a subjective standard of care.[2] It does not take into account the idiosyncrasies of the defendant to ask whether this defendant did the best he or she could under the circumstances, but rather whether this defendant did what society expects of the idealized mythical reasonable person. Although subject to criticism, this approach has endured based on the belief that we are entitled to expect a reasonable uniform level of care from our fellow citizens and that individualized judgments of ability would be legally impracticable.

One modification of this approach has been the law's attempt to distinguish the impact of physical and mental aberrations on the standard of care. In an effort to draw a line that is not well grounded in scientific research, the law posits a mental/physical disorder dichotomy and has been willing to tailor the standard of care to the circumstances of the defendant for physical but not mental disorders or disabilities. Thus, when a defendant suffers from a physical disability or disorder, the metric is whether the defendant behaved as a reasonable person with that physical disability or disorder. Where the defendant suffers from a mental disability or disorder, particularly where it has not manifested itself for the first time without warning in the context of the accident or occurrence giving rise to this claim, it is not legally of consequence to the case.[3] There is no insanity defense to civil liability claims for negligence: 'Unless the actor is a child, his insanity or other mental deficiency does not relieve the actor from liability for conduct which does not conform to the standard of a reasonable man under like circumstances.'[4] Courts, have, however, shown a greater willingness to factor mental disabilities or disorders into the standard of care for contributory negligence when assessing the plaintiff's conduct because the risk assessment is with regard to the risks posed to the plaintiff and not society at large.[4]

Surprisingly, the reported cases addressing civil liability tort claims or defenses arising out of sleep disorders do not discuss the mental/physical dichotomy and its consequences for the standard of care for defendants with sleep disorders. While one might consider praising the courts for ignoring this artificial dichotomy and focusing instead on the reasonableness of the defendant's conduct in light of his or her knowledge, the failure to raise and/or dismiss this dichotomy which courts persist in maintaining elsewhere suggests that they miss the issue here. Given the evolving research that explicates the etiology of many of these disorders, it is curious that this dichotomy has not been an issue in the reported cases. The consequences of categorizing sleep disorders such as sleep apnea as physical disorders within the legal construct would be to transform the inquiry for assessing the parties' behavior. In some regards this transformation would demand less of the actor by acknowledging the impact of sleep disorders on the actor's behavior, and in some regards this transformation would demand more of the actor by imputing to the actor the specialized knowledge that persons with sleep disorders should have of the risks that their disorders pose. Ultimately, whether this transformation would demand more or less of the parties is perhaps not as important as that it would focus the lawyers, judges, and jurors on these questions and demand that they be better informed about the impact of these disorders on behavior.

Before proceeding to a more detailed discussion of the four categories, it is worth noting for those who do not approach this topic from a legal background that the legal system often casts these issues in a very different fashion than sleep specialists might cast them. An interaction of substantive legal principles with the legal claims and defenses raised by the parties may make the existence of a sleep deprivation or disorder relevant in one context but not another because of the impact of a seemingly inconsequential fact. For example, when a person is injured allegedly because a heavy equipment machine operator fell asleep at the wheel, the condition of the operator would be relevant when the operator injures a passing pedestrian whose right to compensation would be governed by tort law in which the central liability inquiry is the operator's negligence, but not when the operator injures a fellow employee whose right to compensation is governed by workers compensation, in which the central liability inquiry is whether the injury arises out of the employment. Other changes in the legal posture of the case, such as a settlement between some but not all of the parties or the bankruptcy of a defendant, may transform a case from one that a sleep specialist sees as turning on a sleep deprivation or sleep disorder to one in which another issue unrelated to sleep deficit or sleep disorder is dispositive.

DEFENDANT PRIMARY LIABILITY FOR SLEEP DEPRIVATION OR DISORDER RELATED HARM

Motor vehicle accidents

Negligence, the usual legal basis for a civil claim against a driver who falls asleep while driving, requires proof of a breach of a duty proximately causing injury. A motor vehicle driver has a duty to drive safely so as to avoid foreseeable harm to others. When that duty is breached by unreasonable unsafe conduct, the driver may be held liable for the harm proximately caused. Thus, it might be assumed that whenever a driver falls asleep at the wheel and causes injury it will necessarily be regarded as negligent. However, with rare exception the courts have held that drivers who cause injury because they lose consciousness are not necessarily thereby regarded as negligent as a matter of law.[5] The question in each case is one of foreseeability, i.e. the driver's notice of the condition prior to loss of consciousness, and the reasonableness of the driver's conduct in light of those foreseeable risks.

Motor vehicle accidents caused by unforeseen and unexpected losses of consciousness are not generally regarded as negligent. Thus, for example, a driver who is rendered unconscious due to an unforeseeable heart attack, stroke, or drug reaction is not considered negligent.[6,7,8] Conversely, foreseen and expected losses of consciousness while driving are regarded as negligent. Driving while insufficiently alert because of sleepiness or drowsiness, like driving while under the use of drugs or alcohol, poses an unreasonable risk of harm to others. Drivers who are aware that they are becoming sleepy have a duty to avoid driving until properly rested and are liable for harm proximately caused if they fail to do so, just as a person with uncontrolled seizures has a legal responsibility to refrain from driving until the seizures have been effectively controlled.[9,10,11]

Courts generally assume 'that ordinarily sleep does not come upon one without warning of its approach'[12] and therefore permit the jury to infer negligence from the act of falling asleep while driving. However, the driver is permitted to rebut this inference with evidence of an absence of warning or premonition of the impending loss of consciousness.[13,14] Thus, the principal question in each case is whether the driver should have realized that he or she was likely to fall asleep considering such factors as how long the driver had been driving before falling asleep, warnings such as yawning or napping, use of drugs or alcohol, and strenuous or tiring activities prior to driving.[15]

This question is transformed by the use of motor vehicle guest statutes that exist in some jurisdictions, which provide that a driver is not civilly liable for injury to a non-paying, social guest for ordinary negligence while operating an automobile. In this context the question becomes whether falling asleep while driving constitutes something more than ordinary negligence, such as gross negligence or recklessness, not barred by guest statutes. Here again, the answer to this question turns on the degree of notice or warning to the driver of the risk of falling asleep while driving. Continuing to drive in the face of an awareness of sleepiness or fatigue constitutes gross negligence that is generally cognizable under guest statutes.[16] Evidence of a driver's falling asleep or losing consciousness, without more, however, does not meet the standard for proving recklessness or gross negligence.[17] 'A driver of an automobile is not guilty of wanton or willful misconduct in falling asleep while driving unless it appears that he continued to drive in reckless disregard of premonitory symptoms.'[18]

The degree of warning of sleep onset may vary according to the sleep disorder and/or sleep deprivation, time of day, or use of alcohol or drugs. The cases fail to articulate specific limits or requirements for drivers and instead treat these considerations as matters for the jury.

Other causes of injury

Because sleep disorders and sleep deprivation may affect the behavior of a host of actors across a variety of activities in society, they have been used to support a negligence claim in other contexts. For example, there has been considerable debate within the medical community in the past decade over the hours of work of physicians in residency training. In a case filed in New York,[19] the plaintiff alleged that substandard medical care resulting in the patient's death occurred because the defendant physicians were sleep weary. While there are few reported cases addressing this issue, its potential to shape negligence claims in an age where professionals are required to work harder and faster for less remuneration is vast. Notwithstanding the demands placed upon professionals, society is unlikely to embrace a model of professional competence that tolerates sleep weary judgment, or, as noted later, employment practices that enhance that risk.

HEALTH CARE PROVIDER LIABILITY TO THIRD PERSON FOR PATIENT INJURY

The cases included in this category involve an accident in which the patient of a health care professional causes injury to a third party, who sues the health care professional claiming that substandard care by the health care professional was a legally responsible cause of the harm. What distinguishes this category of cases from the traditional civil liability claim against a health care professional is that the claimant is not the patient. Thus, these cases pose as a controlling question whether and when health care professionals owe a duty to someone other than a patient they voluntarily agreed to treat or diagnose.

Until approximately the 1970s and decisions such as that of the California Supreme Court in *Tarasoff* v. *Board of Regents of the University of California*,[20] holding that mental health professionals owe a duty to protect a person they know or should know is endangered by their patient, the dominant legal thinking was that, except in very narrowly defined categories of cases, health care professionals only owed enforceable duties to those persons they voluntarily chose to take on as patients. Thus, in general, where a health care professional negligently diagnosed or treated a patient leading to a motor vehicle accident, common practice was to consider a claim by the patient against his or her health care professional or by the injured third person against the patient/driver. Although *Tarasoff* was only the decision of a state supreme court, it was emblematic of a conceptual legal transformation that was nationwide in scope recognizing that health care professionals owe duties to act competently not only to their patients but also to third persons foreseeably endangered by their actions.

The cases that fall within this category involve both allegations of a negligent failure to diagnose an illness that may affect loss of consciousness and a negligent failure to inform the patient about the risks of loss of consciousness or attentiveness that are consequences of treatment. Society expects health care professionals to diagnose sleep disorders and to inform patients of the risks these disorders pose, utilizing the skill and judgment of reasonable members of their profession. Typical of the cases involving claims of negligent failure to diagnose is *Freese* v. *Lemmon*,[21] in which the court held that a physician who treated a patient for a seizure may be liable to a third party injured when the patient suffered a subsequent seizure while driving, for a negligent failure to diagnose the cause of that first seizure properly or negligent failure to advise the patient not to drive until the cause of the seizure had been determined.

Typical of the failure to warn of the consequences related to treatment is *Calwell* v. *Hassan*,[22] in which Calwell and Hall alleged that they were seriously injured while riding their bicycles when an automobile driven by Rylant struck them after Rylant fell asleep while driving and crossed the center lane. Calwell and Hall also sued Dr Hassan, who had been treating Rylant 'for what she [Rylant] described as a problem of falling asleep during the day,' alleging a negligent failure to treat Rylant's disorder properly, monitor Rylant's medication, and warn her not to drive given her condition and the medication he had prescribed.

Dr Hassan, a neurologist who had treated Rylant for three years before the accident, determined that she had Disorder of Excessive Sleep (DOES). He prescribed Elavil, which it was subsequently necessary to increase from 25 mg per dose to 50 mg, 75 mg, and ultimately to 100 mg. When that dosage did not produce the desired effects and Rylant became depressed, Dr Hassan also prescribed Prozac. Rylant did not see Dr Hassan for one year until a month before the accident, when she complained of 'fighting sleep and dozing off at work.' Dr Hassan advised her to avoid sugar and caffeine and continued her prescriptions of Elavil and Prozac.

The trial court granted Dr Hassan's motion to dismiss, finding that he owed no 'duty to the driving public to advise Rylant not to drive her vehicle,' in part because a warning would only have told Rylant what she already knew, that she had a problem remaining awake during the daytime and that she should pull off the road when she became drowsy. The Court of Appeals reversed, relying in part on the Restatement (Second) of Torts s. 315, which provides that there is no duty to control the conduct of a third person to prevent that person from causing harm unless a special relationship exists between the third party and the actor which imposes on the actor a duty to control the third person's conduct, the same section of the Restatement relied upon by the California Supreme Court in *Tarasoff*. Finding the doctor–patient relationship between Rylant and Hassan a special relationship for purposes of s. 315, the Kansas Court of Appeals reasoned that if the facts alleged in the Complaint were proved at trial, Dr Hassan owed Rylant a duty to warn her not to drive that would subject Hassan to liability to members of the public proximately injured by the negligent failure to warn Rylant not to drive.

Courts do, however, require a proximal nexus between the negligent failure to diagnose and resulting injury. For example, in *Duvall* v. *Mangelsdorf*,[23] suit was brought following an automobile accident against a physician who, fifteen years earlier, had discontinued treating an epilepsy patient with an anticonvulsive drug and failed to warn him of the danger of driving without medication. When the driver (now ex-patient) suffered an epileptic attack while driving fifteen years later, causing serious injury to a third person, the injured third person brought suit against the physician for negligent failure to warn. The court dismissed, finding an absence of a proximal relationship given not only the temporal gap between the alleged failure to warn and the accident, but also the expectation that the patient would seek medical advice from another physician during this period.

Moreover, in the opinion of some courts, a sufficient proximal nexus requires that the failure to warn a patient arise out of the risks of treatment prescribed by the physician. For example, in *Flynn* v. *Houston Emergicare*[24] the court was unwilling to hold a physician liable to a third party injured by the patient's driving under the influence of cocaine for failure to advise the patient of the risks of driving under the influence of cocaine. The physician had treated the patient for chest pains and concluded that they were caused by cocaine use. However, the physician did not discuss the risks of driving under the influence of cocaine. The court reasoned that because the physician had not prescribed the cocaine, the physician's failure to warn the patient about the risks of driving under the influence of cocaine was too attenuated to permit the physician to be considered a legally responsible cause of the harm. It is not clear that the court would have reached the same result if the physician had been treating the patient for cocaine dependence.

This category of claims also involves treatment for other conditions that affect alertness and/or the ability to drive safely. For example, in *Gooden* v. *Tips*[25] the plaintiffs, who were injured in an accident with Goodpasture, joined as a defendant Dr Tips, who had been treating Goodpasture for various problems, including depression and drug abuse, alleging that Dr Tips had prescribed the drug Quaalude for Goodpasture without informing her not to drive while under the influence of the drug. Dr Tips persuaded the trial court to dismiss the lawsuit against him because there was no doctor–patient relationship between him and the plaintiff. However, the Court of Appeals reversed, holding that Dr Tips had a duty to warn his patient not to drive under the influence of the prescribed medication, the breach of which may serve as the basis for a claim by a third party consequentially injured by that failure.

A related duty of a health care professional to act to reduce the risk of harm to others on the road from patients' sleep disorders is the duty to report such disorders to public health officials, with the corresponding potential of civil liability to a person injured in the wake of a failure to make a report, and the conflicting duty to preserve patient confidences. Based on the assumption that confidentiality plays an important therapeutic role in the physician–patient relationship, physicians are ethically bound to keep the confidences of their patients.[26] Unauthorized disclosures of patient confidences may give rise to actions for professional discipline or breach of privacy tort claims. The duty of confidentiality has never been regarded as absolute, however, and in the face of a significant risk of harm, a physician may be required to disclose a confidential communication.

Responding to this tension between confidentiality and public safety concerns for physicians treating patients with sleep disorders, a number of states have enacted statutes that require physicians to breach confidentiality, investigate, and report to public health officers the name and address of any patient diagnosed with a 'disorder characterized by lapses of consciousness'[27] or 'a disorder characterized by momentary or prolonged lapses of consciousness or control that is or may become chronic.'[28] Other states have enacted an exception to the physician's duty of confidentiality or an immunity provision that permits but does not require a physician to report such patients.[29,30,31] Most states, however, provide no explicit legal guidance, leaving physicians facing the question of whether or when to report to choose between the risk of a lawsuit for breach of the duty of confidentiality[32] or a lawsuit for breach of a duty to protect third persons for failing to report.[33]

Common sense suggests that physicians utilize the gold standard of practice to identify patients with sleep disorders who pose a serious risk of motor vehicle accidents, prescribe appropriate treatment, and warn these patients of the risks their condition poses. When the disorder presents an immediate and substantial risk, the patient should be warned not to drive and if state law permits or requires reporting, a report should be made to the appropriate public health officer.[34]

Given that the effect of sleep disorders exist on a continuum requiring the exercise of discretion to decide where on that continuum the risks are significant enough to consider restricting driving privileges, it is important to define the triggering requirement for mandatory reporting statutes. Unfortunately, most of the statutes and regulations that require reporting offer little additional guidance. For example, the California regulations define disorders characterized by lapses of consciousness that are required to be reported as follows:

> Persons subject to lapses of consciousness or episodes of marked confusion resulting from metabolic or neurological disorders, including but not limited to, Alzheimer's disease and related disorders, uncontrolled diabetes mellitus, cardiovascular or cerebrovascular disease, alcoholism or excessive use of alcohol sufficient to bring about blackouts (retrograde amnesia for activities while drinking) shall be reportable.[35]

This regulation does not address, for example, whether sleep apnea or narcolepsy are included in the disorders that are required to be reported, the relevance of functional considerations in assessing impairment, or whether reporting should apply only to untreated or untreatable sleep disorders or to any sleep disorders.

The California Medical Association has advised its members addressing these issues to err in favor of reporting: 'Unless the physician can categorically state that the condition cannot possibly cause recurrent lapses, it should

be reported.'[36] The American Thoracic Society, addressing this question more generally, has advised a response that seeks to balance the importance of confidentiality with the risks posed by drivers with sleep disorders. It has recommended that in states where sleep apnea is required to be reported, physicians should report patients with excessive daytime sleepiness who have a history of motor vehicle accidents or equivalent historical concerns, and either a condition that is not amenable to short-term treatment (within two months) or patient unwillingness to accept treatment.[37] While the California Medical Association approach to reporting gives too little weight to the risks of discouraging patients from seeking treatment by concluding that reporting should occur in practically all cases, the American Thoracic Society approach to reporting gives too little weight to public safety by concluding that reporting should occur only after a history of motor vehicle accidents or equivalent concerns. While this historical evidence no doubt increases predictive accuracy, it comes at too great a potential cost. A more exacting accommodation would require reporting whenever a risk assessment indicates a serious risk of harm without waiting for accidents to occur.

Requiring physicians to report to public health officials disorders characterized by lapses of consciousness assumes that the risk to others on the road will be decreased by reporting because, where appropriate, driver's licenses will be denied or suspended for those who are unable to drive safely because of a sleep disorder, who will then cease driving. Yet, reporting statutes raise the risk that people will be dissuaded from seeking effective treatment for sleep disorders for fear that their driver's license will be denied or revoked and that they will continue to drive without obtaining treatment.[37] There is a paucity of empirical evidence of the risks and benefits of required reporting disorders characterized by lapses of consciousness. One study examining the impact of mandatory reporting on patients with epilepsy reports that 28% of those currently driving and 16% of those surveyed would not report a breakthrough seizure to their physician if their physician was required to report that information to the state department of motor vehicles.[38] While not dramatic, the results of this study suggest risks of blanket or automatic reporting that caution in favor of a more measured response tailored to a specific assessment of a risk of serious harm.

EMPLOYER LIABILITY FOR THE CONSEQUENCES OF EMPLOYEE SLEEP DEPRIVATION OR SLEEP DISORDERS

Common law liability for employees' harm to third parties

Employers are civilly liable, without regard to their fault, under the common law tort principle of vicarious liability, for the negligent acts of their employees committed within the scope and in the furtherance of their employment. Thus, for example, if an employee suffering from sleep deprivation negligently causes injury while driving his or her employer's vehicle while delivering a product for the employer, the employer is vicariously liable for the harm caused, without regard to the employer's care in selecting, training, or supervising the employee. The newest round of cases has, however, sought to expand the scope of employer liability for injuries that occur without the traditional scope of the employment relationship, alleging employer negligence in unreasonable employment policies that result in sleep deprivation, which increase the risk of harm to third persons.

For example, while employers are not ordinarily civilly liable under vicarious liability for their employees' negligence driving to and returning from work, a number of recent cases have sought to hold employers liable for negligence to third parties for accidents caused by unreasonable employment practices that involve excessive work causing sleep deprivation resulting in accidents returning from work. In *Faverty* v. *McDonald Restaurants of Oregon*,[39] a jury awarded damages against McDonald's Restaurant in favor of a man who was struck by an automobile driven home from work by a McDonald's employee who had worked a consecutive double shift from 3:30 p.m. to 8:21 a.m. the following day. The court of appeals affirmed imposition of liability upon the employer for negligence, reasoning that the accident was a foreseeable risk of working an employee unusually long shifts. Not only had the employer violated its own policies prohibiting employees from working two consecutive shifts, but the employee had shown visible signs of fatigue on the shift that preceded the accident, and the employer was aware that two other employees had recently been involved in accidents under similar circumstances.

Similarly, in *Idilbi* v. *Domino's Pizza*,[40] defendant Domino's Pizza was sued for the actions of an employee returning home from work who struck and killed a California Highway Patrol Officer. The plaintiff claimed that the accident was caused by excessive fatigue that resulted from supervisory and compensation practices leading to excessive hours of work and employee fatigue.

Workers compensation

Workers compensation programs are statutory systems that administratively provide compensation for injuries that arise out of work related injury, in exchange for legislative abrogation of the workers' right to bring common tort claims. Thus, injuries that occur from sleep deprivation and sleep disorders within the workplace are ordinarily subsumed by the workers compensation system. Reported cases discussing these claims are unlikely as the employer is responsible to provide compensation for injuries arising out of the employment without regard to fault.

Rather, the role of sleep deprivation and sleep disorders in workers compensation cases has been to test the limits of the scope of workplace injuries. These cases seek workers compensation for sleep deprivation and sleep disorder related harm manifested outside the workplace that the claimant alleges are caused by acts that occurred within the workplace. Typical of this sort of workers compensation claim is *Henley* v *Roadway Express*,[41] in which the claimant sought workers compensation benefits for sleep deprivation and related serious emotional problems after being required to work during the night and sleep during the day. The trial court concluded that:

> In this case, it appears that the plaintiff was required to work on the third shift, with all the problems that working on the third shift carries with regard to sleeping and resting during daylight hours. The plaintiff was unable, for one reason or another, to sleep or rest during daylight hours, which resulted in him being physically exhausted and led to the development of a severe depression and a subsequent nervous breakdown and mental impairments resulting therefrom. In the court's opinion, the nervous breakdown was caused by working on the third shift, which was a condition of employment under which he worked, and therefore arose out of his employment and he is entitled to worker's compensation benefits for the disabilities resulting therefrom.[42]

The state Supreme Court reversed, disagreeing that this was an employment related disability that arose out of the course of employment. It was unwilling to find that the impact of the shift or hours on sleep at home that an employer dictates was a 'hazard incident to the employment relationship.'[43] This tension at the boundaries of workers compensation is likely to increase as employers require greater efficiencies to survive in the marketplace, employees face a shrinking job market, and sleep research further explicates the relationship between sleep deprivation or disorders and other aspects of behavior. The crucial question is whether the costs of these harms should be borne by the products and services to which these workers contribute, or are so unrelated that they should be borne by society more generally.

Sleep deprivation and sleep disorders have also been used in attempts to expand worker claims for work related injuries beyond the limits imposed by workers compensation. Workers compensation programs do not address worker claims for harm caused by the actions of those who do not stand in the role of employers. Sleep deprivation and sleep disorders have been used to raise claims against others for worker injuries. As noted above, in general, commuting to and from employment in the employee's private vehicle is not regarded as an activity occurring within the course of employment. Therefore, employee injuries during commuting are not generally compensable under workers compensation plans. *D.T.* v. *J.H. Kelly Construction Co.*[44] is an example of an attempt to expand employee claims for injuries occurring during commuting as the result of workplace sleep deprivation. The plaintiff was injured in an automobile accident that occurred while driving home after working a 39-hour shift demanded by the general contractor for whom his employer was a subcontractor. The plaintiff sought, among other claims, to hold the general contractor liable under common law tort principles for creating an unreasonable risk of harm that their demanding schedule posed to the plaintiff. Although the case settled before trial and therefore does not resolve whether the courts would find this attempt to expand the plaintiff's remedies legally cognizable, it is an example of the contemporary use of sleep deprivation and sleep disorders to change the contours of liability for injuries arising out of the employment relationship.

CONTRIBUTORY NEGLIGENCE RELATED TO SLEEP DISORDER OR DEPRIVATION

As noted above, negligence is the breach of a duty that proximately causes injury to another. Either under the label of causation (which requires that the defendant's conduct play a significant role in the harm) or contributory negligence (which bars recovery when the plaintiff's negligence contributed to his or her harm) or comparative negligence (which reduces the plaintiff's recovery when the plaintiff's negligence contributed to his or her harm), a defendant may argue that it was the plaintiff's conduct that was the legally responsible cause of his or her injuries. These concepts are well recognized in tort law for limiting the tort liability of defendants, and sleep deprivation and disorders have long supplied support for such arguments. For example, in a turn of the century case, *St. Louis Southwestern Railway Co. v. Shiflet*,[45] Shiflet's parent sued the railroad when he was run over and killed by one of their trains at a location commonly used by pedestrians. The railroad raised and the the court charged the jury to consider as an issue of contributory negligence whether Shiflet fell asleep on the tracks.

A contemporary application of this concept is *Silva v. Freuhauf Trailers*,[46] a products liability claim against the manufacturer of a tractor–trailer rig for failing to equip it with adequate lights or reflective tape that allegedly caused an accident resulting in the death of nine people who were riding in a vehicle that collided with the tractor–trailer. The defendant successfully persuaded the jury that the driver of the vehicle with the people who were killed, who had had less than eight hours sleep in the preceding three days because of a lengthy transcontinental drive to a family funeral, suffered from sleep deprivation and likely fell asleep while driving, thereby causing the accident.

And, in *Walker v. State*,[47] a wrongful death action against the state for negligence in the design, construction, and maintenance of the highway on which the decedent was killed when his vehicle left the road and struck a tree in a one-car accident, the defendant introduced expert testimony that the decedent's vehicle left the road because he fell asleep while driving. The jury found that the defendant had been negligent but that the decedent was 70% responsible for the accident. The Supreme Court of Washington rejected the plaintiff's challenge to the foundation for the expert's testimony, finding that reliance on scientific studies, a review of the statement of the driver in the car following the decedent, the report of the investigating officer, the toxicology report, a videotape and photographs of the highway supplied an adequate foundation for the expert's opinion. The appropriate qualifications for an expert on this issue was not raised in the appeal.

CONCLUSION

Tort liability seeks to reduce harm by deterring unreasonably unsafe behavior and compensating those injured by such behavior.[48] While there is good reason to question how effectively tort law shapes behavior,[49] it seems particularly important for tort law to try to address the significant risks posed by persons with sleep deprivation and sleep disorders. The deterrent impact of tort law on legally unsophisticated actors such as automobile drivers may be minimal, particularly in light of automobile liability insurance and other incentives to drive safely, including self-preservation. However, the impact of tort law on the behavior of legally sophisticated actors such as trucking companies and large employers, who are repeat players in tort law and are increasingly self-insured or carry large deductibles, holds greater promise for positive change. The challenge is to bring the evolving research and knowledge about sleep deprivation and sleep disorders to bear in significant legal decisions that address issues of risk and responsibility.

ACKNOWLEDGMENT

The author gratefully acknowledges a grant from the M.D. Anderson Foundation that supported this research.

REFERENCES

1. Shapiro, C.M., Heslegrave, R., Beyers, J. and Picard, L. (1997) *Working the Shift.* Toronto, Joli Joco Publications.
2. Seavey, W.A. (1927). Negligence: objective or subjective? *Harvard Law Review* **41**:1–28.
3. *Breunig* v. *American Family Ins.*, 173 N.W. 2d 619 (Wis. 1970).
4. Restatement (Second) of Torts s. 283(B); 464 (1965).

5. *Theisen* v. *Milwaukee Automobile Mutual Insurance Co.*, 118 N.W. 2d 140 (Wis. 1962).
6. *Cohen* v. *Petty*, 65 F. 2d 820 (D.C. Cir. 1933).
7. *Goodrich* v. *Blair*, 646 P. 2d 890 (Ariz. App. 1982).
8. *Slattery* v. *Haley*, 52 O.L.R. 95 (1923).
9. *Knight* v. *Miller*, 503 So. 2d 120 (La. App. 5th Cir. 1987).
10. *Soule* v. *Grimshaw*, 253 N.W. 237 (Mich. 1934).
11. *Storjohn* v. *Fay*, 519 N.W. 2d 521 (Neb. 1994).
12. *Bushnell* v. *Bushnell*, 131 A. 432 (Conn. 1925).
13. *Bernosky* v. *Greff*, 28 A. 2d 35 (Pa. 1944).
14. *Edwards* v. *Washkuhn*, 119 P. 2d 905 (Wash. 1941).
15. Physical Defect, Illness, Drowsiness, or Falling Asleep of Motor Vehicle Operator as Affecting Liability for Injury, 28 ALR 2d 12, at 3.
16. *Richards* v. *Parks*, 93 S.W. 2d 639 (Tenn. Ct. App. 1935).
17. *La Vigne* v. *La Vigne*, 158 P. 2d 557 (Or. 1945).
18. *Lankford* v. *Mong*, 214 So. 2d 301 (Ala. 1968).
19. *Zion* v. *New York City Hospital*, 183 A. 2d 386 (N.Y. App. Div. 1992).
20. *Tarasoff* v. *Board of Regents of the University of California*, 551 P. 2d 334 (Cal. 1976).
21. *Freese* v. *Lemmon*, 210 N.W. 2d 576 (Iowa 1973).
22. *Calwell* v. *Hassan*, 1995 WL 739852 (Kan. App.).
23. *David* v. *Mangelsdorf*, 673 P. 2d 951 (Ariz. Ct. App. 1983).
24. *Flynn* v. *Houston Emergicare*, 869 S.W. 2d 403 (Tex. App. – Houston [1st Dist.] 1993, writ. denied).
25. *Gooden* v. *Tips*, 651 S.W. 2d 364 (Tex. App. – Tyler [12th Dist.] 1983).
26. Medical Association (1981). The principles of medical ethics. *JAMA* 246:2187–88.
27. Cal. Code. Regs. Tit. 17 s. 2572(2) (1995).
28. Or. Rev. Stat. s. 807.710 (1994).
29. Me. Rev. Stat. Ann. Tit. 29, s. 1258(b) (1995).
30. Md. Transp. Code Ann. s. 16–119 (1995). (Note that while Maryland permits the physician to report it states in somewhat confusing language that in the absence of written patient consent, the report may not be made from information derived from a relationship which the law regards as confidential or privileged.)
31. 1995 Tex. Gen Laws 165 s. 12.096.
32. *Doe* v. *Roe*, 93 Misc. 2d 201, 400 NYS 2d 668 (1977).
33. *Lopez* v. *Hudgeons*, 115 Cal. App. 3d 673 (1981).
34. Findley, L.J. and Bonnie, R.J. (1988). Sleep apnea and auto crashes: what is the doctor to do? *Chest* **94**:225–226.
35. Cal. Code Regs. Tit. 17 s. 2572(2) (1995).
36. California Medical Association Legal Counsel, *Lapses of Consciousness*, San Francisco, California Medical Association; 1994. 17 Cal. Code Reg. s. 2572.
37. American Thoracic Society (Strohl, K.P., Bonnie, R.J., Findley, L., Fletcher, E.C., Getsy, J., Kryger, M.H., Millman, R., Novak, R., Roth, T., Walsleben, J. and Williams, A.) (1994). Sleep apnea, sleepiness, and driving risk. *Am. J. Respir. Crit. Care Med.* **150**:1463–1473.
38. Salinsky, M.C., Wegner, K. and Sinnema, F. (1992). Epilepsy, driving laws, and patient disclosures to physicians. *Epilepsia* 33:469–417.
39. *Faverty* v. *McDonald Restaurants of Oregon*, 892 P. 2d 703 (Or. Ct. App. 1195).
40. *Idilbi* v. *Domino's Pizza* [Los Angeles County, California Superior Court, 1991, Case No. EAC 78877].
41. *Henley* v. *Roadway Express*, 699 S.W. 2d 150 (Tenn. 1985).
42. At pages 153–154.
43. At page 155.

44. *D.T.* v. *J.H. Kelly Construction Co.* (No. 92-2-00983-6 Lewis City, Wash., Super. Ct.) (plaintiff's name withheld at the request of the party).
45. *St. Louis Southwestern Railway Co.* v. *Shiftlet*, 83 S.W. 677 (Tex. 1904).
46. *Silva* v. *Freuhauf Trailers* (1990 – 7752 Star Cty. Dist. Ct., Texas).
47. *Walker* v. *State* (848 P. 2d 721 (Wash. 1993).
48. Shuman, D.W. (1993). Making the world a better place through tort law? Through the therapeutic looking glass. *New York Law School Journal of Human Rights* **X**:739–758.
49. Shuman, D.W. (1993). The psychology of deterrence in tort law. *University of Kansas Law Review* **42**:115–168.

6

Regulations for Driving for Patients with Sleep Disorders

*A.I. Pack, *S.J. Pakola and ‡L.J. Findley

*University of Pennsylvania Medical Center and ‡Aspen Medical Center

INTRODUCTION

One of the most important legal issues that patients with sleep disorders face is the issue of driving privileges. It is an issue that is causing patients concern. They are frightened that one response to current public awareness campaigns to inform the public about the dangers of drowsy driving, e.g. the 'Drive Alert . . . Arrive Alive' campaign of the National Sleep Foundation in the United States, will be severe limitations on their ability to drive. For some patients such actions could threaten their livelihood.

These concerns are not unwarranted. There is clearly an increasing move in several countries and in individual states in the United States to have such regulations in place. Currently, however, we do not know the effect of such regulations. We do not know whether the regulations are being followed in these areas by physicians who treat patients with sleep disorders. We also do not know whether patients themselves are aware of them and hence do not seek treatment, or at least keep their condition unknown to others. We also do not know whether the regulations are having a positive impact in reducing the adverse outcome, i.e. vehicular crashes due to the driver falling asleep as a result of a sleep disorder. It would seem essential that, as in other interventions, such regulations are put in place with clear plans to evaluate how they operate in practice and their efficacy.

There are clearly societal issues in addition to the rights of individual

Forensic Aspects of Sleep. Edited by C.M. Shapiro and A. McCall Smith.
© 1997 John Wiley & Sons Ltd.

patients with sleep disorders since the public at large needs to be protected from unreasonable risk. For example, would anybody want to be driving down the highway with a truck filled with a highly flammable material driven by a driver with severe sleep apnea and a mean sleep latency of less than 1.0 minute?

Thus the issue here is how we move to adopt a balanced approach. Such an approach should be based on firm scientific evidence and should be subject to scientific evaluation. In this chapter we provide information to inform this debate. We review data as to whether there is an increased crash risk in patients with sleep disorders, and the effects of treatment on this risk. We also provide the regulations that are currently used in many countries. The latter material is taken from an article that was recently published in *Sleep*.[1]

There are several dimensions to this issue. First, we must differentiate between the risk and potential regulations for patients with untreated sleep disorders from those with successfully treated disorders. Success itself needs to be defined. Moreover, one needs to differentiate what is appropriate for patients who simply drive their cars from those who are engaged in the commercial transportation industry. We first review data on driving performance and crash risk.

DO SLEEP DISORDERS RESULT IN IMPAIRMENT IN DRIVING PERFORMANCE?

This question has been addressed to some extent for patients with obstructive sleep apnea and to a lesser extent for patients with narcolepsy. These studies have been in relatively small numbers of subjects with a variety of methodologies. Studies have shown that patients with sleep apnea perform more poorly on driving simulators than do control subjects.[2,3] In the study of Haraldsson et al.,[3] 8 of 15 patients with habitual sleepiness and heavy snoring had at least one episode of driving off the road during a 60–90 minute simulated drive, while only 1 of 10 control subjects did so. In total, the 15 sleep apnea patients drove off the road a total of 101 times while the controls had a total of only 2 such off-road episodes.

Studies have also been done with the divided attention tracking task that is widely used in the investigation of alcohol impaired driving. Such studies show that patients with sleep apnea can perform as poorly as subjects who are over the legal limit for alcohol.[4] There is considerable individual variability in the effect of sleep apnea on driving performance. There are only weak correlations between the degree of sleep apnea as measured by the respiratory disturbance index and driving impairment. Moreover, the degree of sleepiness as measured by the multiple sleep latency test is also weakly correlated with driving impairment.[4]

This individual variation in level of driving impairment that seems not to be predictable from commonly used clinical metrics of disease, such as the respiratory disturbance index, has obvious implications for policy makers. It has led to efforts to develop simpler methods to assess driving impairment. One such method is called Steer Clear.[2] It is essentially a simple reaction time task implemented on a personal computer rather than being a driving simulator. The task is to avoid obstacles that appear at random times on the computer screen. Studies have shown that patients with untreated sleep apnea hit a larger number of obstacles.[2] Likewise, there are data for narcolepsy, again in small numbers of subjects (eight patients, eight controls), that show that patients with narcolepsy perform worse than controls.[5]

These studies show, therefore, the not unexpected result, i.e. that patients with sleep disorders have impairment in driving skills. They document that the impairment can be severe and of a similar magnitude to that in drunk drivers. They also show that there is considerable variation in the level of impairment, and there is no simple way to predict the degree of impairment from commonly used clinical measures of abnormality. Clearly, further studies in this area are needed so that we can reliably identify the sleep disorders patients who are at risk. It appears that while on average such patients have impairment in driving performance, this may not be the case in an individual patient.

DO PATIENTS WITH SLEEP DISORDERS HAVE AN INCREASED RISK OF VEHICULAR CRASHES?

Again, there are studies that document an increased crash risk in patients with sleep disorders. The studies are in small numbers of patients and, in general, retrospective. (Prospective data will, however, be available soon, at least for obstructive sleep apnea, from the large Wisconsin Sleep Cohort study.) One of the most common sleep disorders is insomnia. Chronic insomnia is estimated to affect about 9% of the population.[6] By self-report in a Gallup survey, individuals with chronic insomnia reported 2.5 times as many fatigue-related auto crashes as normal sleepers.[6]

Likewise, for narcolepsy there are self-report data that such patients have difficulty driving before being effectively treated. Joseph A. Piscopo, a narcolepsy patient, reports that he had nine auto accidents between the ages of 16 and 20, all from falling asleep while driving.[7] Various studies reveal that 40%,[8] 73%,[9] and 67%[10] of patients with narcolepsy report having fallen asleep while driving. While this is high, one needs to remember that 25% of the general population also report having fallen asleep while driving.[11] In one study it was reported that 37 of 180 patients with narcolepsy had at least one vehicular crash. This is significantly greater than an age- and sex-matched control group.[10] Thus, not surprisingly, patients with narcolepsy do seem to have an increased crash risk. But the data are sparse. We know little about individual variation in risk and how to identify those patients most at risk.

There are more data about obstructive sleep apnea. One questionnaire study based on self-report[12] found that 13% of patients with sleep apnea reported at least one crash due to falling asleep but this was not significantly greater than a control group. Other studies[13,14,15] have, however, found a significantly higher crash rate in sleep apnea patients. Findley et al.[14] compared, for example, the state driving records for the previous five years for 29 patients with sleep apnea and 35 controls. They found that patients with apnea had a seven-fold greater crash rate than controls and almost three times the rate of all drivers in the state (Virginia). There is some evidence that the crash risk is related to the severity of disease. Findley et al.[15] investigated the crash records of patients with mild, moderate and severe sleep apnea. They found that the increased crash rate was only significant in those with the most severe disease (a respiratory disturbance of greater than 50 events per hour). But the number of patients in these groups are small: mild (16 patients), moderate (17 patients), severe (13 patients).

Sleep apnea may also be an issue for the commercial driver. There is suggestive evidence that obstructive sleep apnea is common in this group,[16] although the sampling scheme employed is not rigorous from an epidemiological viewpoint. Commercial drivers with sleep apnea had twice the crash rate in this study, a result reported widely in the press in the United States.[16] But the statement is misleading since there was no significant difference in crash rates in commercial drivers with sleep apnea as compared to those without apnea ($p = 0.14$).[16] Thus, currently there are no definitive data that commercial drivers with sleep apnea have an increased crash risk. It would seem likely that this is the case but clearly more studies are urgently needed.

DOES TREATMENT OF SLEEP DISORDERS IMPROVE DRIVING PERFORMANCE?

There are some data, in very small numbers of subjects, that treatment of sleep disorders improves driving performance. This has been shown for patients with narcolepsy using the Steer Clear test described above. They performed significantly better when taking amphetamine than while on placebo.[5] Likewise, treatment of sleep apnea with nasal CPAP also improves performance on Steer Clear,[2] although very few patients were included in this study ($n = 6$). Surgical treatment of sleep apnea with uvulopalatopharyngoplasty has also been shown to improve driving performance.[17] Thus, there are some data that treatment of sleep disorders improves driving 'performance' although the data are scant and there is no evidence that performance on simple tasks such as Steer Clear are related to crash risk in real-life situations.

DOES TREATMENT OF SLEEP DISORDERS REDUCE CRASH RATES?

There are almost no data that treatment of sleep disorders reduces crash rates. There are some self-report data that the majority of patients with narcolepsy after treatment no longer have sleepiness while driving.[8] For sleep apnea there are also studies based on interviews which indicate that successful treatment reduces the number of crashes. Suratt and Findley[18] reported that 41% of 22 patients reported at least one crash during the two years before diagnosis but only 5% had a crash during the two years after inception of treatment. Minemura *et al.*[19] also reported a reduction in self-reported crashes following treatment. But these studies have not been carried out in a rigorous fashion with objective documentation of crash risk. Thus, in this area, as in other aspects of sleep disorders, there is a lack of outcomes data. Such outcomes data are urgently needed.

There are data within each of the areas of interest. The data are, however, sparse.

CURRENT REGULATIONS ABOUT DRIVING AND SLEEP DISORDERS

Although, as noted above, there are limited data, there are increasing regulations in this area. The regulations used in the different states in the United States and in different countries vary considerably. Many of the stipulations seem arbitrary and are not based on firm scientific evidence.

In March 1994, we conducted a survey of all regulations that existed at that time.[1] We contacted relevant authorities in all states of the United States, individual provinces in Canada and authorities in Australia, the Netherlands, Sweden and the United Kingdom.

Regulations in the United States

In the United States we found that there are no specific regulations at a federal level. The federal regulations regarding commercial motor carrier safety for interstate commerce are delineated in the Federal Motor Carrier Safety Regulations (49 CFR 390–399).[20] Section 391.41 delineates the specific disorders or illnesses that would disqualify a person from driving a motor vehicle. No sleep disorder, including sleep apnea or narcolepsy, is contained within this part or any other part of the Federal Motor Carrier Safety Regulations. Part 391.41(b) does contain the following: 'A person is physically qualified to drive a motor vehicle if that person . . . (5) Has no medical history or clinical diagnosis of a respiratory dysfunction likely to interfere

Table 1. Comparison of the seven US states with regulations or guidelines for all motor vehicle operators dealing with sleep apnea and/or narcolepsy, with regard to length without symptoms before resumption of driving (time controlled) and recommended frequency of medical review (review interval)

State	Sleep apnea	Narcolepsy	Time controlled	Review interval
California	Yes	Yes	Not mentioned	Not mentioned
Maine	Yes (proposed)	No	Not mentioned	12 months
Maryland	No	Yes	12 months*	Not mentioned
North Carolina	No	Yes	12 months[†]	Not mentioned
Oregon	No	Yes	Not mentioned	6 months
Texas	Yes	Yes	6 months[‡]	12 months
Utah	No	Yes	12 months	Not mentioned

* 'for any class of license . . .'; [†] 'for personal vehicles . . .' [‡] 'only private operator in class C if without symptoms for 6 months (review annually) . . .'. Either sleep apnea or narcolepsy precludes operation of cargo and passenger transport vehicles in classes A, B, and C.

with his ability to control and drive a motor vehicle safely; . . . (8) Has no established medical history or clinical diagnosis of epilepsy or any other condition which is likely to cause loss of consciousness or any loss of ability to control a motor vehicle; . . . (9) Has no mental, nervous, organic, or functional disease or psychiatric disorder likely to interfere with his ability to drive a motor vehicle safely.' It might be argued that obstructive sleep apnea could be covered under (5) since it involves recurrent obstruction of the airway with decrements in oxygen saturation; under (8) since it can lead to microsleeps and falling asleep at the wheel; or under (9) since there is evidence of an increased risk of driving accidents. Likewise, narcolepsy could be considered under (8) and (9).

Commercial vehicle licensing, safety or enforcement authorities from 50 states were also asked about any regulations or guidelines developed specifically for commercial vehicle operation that dealt with medical qualifications. None of the authorities contacted was aware of any documents developed specifically for commercial vehicle operation that specifically mentioned any sleep disorder. However, the commercial regulations in New Hampshire do indicate that it is prohibited to drive while sleepy. No indication is given as to how sleepiness is to be defined or evaluated.

There are, however, Departments of Motor Vehicles in some states that do have regulations or guidelines that specifically mention sleep apnea and/or narcolepsy as conditions that can prohibit driving (see Tables 1 and 2). There is, as can be seen, considerable variation in the regulations even in the few states that currently have regulations.

First, some states have regulations for both narcolepsy and sleep apnea

Table 2. Summary of guidelines from different states in the United States that have guidelines relating to sleep apnea or narcolepsy.

State	Guideline
California	**Narcolepsy** and Cataplexy (a. **Sleep Apnea**, b. Other sleep disorders) *Range of Actions:* No Action – stable and controlled so that it does not affect driving; Probation Type II – Control only recently achieved for three months with potential for instability; Probation III – Control for ≥ six months with potential for instability due to contributing factors; Suspension – Uncontrolled pathological sleep which could affect ability to safely operate vehicle; Revocation – Condition not likely to ever be controlled.
Maine	**Sleep Apnea**: Fully recovered (post effective treatment and without significant apneas on PSG*) – No review needed; Active Impairment – Minimal to moderate ([†]MSLT <15 minutes and/or presence of apneas) – 1-year review; Severe (unresponsive or non-compliant to therapy) – No driving; Condition under investigation – No driving.
Maryland	**Narcolepsy**. An individual under treatment may not be considered for any class of license until he has been symptom free for at least 1 year without side effects from medication.
North Carolina	**Narcolepsy**: Patients suspected of suffering from **narcolepsy** should be given special studies to rule out **sleep apnea** . . . If symptoms can be controlled through medication, patients may be allowed to drive their personal vehicles after one year of being symptom free.
Oregon	**Narcolepsy**: Should not be permitted to drive until the underlying condition has been resolved or sufficiently stabilized, as recommended by a physician. Recertification should be done every 6 months for 2 years. If no LOC[‡], then no more surveillance required.
Texas	History of **narcolepsy**, excess daytime sleeping or **sleep apnea** precludes operation of cargo and passenger transport vehicles in classes A, B and C. Private vehicle operator licensing in class C is dependent upon absence of episodes for a 6 month observation period prior to medical review and physician recommendation. Applicants should be reviewed annually.
Utah	**Narcolepsy**: Commercial intrastate – must be episode free for 1 year, with medical review every 1–2 years. Private Vehicle – episode free 1 year, require medical review every year; episode free 3–6 months, require review every 6 months, with speed, area and time of day limitations for 5, 4, and 3 month episode free intervals, respectively; episodes uncontrolled – no driving.

* PSG, Polysomnogram; [†] MSLT, multiple sleep latency test; [‡] LOC, loss of consciousness.

(California and Texas), others for only narcolepsy (Maryland, North Carolina, Oregon and Utah), while others for only sleep apnea (Maine).

Some states (North Carolina, Texas, and Utah) have recommendations that are different, or seem to be different, for different classes of license holder. In Texas, either narcolepsy or sleep apnea precludes operation of cargo or passenger vehicles. The North Carolina guidelines state that for patients with narcolepsy a one-year symptom-free period is recommended before licensure 'to drive their personal vehicles.' In Utah commercial drivers with narcolepsy must be episode-free for one year (medical review every 1–2 years) while private vehicle operators must be without symptoms for more than three months.

The different regulations also vary with respect to how quickly a driver with a sleep disorder, who is stopped from driving, can resume driving once he or she is successfully treated. This seems to vary from three to twelve months. Moreover, the interval that the driver needs to be reviewed medically for fitness to drive also varies considerably (see Tables 1 and 2).

Regulations in Canada

These differences in regulations within the states of the United States also are found in the regulations in different countries. In Canada there are guidelines in the Canadian Medical Association's (CMA) 'Physician's Guide to Driver Examination' (last published in 1991). It contains guidelines for both sleep apnea and narcolepsy. It states that:

> patients with severe sleep apnea or other syndromes that chronically interfere with sleep are at increased risk of an accident or injury while driving because of daytime sleepiness. Sleep apnea is often accompanied by obesity, a condition affecting many professional drivers. Patients with a history of pathologic daytime sleepiness should be referred to a consultant for further assessment. If their condition is severe enough to impair driving ability, they should not be allowed to drive any class of motor vehicle until the condition has been treated and controlled.
>
> Patients who suffer attacks of narcolepsy also should not be allowed to drive any type of motor vehicle. If they respond favorably to treatment and experience no side effects from the medication, they may drive Class 5 or 6 vehicles after 3 months. However, they should not be allowed to hold a Class 1, 2, or 3 license (vehicles of any size) or Class 4 license (passenger vehicles) (Part 8.3).*

---

*Summary of Canadian driver license classification: Class 6 – motorcycle or bicycle; Class 5 – Class 6 plus any two-axle vehicle; Class 4 – Class 5 plus buses (25 person maximum), taxis, ambulances; Class 3 – Class 5 plus three- or more axle vehicles and combinations of vehicles; Class 2 – Class 4 and 5, without a limit on number of passengers; Class 1 – any motor vehicle or combination of vehicles except motorcycles.

The National Safety Code for Motor Carriers (NSC),[21] last updated in September 1993, adopted these guidelines from the CMA. The NSC stipulated three months as the time of control necessary for people with narcolepsy before they may be eligible to operate a private vehicle. For sleep apnea, the document states '[sufferers] may operate any class of vehicle after the condition has been adequately treated and controlled.'

Nine of the twelve provinces in Canada confirmed use of the CMA and/or NSC guidelines. There are some minor differences in some provinces. For example, in Manitoba their regulations contain the same regulations as the NSC with respect to narcolepsy. However, the Manitoba act does not list sleep apnea as a disqualifying condition for any class of license.

Regulations in Other Countries

United Kingdom

In the United Kingdom there are different regulations for narcolepsy and obstructive sleep apnea.

Under 'neurological disorders' is listed the following heading and description: '*Narcolepsy/Cataplexy* and Other Sleep Disorders, causing excessive wake time somnolence.' For this category of conditions, the manual recommends 'permanent refusal or revocation' of Group 2 (commercial) entitlement. For Group 1 (private) entitlement, driving will only be permitted when 'satisfactory control of symptoms achieved, then 1/2/3/year license with regular medical review.'

Under 'respiratory disorders' is listed the following heading and description: '*Sleep Apnoea Syndrome (Obstructive Sleep Apnoea)* causing excessive awake time somnolence.' For this condition and the issue of Group 2 (commercial) entitlement, the manual states the following: 'Recommendation to cease driving. When it is confirmed by specialist assessment that condition adequately controlled for at least 12 months, driving may be resumed subject to annual review.' For this condition and the issue of Group 1 (private) entitlement, driving is permitted when satisfactory control of symptoms is achieved (no length of control or required periodic review are stated).

The Netherlands

Regulations from the Netherlands were obtained from the chief physician employed by the Transport Division of the Ministry of Transport. From this document are quoted the following excerpts:

Chapt. VI 2.2
    narcolepsy and cataplexy:
    in general unfit for driving for all categories of the driving license.

Chapt. VII 6.1
states of narrowing of the mind (dullness or sleepiness), caused by medi-
cines/drugs or not, indicate a temporary unfitness to participate in motorized
traffic.
If these states occur recurrently or psychoreactively is to be considered a
restriction in the period of validity of the driving license, or a permanent unfitness to drive.

There is no mention elsewhere in this regulation of other sleep disorders,
including sleep apnea.

Sweden

Currently Sweden's regulations for medical qualifications of commercial
vehicle drivers does not include sleep disorders. However, the medical
requirements were being updated. This updated version, according to the
chief physician developing these regulations, does contain a segment prohibiting persons with untreated sleep apnea from driving commercial vehicles. It is also being proposed that persons without apneic episodes but with
heavy snoring and daytime sleepiness who are not successfully treated be
prohibited from driving commercial vehicles.

Australia

A copy of the Federal Office of Road Safety's 'National Guidelines for
Medical Practitioners in Determining Fitness to Drive a Motor Vehicle' was
obtained. It contains the following section:

7.3 NARCOLEPSY
Applicants who are subject to attacks of narcolepsy cannot drive any type of
motor vehicle safely. If they respond favourably to treatment and have no
periods of uncontrolled sleepiness for a period of three (3) months and are experiencing no side effects from their medication, they may be able to drive a private
motor vehicle safely, but some neurologists advise total prohibition.
Applicants with narcolepsy, whether adequately treated or not, cannot drive a
passenger transport or heavy commercial vehicle safely because the risk of a crash
is too great to accept should they run out of or neglect to take their medication.

In its current form, this document does not discuss sleep apnea.
In addition, there is in Australia a comprehensive document entitled
'Medical Examinations of Commercial Vehicle Drivers.' It mentions both
sleep apnea and narcolepsy. For sleep apnea it states that criteria for commercial driving are *not* met in the following circumstances:

• If the person has established sleep apnea until treatment is effective.
Consideration should be given to how long-distance drivers will comply with
treatment such as CPAP.

A conditional license (with periodic review) should be recommended:
- If the person has a combination of daytime sleepiness and a BMI in excess of 30 and a reddened, oedematous narrow oropharynx; and
- if the person has a history of snoring and witnessed apneas, unless sleep apnea can be reasonably excluded. The certifying practitioner should arrange investigation.

For narcolepsy, it simply states that criteria for commercial driving are *not* met if narcolepsy is confirmed.

Thus, in Australia, the Netherlands, the United Kingdom and Texas patients diagnosed with narcolepsy cannot engage in commercial driving.

ISSUES TO BE RESOLVED

This description of different regulations indicates that there is currently no common opinion of what needs to be done in this area. This is hardly surprising since, as pointed out earlier, there are very limited data. In particular, the data are extremely limited as to whether patients with sleep disorders, once treated, have any increased risk of crashes.

The first important issue to be resolved is whether specific regulations are needed in this area. There is a concern that the issue is a relatively complex one that is not amenable to simple regulations. This was considered in a recent, excellent and thoughtful, official statement of the American Thoracic Society on sleep apnea, sleepiness and driving risk.[22] This report argues against categorical reporting. It states that:

> The problem with this strategy is that it would affect many patients who do not pose a risk and be potentially harmful to medical care. It can be expected that risk assessments by the licensing authority would tend to err heavily on the side of public safety and that many patients would be unnecessarily disadvantaged. Moreover, the fear of being reported might lead patients to withhold medical information, thereby compromising recognition and treatment, eroding the physician–patient relationship, and frustrating the regulatory goal as well.

On the other hand, the report recognizes that there will be situations when reporting of patients to driving authorities is warranted. They provide guidelines but largely envisage that this is a judgment call for individual physicians. This may not be something that physicians are comfortable with. But, as pointed out by the American Thoracic Society report, the only way to avoid this responsibility is to report all patients diagnosed with sleep disorders. This, too, is something that physicians are unlikely to support. Physicians alone, however, cannot assume responsibility. Their judgments are based on the self-report of the patient and they are dependent on that patient using the prescribed therapy. Thus, it is important that the patients, i.e. the drivers themselves, assume responsibility. The physician needs to fully inform the patient and document that this has been done.

An important distinction if regulations are to be developed needs to be between the treated and the untreated patient. It seems likely that all would agree that untreated high-risk patients with known sleep disorders should not be allowed to drive. This was one of the conclusions of the American Thoracic Society report. It advocated reporting when a high-risk patient's condition is 'untreatable or not amenable to expeditious treatment within 2 months when the patient is not willing to accept treatment or is unwilling to restrict driving until effective treatment has been instituted.' It is unfortunate that no such statement has been developed by the Academy of Neurology for similar issues for patients with narcolepsy.

If we consider that there need to be different regulations for treated and untreated patients, then this raises questions about how long it takes to have effective treatment and how efficacy of therapy can be judged. Current regulations envisage months to one year. But what is the basis of this? In sleep apnea, if individuals respond to nasal continuous positive airway pressure (CPAP) they do so quickly and should be effectively treated in days to a few weeks. Why should such individuals be barred from driving for much longer periods? For narcolepsy, however, it is likely to take longer to appropriately adjust medication to achieve the optimal regimen. It needs to be remembered, moreover, that patients with sleep disorders are only effectively being treated as long as they are using their therapy. Studies, for example, with nasal CPAP show that if individuals do not use their therapy for a single night they are just as sleepy the next day as they were before any treatment.[23] It is essential, therefore, that individual patients are informed of this and the resulting risk. We cannot burden physicians with the responsibility not only of diagnosing and treating patients with sleep disorders but also of ensuring that such patients use their treatment every day.

Nevertheless, the technology does exist to monitor patients' use of their therapy. For example, systems are now available to monitor CPAP use.[24] The precise role, if any, of this technology in assessing ability to drive has not been established. It could, however, have a role if patients with sleep apnea on CPAP are allowed to drive commercial vehicles. It is a tool that could be employed by the owners of commercial driving companies in comprehensive alertness management programs.

Another issue that needs to be considered if regulations are to be contemplated is whether regulations should be different for the commercial as compared to the private vehicle driver. This question has currently not been addressed by any of the professional societies. Indeed, the recent report of the American Thoracic Society[22] specifically did not address the commercial driving issue. Here, too, there is a balance to be struck. On the one hand, there is clearly the issue of exposure, i.e. commercial drivers are much more likely to have more crashes due to the high number of miles driven. On the other hand, if all patients with sleep disorders cannot engage in this employment should they be eligible for disability payments? The costs for sleep apnea, which is estimated to affect at least 4% of the middle-aged male population,[25] would be staggering. It would seem that the best initial approach would be for commercial driving companies to put mechanisms in place to screen their drivers for sleep apnea in a cost-effective way. Expensive polysomnograms, carried out in the sleep laboratory, which are advocated by some, are neither a cost-effective nor a viable approach. For narcolepsy the situation is different and we personally agree with the regulation in certain countries that patients with this disorder would be better employed in other ways.

If regulations are to be developed, they need to address, moreover, the issue that a sleep disorder is not an all-or-none phenomena; rather there is a continuum of abnormality. This is true for both narcolepsy and obstructive sleep apnea. For sleep apnea this continuum appears to be easier to define since it is based on the respiratory disturbance index. But, as pointed out earlier, this index is a poor predictor of driving impairment.[4] For sleep apnea, the epidemiology shows that the number of individuals with milder disease are much greater than those with severe disease.[25] Thus, regulations would likely deny the ability to drive to large segments of our population in whom this is not warranted. Ideally, we should be able to develop criteria to help in this regard but simple algorithms based on the respiratory disturbance index and/or result of the multiple sleep latency, as proposed in Maine, are not supported by the available data. Attempts need to continue to be made to better identify the high-risk patient, perhaps based on approaches such as performance on the divided attention driving simulation task.

CONCLUSION

The issue of driving privileges is perhaps the most important of the legal issues for patients with sleep disorders. It is a complex issue for which there are currently limited data. There are areas of debate but also areas of consensus.

We believe that everybody would agree to the following: (i) there is a need for increased awareness of the issues among all relevant groups – lay public, physicians conducting physical examinations for commercial drivers, policy makers, police officers; (ii) there is a need for a shared responsibility between the patient and the physician to address this problem, although the exact balance might be debated; (iii) there is a need for more research to better identify the patient with a sleep disorder who has an increased risk of vehicular crashes; and (iv) there is a need to develop programs to routinely 'screen' commercial drivers for sleep disorders, albeit in a cost-effective way.

An area of controversy relates to regulations. There is a sense that simple 'blanket' regulations cannot address the complexity of the issue. Given the high prevalence of these disorders, large segments of our society will be affected. Professional societies should be encouraged to develop task forces such as that of the American Thoracic Society[22] to develop guidelines. These task forces should include input from all with expertise and/or a stake in the issue – sleep professionals, lawyers, regulators, patients with the disorder, owners of commercial vehicle companies, etc. They should address the issues for the different sleep disorders, i.e. at this time narcolepsy and obstructive sleep apnea, and consider separately the problem for the non-commercial and commercial driver. Without our societies taking this step, we face increasing regulations being put in place by individuals who are likely to be less well informed.

ACKNOWLEDGMENTS

We are grateful to Mr Daniel C. Barrett for help in preparation of this manuscript. The original research was supported by SCOR grant HL-42236 and a grant from the Trucking Research Institute.

REFERENCES

1. Pakola, S.J., Dinges, D.F. and Pack, A.I. Review of regulations and guidelines for commercial and noncommercial drivers with sleep apnea and narcolepsy. *Sleep* **18**:787–796, 1995.
2. Findley, L., Fabrizio, M.J., Knight, H., Norcross, B.B., Laforte, A.J. and Suratt, P.M. Driving simulator performance in patients with sleep apnea. *Am. Rev. Respir. Dis.* **140**:529–530, 1989.
3. Haraldsson, P.O., Canenfelt, C., Laurell, H. and Tornros, J. Driving vigilance simulator test. *Acta Otolaryngol (Stockh)* **110**:136–140, 1990.
4. George, C., Smiley, A., Flaherty, B. and Boudreau, A. Simulated driving and sleep apnea. *Am. J. Respir. Crit. Care Med.* **150**:A748, 1994.
5. Mitler, M.M., Hajdukovic, R. and Erman, M.K. Treatment of narcolepsy with methamphetamine. *Sleep* **16**:306–317, 1993.
6. Gallup. *Sleep in America: A National Survey of US Adults*. A report prepared for the National Sleep Foundation, Los Angeles, CA, 1991.
7. Piscopo, J.A. Foreword, in *Principles and Practice of Sleep Medicine*, edited by Kryger, M.H., Roth, T. and Dement, W.C. W.B. Saunders, Philadelphia, PA, 1994, pp. xxi–xxii.
8. Bartels, E.C. and Kusakcioglu, O. Narcolepsy: a possible cause of automobile accidents. *Lahey Clin. Foundation Bull.* **1**:21–26, 1965.
9. Broughton, R.J., Guberman, A. and Roberts, J. Comparison of psychosocial effects

of epilepsy and narcolepsy/cataplexy: a controlled study. *Epilepsia* **25**:423–433, 1984.

10. Broughton, R., Ghanem, Q., Hishikawa, Y., Sugita, Y., Nevsimalova, S. and Roth, B. Life effects of narcolepsy in 180 patients from North America, Asia, and Europe compared to matched controls. *Can. J. Neurol. Sci.* **8**:299–304, 1981.

11. McCartt, A.T., Ribner, S.A., Pack, A.I. and Hammer, M.C. The scope and nature of the drowsy driving problem in New York State. *Accident Analysis and Prevention* **28**(4):511–517, 1996.

12. Aldrich, M.S. Automobile accidents in patients with sleep disorders. *Sleep* **12**:487–494, 1989.

13. George, C.F., Nickerson, P.W., Hanly, P.J., Millar, T.W. and Kryger, M.H. Sleep apnoea patients have more automobile accidents. *Lancet* **8556**:447, 1987.

14. Findley, L.J., Unverzadt, M.E. and Suratt, P.M. Automobile accidents involving patients with obstructive sleep apnea. *Am. Rev. Respir. Dis.* **138**:337–340, 1988.

15. Findley, L.J., Fabrizio, M., Thommi, G. and Suratt, P.M. Severity of sleep apnea and automobile crashes. *N. Engl. J. Med.* **320**:868–869, 1989.

16. Stoohs, R.A., Guilleminault, C., Itoi, A. and Dement, W.C. Traffic accidents in commercial long-haul truck drivers: the influence of sleep-disordered breathing and obesity. *Sleep* **17**:619–623, 1994.

17. Haraldsson, P.O., Carenfelt, C., Lysdahl, M. and Tornros, J. Long-term effect of uvulopalatopharyngoplasty on driving performance. *Arch. Otolaryngol. Head Neck Surg.* **121**:90–94, 1995.

18. Suratt, P. and Findley, L. Effect of nasal CPAP treatment on automobile driving simulator performance and on self reported automobile accidents in subjects with sleep apnea. *Am. Rev. Respir. Dis.* **145**:A169, 1992.

19. Minemura, H., Akashiba, T., Yamamoto, H., Suzuki, R., Itoh, D., Kurashina, K., Yoshizawa, T. and Horie, T. Traffic accidents in obstructive sleep apnea patients and effect of nasal CPAP treatment. *Jpn. J. Thorac. Med.* **31**:1103–1108, 1993.

20. Federal Motor Carrier Safety Regulations. US Department of Transportation. Federal Highway Administration. Title 49.391.41–391.49, September 1993.

21. National Safety Code for Motor Carriers. Canadian Council of Motor Transport Administrators (CCMTA). September 1993.

22. American Thoracic Society (Strohl, K.P., Bonnie, R.J., Findley, L., Fletcher, E.C., Getsy, J., Kryger, M.H., Millman, R., Novak, R., Roth, T., Walsleben, J. and Williams, A.). Sleep apnea, sleepiness, and driving risk. *Am. J. Respir. Crit. Care Med.* **150**:1463–1473, 1994.

23. Kribbs, N.B., Pack, A.I., Kline, L.R., Getsy, J.E., Schuett, J.S., Henry, J.N., Maislin, G. and Dinges, D.F. Effects of one night without nasal CPAP treatment on sleep and sleepiness in patients with obstructive sleep apnea. *Am. Rev. Respir. Dis.* **147**:1162–1168, 1993.

24. Kribbs, N.B., Pack, A.I., Kline, L.R., Smith, P.L., Schwartz, A.R., Schubert, N.M., Redline, S., Henry, J.N., Getsy, J.E. and Dinges, D.F. Objective measurement of patterns of nasal CPAP use by patients with obstructive sleep apnea. *Am. Rev. Respir. Dis.* **147**:887–895, 1993.

25. Young, T., Palta, M., Dempsey, J., Skatrud, J., Weber, S. and Badr, S. The occurrence of sleep-disordered breathing among middle-aged adults. *N. Engl. J. Med.* **328**:1230–1235, 1993.

Chronobiologic and Medical Aspects of Alertness

M.M. Mitler and J.S. Poceta
Scripps Clinic and Research Foundation

CIRCADIAN RHYTHMS AND ALERTNESS

Human error accidents on the road and in the workplace are increasingly the subject of litigation. Understanding the biological factors that affect alertness and ability to work is fundamentally important for litigators and policy makers who deal with round-the-clock operations. This chapter is intended to familiarize the reader with the basics of 24-hour changes in human function, what can go wrong, and how abnormalities in alertness are measured.

We are all aware of daily ups and downs in our abilities. Such normal fluctuations in performance have been documented for many years[1,2] and are not random throughout the 24-hour day.[3,4] In 1955, Bjerner *et al.* reported on diurnal performance fluctuations for employees at a Swedish gas company whose work was monitored over a 20-year period.[2] Figure 1 shows the distribution throughout the 24-hour day of 74 927 meter reading errors made by these workers. Note that more errors occurred during the night, with a major peak between 1 and 3 a.m., and a smaller afternoon peak in errors occurred between 1 and 3 p.m.

Since these early observations, other more destructive human error events have also been shown to occur with this same two-peak pattern. Figure 2 shows the 24-hour distribution of 6052 vehicle crashes attributable to fatigue (i.e. crashes for which investigation disclosed no mechanical failure and no alcohol or substance-related causal factors). These data were

Forensic Aspects of Sleep. Edited by C.M. Shapiro and A. McCall Smith.
© 1997 John Wiley & Sons Ltd.

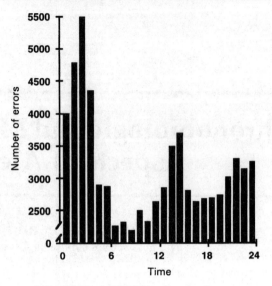

Figure 1. The temporal distribution of 74 927 meter reading errors recorded for Swedish gas workers over a 20-year period. Data are plotted from the report of Bjerner et al.[2] The horizontal axis represents clock time of a 24-hour day beginning at midnight

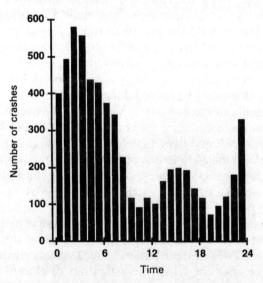

Figure 2. The temporal distribution of 6052 fatigue-related automobile crashes.[6-8] The horizontal axis represents clock time of a 24-hour day beginning at midnight. See also figure 4 in Mitler et al.[5]

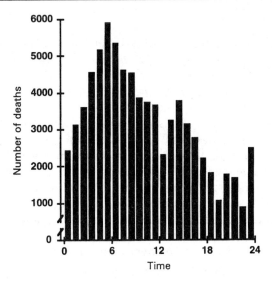

Figure 3. Temporal distribution of 437 511 disease-related deaths.[11,12] The horizontal represents clock time of a 24-hour day beginning at midnight. See also figure 2 in Mitler *et al.*[5]

originally compiled and plotted by Mitler *et al.*[5] Note the two-peak pattern in this distribution is similar to that in Figure 1. The number of crashes is elevated between about midnight and 6 a.m. and again between about 1 and 4 p.m.

Numerous studies have now demonstrated that human 24-hour rhythms in many measures of performance and physiologic activity have a two-peak diurnal pattern.[5,6,7] Broughton[3,4] was the first to bring this robust characteristic of human performance to the attention of researchers.

The 'biological' rather than 'behavioral' nature of this two-peak temporal pattern is evidenced by the fact that identical patterns also exist in the timing of human mortality attributable to disease.[8] Figure 3 shows the temporal distribution of 437 511 disease-related deaths compiled by Mitler *et al.*[8] and Smolensky *et al.*[9] The strength of the two-peak pattern is noteworthy in spite of the imprecision that must be associated with the process of combining deaths from all types of diseases. Breaking down disease-related deaths according to type of disease, age and sex suggested that the two-peak temporal pattern is most prominent in deaths due to ischemic heart disease in both men and women over the age of 65.[8]

With the application of continuous electroencephalographic (EEG) monitoring techniques for the measurement of cycles in sleep and wakefulness,[10] it became apparent that physiologic sleep tendency also has its ups and downs throughout the 24-hour period.[11-16]

EEG monitoring of sleep

There have been few multi-day studies on humans using continuous EEG monitoring of sleep and wakefulness that are actually relevant to measurement of sleep tendency. The two main purposes of such studies are to capture episodic abnormalities in the EEG, such as epileptic seizures,[17] or to study circadian cycles in sleep and/or wakefulness.[18] While all of these studies accomplish their purposes and also show objective and reproducible diurnal alternations of wakefulness and sleep in patients and normals, none have demonstrated definitive technology for quantitatively differentiating one person's sleep tendency from that of another or for detecting the presence of abnormal sleep tendency. In one of the earliest studies that permitted naps during the 'day' in subjects living under time isolation, Schaefer et al.[19] documented the propensity of humans to sleep up to 212 minutes in the 'afternoon'. While it might seem that circadian EEG studies should be helpful in quantifying individual sleep tendency, this has not been the case. For methodological and scientific reasons, subjects in these types of studies are encouraged to have only one sleep period for each circadian cycle.[20]

Thus, most circadian studies are designed to measure overall circadian patterns, not the fine structure of a person's sleep cycles or how sleepy one person is compared with another. However, in 1976 Kripke[21] suggested that circadian studies might yield insights for understanding sleep disorders such as narcolepsy. Some clinical studies were done using round-the-clock EEG monitoring of sleep tendency in patients with sleep disorders. Several studies suggest that patients with narcolepsy, who characteristically complain of excessive sleepiness, do not sleep significantly more than normal when studied for 24–48 hour periods.[22–24] Rather, the sleep of narcoleptics is less consolidated than that of normals and occurs in multiple short naps. Pollak and his colleagues[25,26] extended this circadian clinical research by evaluating narcoleptic subjects in true temporal isolation and found that narcoleptics did have more sleep periods per circadian cycle than controls but that their total sleep time was not greater than that for normal subjects.

Modern EEG techniques for measuring sleep tendency did not grow out of circadian studies, but out of sleep research on the properties of the nominal human sleep fraction of 1:2 (i.e. 8 hours of sleep for every 16 hours of wakefulness).[11–13,27] Sleep researchers would measure sleep tendency round-the-clock by allowing 1 hour of sleep for every 3 hours of time, or 30 minutes for every 90 minutes, or 3 hours for every 9 hours. Lavie and colleagues have extended and refined this approach by preserving the basic sleep fraction but moving to ultra-short multiples (e.g. 7 minutes of every 20).[14–16,28] With such ultra-short naps, the measurement of sleep tendency at any given time in the 24-hour day is not greatly influenced by sleep that may accumulate on previous naps in protocols that allow longer sleeping times.

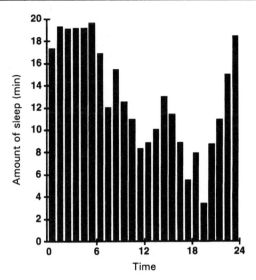

Figure 4. The amount of sleep obtained each hour for nine subjects permitted to sleep for up to 7 of every 20 minutes throughout the 24-hour day. The data were taken from figure 8 of Lavie.[28] The horizontal axis represents clock time of a 24-hour day beginning at midnight

The typical result of such studies is depicted in Figure 4, which is a recalculation and replotting of the amount of sleep that nine of Lavie's subjects obtained each hour when they were allowed 7 minutes out of every 20 to sleep. Note that the two-peak pattern is again apparent. There is a rapid rise in sleep tendency, which Lavie refers to as the rapid opening of the nocturnal sleep gate, beginning at about 8 p.m. with a broad plateau from about midnight to 6 a.m. There is a smaller mid-afternoon increase in sleep tendency between 1 and 3 p.m. and a period when almost no sleep occurs at about 6–7 p.m., which Lavie refers to as the 'forbidden zone'. The general pattern of this elegant work fits very well with that found by Carskadon and Dement[12] in their 90-minute day studies (30 minutes of sleep every 90 minutes round the clock) and with the temporal pattern of unintended sleep episodes described for subjects trying to stay awake throughout a 24-hour period.[29,30] The coincidence of the peak times for errors in Figure 1, crashes in Figure 2, disease-related deaths in Figure 3 and sleep tendency in Figure 4 is obvious.

MEDICAL CONDITIONS AND DAYTIME ALERTNESS

Alertness, in its objectively observable form, is a result of many functional systems and can be influenced by many factors. The circadian aspects and the

Table 1. Conditions associated with excessive daytime sleepiness

Sleep disruption	Obstructive sleep apnea
	Periodic limb movement disorder
	Sleep stage abnormality
	Nightmares
Circadian rhythm	Insufficient sleep in a long sleeper
	Sleep deprivation (total or partial)
	Age (childhood to adulthood)
	Delayed sleep phase syndrome
	Advanced sleep phase syndrome
Neurological disorders	Narcolepsy
	Idiopathic hypersomnia syndrome
	Psychomotor epilepsy
	Kleine–Levin syndrome
	6–18 months post-head trauma
	Early symptom of progressive hydrocephalus
	Intracranial space-occupying lesions
Psychological disorders	Depression
	Malingering
	Somatoform disorders
Bio-medical/physical disorders	Hypoglycemia
	Myotonic dystrophy
	Hypothyroidism
	Alcoholism
	Prader–Willi syndrome
	Drug withdrawal (especially from CNS stimulants)
	Long half-lives of sedatives

effects of physiologic sleep tendency modulate alertness within a certain range. These intrinsic biological influences interact with other physiologic and pathophysiologic conditions to produce a level of alertness at a specific time or in a specific situation. Table 1 lists many physiologic and pathophysiologic conditions that can produce excessive daytime sleepiness, reduced alertness and impaired performance.

The medical status of a person can overwhelm even the most vigorous circadian influences. For example, a person who has suffered a destructive ischemic stroke in the brainstem may be stuporous or comatose, and be unable to stay awake at any time. A person under acute stress or on stimulant drugs may be quite alert at times when he or she would normally sleep. Thus, the medical status of a person must be considered when making an assessment of alertness in any particular instance. Certain medical conditions are more likely than others to influence alertness, and some of these are reviewed below. Narcolepsy, idiopathic hypersomnolence, and obstructive sleep apnea are discussed elsewhere.

Cerebrovascular disease and structural brain lesions

It has been recognized for many decades that brain lesions such as tumors and strokes can produce relatively specific alterations in sleeping and waking behaviors. For example, lesions in the region of the third ventricle have been described to produce excessively long sleep periods and diminished daytime alertness.[31] Ischemic lesions in several areas can also produce excessive sleepiness. Potential mechanisms involve the size and specific area of the stroke, and the influence of the lesion on intracranial pressure.[32] Closed head injury is another common cause of an encephalopathy with a decreased state of alertness.[33] Large or sudden lesions are easily recognized and present no problem identifying a major, disabling level of alertness. However, smaller or more insidious processes such as small vessel ischemic disease or demyelination might affect alertness in a manner that would not be easily identified without specific testing.

Epilepsy and seizure disorders

Many persons with epilepsy are completely normal in between seizures. In fact, there is little to suggest that during the inter-ictal period there would be any lasting neurologic sequelae from the seizure, and therefore patients with epilepsy in general have no more or less risk for diminished alertness than non-epileptics. However, certain associated aspects of epilepsy might increase this risk. For example, the seizure itself can produce an alteration or loss of consciousness, and a person might not be fully alert during many types of seizures. Many seizures also produce a transient sleepiness after the seizure, so if seizures are occurring frequently, the patient may have diminished alertness with reduced capability to perform certain tasks. In addition, nocturnal seizures can produce daytime sleepiness by disrupting sleep at night.[34] Importantly, the majority of medications used to treat seizures have sedative effects, as discussed elsewhere in this book.

Cheyne–Stokes respiration

Cheyne–Stokes respiration (CSR) is a form of sleep-disordered breathing occurring in patients with congestive heart failure from cardiomyopathy or in certain other conditions.[35] CSR can sometimes be primarily neurologic in origin. The pattern of respiration is one of a gradual decrease in respiratory effort, leading to complete cessation of respiratory effort. After a period of time, perhaps 30–60 seconds, breathing gradually resumes, reaching a peak after 30–60 seconds, and then beginning to diminish again. This pattern is classically described as a crescendo–decrescendo breathing. Often, there is oxyhemoglobin desaturation caused by the apnea. Frequent arousals and poor quality sleep result, often with secondary impairment of daytime alertness. This condition should be suspected in any patient with a history of congestive heart failure and complaints of poor sleep quality. The condition can be transient, and can often be altered by altering the underlying cardiac status. Although not well studied at this time, it is possible that patients with cardiovascular conditions that are associated with increased risk of mortality may be excessively sleeply.

Alcholism

We are not aware of studies which have specifically addressed the state of alertness/sleepiness in alcoholics or abstinent alcoholics. However, the soporific effects of acute alcohol ingestion are well accepted.[36] A more difficult situation is a former alcoholic who complains of fatigue or poor sleep. Abstinent alcoholics have been shown to have disrupted sleep for years after the cessation of drinking. This can result in a complaint of insomnia with negative daytime consequences on alertness.

Other medical conditions

There are a large number of medical conditions that can diminish alertness on an acute or chronic basis. Virtually any condition that can cause a delirium or encephalopathy can produce diminished alertness. Some typical conditions include hepatic failure, uremia from kidney failure, or elevated calcium in bony cancer. Hypothyroidism is particularly common and amenable to treatment. HIV infection can produce subtle neurocognitive problems including fatigue, and these problems may occur very early in the course of the condition.[37]

Pain from virtually any cause can disrupt sleep and produce symptoms of daytime fatigue and sleepiness. This certainly includes conditions such as acute low back pain, but also chronic conditions such as rheumatoid arthritis.[38] There is also a well documented sleep disorder in fibromyalgia, a non-inflammatory musculoskeletal pain syndrome.[39]

MEASURES OF DAYTIME ALERTNESS AND SLEEPINESS

Telling abnormal from normal

Multiple-nap studies of the kind shown in Figure 4 have focused on normal populations. Such studies will undoubtedly continue and should refine our understanding of the normal temporal interrelationships between sleep and performance. However, what about the abnormal? Recently, the timing of ups and downs in human sleep tendency have been associated with, if not causally linked to, the timing of industrial and transportation catastrophes and mishaps caused by human error.[5] The Office of Technology Assessment of the US Congress has reviewed the impact that diurnal variation in sleep and performance have on safety and productivity in a variety of industries worldwide[6] and provided lawmakers with a number of legislative options aimed at limiting loss of life and property. Thus, problems relating to human sleep tendency are being addressed at all levels of our society and government. Among the most challenging public policy issues are: (i) the rate and temporal distribution of human error catastrophies that should be considered unavoidable and normal, (ii) the degree to which a person's sleep tendency must rise before it is considered a risk to the person or to the public and (iii) to what extent human error caused by abnormal or normal levels of sleepiness can be reduced. With so great a degree of interest in sleepiness, it is appropriate to review critically the various methods of measuring sleep tendency and our current concepts regarding what is normal and abnormal sleep tendency.

Self-report techniques

The first attempts to assess sleepiness were probably subjective and self-report in nature, and consisted of documenting the subject's spontaneous thoughts and comments concerning level of energy, ability to function and desire for sleep.[40] Interview and questionnaire techniques were developed to standardize the process and better delineate the time of each measurement. Among the best known of the questionnaire techniques is the Stanford Sleepiness Scale (SSS).[41] Subjects complete this measurement by choosing one of seven statements describing their state of sleepiness from the following: (i) Feeling active and vital; alert; wide awake; (ii) Functioning at a high level, but not at peak; able to concentrate; (iii) relaxed; awake; not at a full alertness; responsive; (iv) A little foggy, not at peak; let down; (v) Fogginess; beginning to lose interest in remaining awake; slowed down; (vi) Sleepiness; prefer to be lying down; fighting sleep; woozy; (vii) Almost in reverie; sleep onset soon; lost struggle to remain awake. Major strengths of the SSS are that it can be administered many times per day, that it correlates with standard measures of performance and that it reflects the effects of sleep loss. However, throughout the 24-hour day, all levels of the SSS can be recorded in normal subjects, experimentally sleep deprived normal subjects and patients with sleep disorders. Thus, there is no clear procedure for determining what is normal and what is abnormal on the SSS. Furthermore, Dement and colleagues have documented glaring discordance between high SSS ratings of 1 or 2 and gross behavioral indicators of sleep such as closed eyes and snoring in patients with sleep apnea, and suggest that such discordance stem either from the subject's loss of a proper frame of reference as to what normal alertness really is or from simple denial.[42] Another possible explanation for discordance is that the SSS and behavioral indicators of sleep reflect different things.

Another common self-report instrument is the Epworth Sleepiness Scale (ESS) devised by Johns at Epworth Hospital in Melbourne Australia.[43] The ESS asks subjects to use a number from 0 to 3 corresponding to the likelihood ('never', 'slight', 'moderate', and 'high') that they would fall asleep in eight situations: (i) Sitting and reading, (ii) Watching TV, (iii) Sitting, inactive in a public place, (iv) As a passenger in a car for an hour without a break, (v) Lying down to rest in the afternoon when circumstances permit, (vi) Sitting and talking to someone, (vii) Sitting quietly after a lunch without alcohol, (viii) In a car, while stopped for a few minutes in the traffic. After administration, an ESS score that can range between 0 and 24 is tallied. The ESS statistically distinguishes normal subjects from patients with sleep disorders leading to the symptom of excessive sleepiness. The ESS also correlates with electroencephalographically determined sleep latencies measured at night or during the day and does reflect changes in sleepiness associated with treatment-related improvement in sleep apnea.[44] The ESS is considered to be a validated and reliable self-report measure of sleepiness. However, the ESS is not designed to be used on multiple occasions during the day or in the presence of short-term conditions that might influence sleep tendency, such as acute sleep loss.

Pupillography

Pupillography is an objective, laboratory-based method of electronically monitoring the size of a person's pupil.[45] Studies have shown that the diameter of the pupil as well as the degree of stability of pupil size is inversely related to the complaint of sleepiness. Pupillography has been used as a clinical measure of sleep tendency.[46,47] However, the technique has not come into widespread use because modern pupillographic equipment is not generally available and the pupillographic indicators of sleepiness are not specific to whether the sleepiness is the normal result of circadian variation in alertness or the symptomatic consequence of sleep disorders such as sleep apnea and narcolepsy.

EEG-based techniques

Common sense dictates that when asked to fall asleep, someone who is not sleepy will take longer to produce EEG waves of sleep than someone who is sleepy. However, in 1976, Carskadon and her colleagues[48] studied the nocturnal sleep of 122 patients who complained of insomnia and found that the time taken to fall asleep by EEG criteria (sleep latency) varied greatly and that the distribution of sleep latencies for the group of insomniacs did not seem much different from groups of people without insomnia. Also striking for these insomniacs was their overestimation of how long it took to fall asleep. Sleep latency was overestimated by more than 15 minutes in 60 subjects and by more than 60 minutes in 15 subjects. This kind of discrepancy between subjective and objective measures of sleep tendency is the basic reason why sleep researchers have pursued and refined EEG-based measures of sleep tendency.

Continuous and round-the-clock studies

We have already mentioned continuous EEG studies of sleep and wakefulness as well as those that follow the nominal one-third sleep to two-thirds wakefulness sleep fraction. Such approaches certainly have the advantage of objectivity. These approaches have shown that the factors of diurnal variation in sleep tendency and sleep deprivation can be objectively separated[14-16,28] and that, in general, sleep loss increases overall sleep tendency but does little to the 24-hour pattern of ups and downs. However, round-the-clock EEG studies are expensive and not easily applicable to diagnostic or screening purposes demanded by the clinical and public safety concerns associated with the problem of abnormal sleep tendency. Furthermore, no guidelines are available as to how to quantify sleep tendency (in terms of total sleep time, number of sleep episodes, amount of certain sleep phase, etc.) or how to differentiate normal from abnormal.

The Multiple Sleep Latency Test

The Multiple Sleep Latency Test (MSLT) is an electroencephalographically-based clinical and research tool that was developed at Stanford University.[49,50] The technique did grow out of studies on the human sleep fraction, namely, the 90-minute day, round the clock studies of sleep tendency by Carskadon and Dement.[12] The MSLT assesses sleep tendency during the day. Details of the protocol have been published elsewhere.[49,51] Essential features are that a subject, who has kept regular sleeping and waking hours prior to the test, spends a night in the sleep laboratyory and is then permitted four, five or six 20-minute long opportunities to sleep offered at two-hour intervals after getting up in the morning. The sleep latency is electroencephalographically determined on each test and an average of a four or five trial MSLT is calculated and interpreted. Other parameters, such as duration and type of sleep, may also be determined, depending on whether the MSLT is being used for clinical or research purposes. Figure 5 presents the average sleep latency for each of the five opportunities to sleep on the MSLT for 17 normal subjects

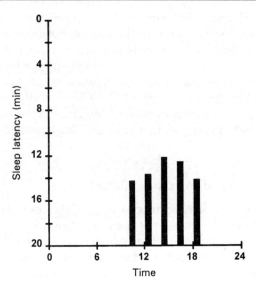

Figure 5. Average sleep latency for each of the five opportunities to sleep on the MSLT for 17 normal subjects from table 1 Mitler *et al.*[52] The order of numbers on the vertical axis has been reversed to make increases in sleep tendency go up. The horizontal axis represents clock time of a 24-hour day beginning at midnight

originally reported by Mitler *et al.*[52] The order of numbers on the vertical axis has been reversed to make increases in sleep tendency (i.e. decreases in sleep latency) go up, thereby facilitating visual comparison among various measures of sleep tendency and performance. By comparing Figures 4 and 5 one can appreciate the fact that the MSLT, while not a round-the-clock measure of sleep tendency, does measure the daytime level of sleep tendency and captures the afternoon rise in sleep tendency as well as its subsequent fall toward what Lavie has termed the 'forbidden zone' in the late afternoon and early evening.

The MSLT is a well-validated research and clinical tool in wide use throughout the world.[53] Normative values for subjects at various ages have been published.[30,54] One of the most important features of the MSLT is that it clearly reflects the effects of experimental sleep deprivation,[55,56] albeit only for the daytime hours. If prior sleep is reduced from baseline levels, the MSLT shows an increase from baseline levels in sleep tendency. Unlike round-the-clock techniques for measuring sleep tendency, the MSLT was the first objective tool that could be used on a standardized widespread basis to address the increased and/or excessive sleep tendency that arises from sleep loss, drugs or disease. The MSLT distinguishes between excessively sleepy patients and normals.[49] The MSLT can detect the daytime carry-over effects of a long-acting sleeping pill.[57] Guidelines for MSLT normalcy have been published such that an average MSLT sleep latency of less than 5 minutes is considered pathological[49] and an average sleep latency of between 5 and 10 minutes may be considered abnormal or borderline depending on clinical complaints.[58] The major drawbacks of the MSLT are that, while less cumbersome to do than a round-the-clock study, it is still quite cumbersome and expensive and not at all suitable for screening to identify abnormally sleepy individuals in a population. Additionally, the MSLT is subject to certain interpretative and conceptual problems when it is used to assess sleep tendency in people who complain of difficulty staying awake: (i) the instructions of the MSLT ('Try to fall asleep') are counterintuitive to people who have trouble staying awake, (ii) a person with a vested interest in appearing normal on the MSLT may ignore the instructions and try to stay awake on each MSLT trial, (iii) the MSLT may not reflect changes in sleep tendency that result from treatment of very sleepy patients with narcolepsy or sleep apnea even though the patient reports improvement.[27]

The Maintenance of Wakefulness Test

The Maintenance of Wakefulness Test (MWT) is a variant of the MSLT originally devised to obviate some of the interpretative and conceptual problems of the MSLT.[59] The MWT subject is asked to remain awake, and is monitored for electroencephalographic sleep onset. Early MWT studies demonstrated a prolonged sleep latency as a result of the instruction to remain awake, compared to asking the subject to go to sleep as is done in the MSLT.[60] The original MWT used a 20-minute trial conducted five times over the course of a day beginning about two hours after nocturnal sleep ends, and was shown to be useful to evaluate the effect of treatment in patients with narcolepsy.[52] Figure 6 is a graphic summary of MWT sleep latencies for eight control subjects offered five 20-minute long opportunities to stay awake at two-hour intervals beginning at 10 a.m. These data were originally published by Mitler et al.[59] and are replotted in the same format as Figure 4 to facilitate comparisons. Note that the afternoon increase in sleep tendency is similarly positioned as in Figures 4 and 5. Also note that all sleep latencies are longer on the MWT than on the MSLT.

In 1984, the group at Scripps Clinic lengthened the original MWT's 20-minute trials to 40 minutes because they observed that patients who had histories of daytime sleepiness were too often able to maintain wakefulness for 20 minutes. This 'ceiling effect' was diminished with trial lengths of 40 minutes. This 40-minute version of the MWT has now been applied to large numbers of patients with obstructive sleep apnea by at least two independent laboratories.[61-63] Because its instructions more directly assess clinical and public safety concerns and because it seems to detect clinical improvement in sleepy patients who are not completely cured, MWT eliminates some of the

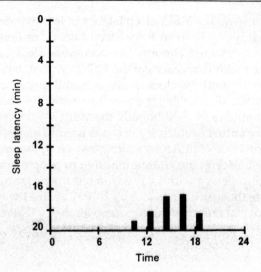

Figure 6. MWT sleep latencies for eight control subjects offered five 20-minute long opportunities to stay awake at 2-hour intervals beginning at 10 a.m. These data were originally published in Mitler et al.[59] and are replotted in the same format as Figure 5 to facilitate comparisons

interpretative problems associated with the MSLT. Furthermore, Poceta et al.[61] and Sangal et al.[62,63] have suggested guidelines for normalcy: an MWT sleep latency of less than 15 minutes is considered dangerous for driving an automobile. The Federal Aviation Administration now calls for use of the MWT in determining whether non-commercial pilots are licensable after the diagnosis of sleep apnea has been made.[64] While the MWT may seem to produce a simple prolongation of daytime sleep latencies, detailed comparisons of the MSLT and the MWT have disclosed that the two tests do not correlate well in patients who complain of excessive sleepiness and may actually measure different abilities.[62,63] For example, some patients with very short MSLT sleep latencies are consistently able to stay awake on 40-minute MWT trials, and others cannot sleep on MSLT trials but fall asleep quickly on MWT trials. Significant limitations of the MWT include: (i) it is as cumbersome and expensive as the MSLT, (ii) there is marked discordance with the primary and most widely used electroencephalographic measure of sleep tendency, the MSLT, and (iii) there are no data as to MWT responsiveness to experimental sleep deprivation. Despite the MWT's limitations, normative values for the MWT that represent both sexes and a wide range of adults are now available in the literature and provide a valuable perspective for the results of therapeutic interventions.[65,66]

There have been other methods for electroencephalographically measuring daytime sleep tendency. Erman and colleagues attempted to obviate the separate problems of the MSLT and the MWT by combining both tests. They studied 20 narcoleptic subjects with the Modified Assessment of Sleepiness Test (MAST), which consisted of three sleep-in-bed conditions interspersed with two reading-in-chair conditions.[67] While ingenious, the problems of expense and lack of normative data are still severe limitations to any such laboratory-based strategy.

Computerized EEG studies

The widespread application of computer technology to EEG monitoring has led to important new approaches for measuring sleep tendency. For example, the quantitative analysis of EEG delta activity has long been thought to reflect the physiological tendency for sleep and does increase in response to experimental sleep deprivation.[68] Hasan et al.[69] have suggested a method of computer analysis that may automatically detect drowsiness in MSLT-like settings. Others, such as Broughton et al.[70] have applied event-related potential technologies to the assessment of sleep tendency. These technologically advanced approaches to measuring sleep tendency hold promise. However, they have not yet shown themselves to be useful in general clinical applications or as screens for abnormally sleepy individuals.

EXEMPLARY LITIGATION

In this section we outline a sampling from many actual legal cases in which chronobiologic and medical aspects of alertness formed the bases of important arguments. Our purpose is to convey the breadth of the interface between the physiology and pathophysiology of fatigue and sleep, on the one hand, and modern litigation, on the other.

In *People* v. *Thompson*[71] the defendant claimed that he was not involved in the early morning stabbing murder of his girlfriend and that he could not stop his male companion from committing the murder because the defendant habitually slept so soundly that only extraordinary physical stimulation could awaken him. The chronobiologic and medical aspects of alertness that were deemed relevant included the time of day of the crime, the influence of alcohol on sleep and the heightened arousal threshold of a young adult who habitually slept soundly and experienced such sleep-related symptoms as sleep walking and enuresis.

In *Vasquez* v. *Southern Pactific*[72] the plaintiff had been disabled in a railroad accident. The plaintiff argued that his track service vehicle crashed into a stationary object because his alertness was too impaired to operate the vehicle safely due to fatigue caused by shift work and excessive hours of service forced on him by the defendant. Relevant chronobiologic and medical aspects of alertness included time-of-day effects on sedentary activities which require sustained attention for safety.

In *Idilbi* v. *Domino's Pizza*[73] a California Highway Patrol officer was struck and killed by the personal car of one of the defendant's truck drivers who was going home after his shift. The plaintiff claimed that the wrongful death of a California police officer was due to excessive fatigue caused by coercive supervisory and compensation practices by the defendant that led to unreasonable hours of service and fatigue. Relevant chronobiologic and medical aspects of alertness included time-of-day effects on sedentary activities which require sustained attention for safety.

In *Miller* v. *Filippi's Pizza*[74] a woman was injured in a fall while on a walkway from the defendant's parking lot to the restaurant. Plaintiff argued that the fall was caused by poor lighting and maintenance. Defendant argued that the plaintiff had been diagnosed with narcolepsy and that the fall was due to a cataplectic attack. Relevant chronobiologic and medical aspects of alertness included the validity of the diagnosis of narcolepsy and the involuntary nature of cataplectic episodes.

REFERENCES

1. Browne, R.C. The day and night performance of teleprinter switchboard operators. *Occup Psychol* 1949; **23**:1–6.
2. Bjerner, B., Helm, A., Swenson, A. Diurnal variation in mental performance: a study of three-shift workers. *Br J Ind Med* 1955; **2**:103–130.
3. Broughton, R.J. Biorhythmic variations in consciousness and psychological functions. *Can Psychol Rev* 1975; **16**:217–230.
4. Broughton, R.J. Chronobiological aspects and models of sleep and napping. In: Dinges D.F., Broughton, R.J. eds. *Sleep and Alertness: Chronobiological, Behavioral and Medical Aspects of Napping*. New York: Raven Press; 1989: pp 71–98.
5. Mitler, M.M., Carskadon, M.A., Czeisler, C.A., Dement, W.C., Dinges, D.F., Graeber, R.C. Catastrophes, sleep and public policy. *Sleep* 1988; **11**:100–109.
6. US Congress Office of Technology Assessment. *Biological Rhythms: Implications for the Worker*. Washington, DC: US Government Printing Office; 1991: pp 1–249.
7. Eastman, C. Are separate temperature and activity oscillators necessary to explain the phenomena of human circadian rhythms? In: Moore-Ede, M.C., Czeisler, C.A. eds. *Mathematical Models of the Circadian Sleep–Wake Cycle*. New York: Raven Press; 1984: pp 81–103.
8. Mitler, M.M., Hajdukovic, R.M., Shafor, R., Hahn, P.M., Kripke, D.F. When people die. Cause of death versus time of death. *Am J Med* 1987; **82**:266–274.
9. Smolensky, M., Halberg, F., Sargent, F. Chronobiology of the life sequence. In: Ito, S., Ogata, K., Yoshimura, H. eds. *Advances in Climatic Physiology*. Tokyo: Igaku Shoin; 1972: pp 281–318.
10. Rechtschaffen, A., Kales A. *A Manual of Standardized Terminology, Techniques and Scoring System for Sleep Stages of Human Subjects*. Los Angeles: UCLA Brain Information Service/Brain Research Institute; 1968.

11. Weitzman, E., Nogeire, C., Perlow, M., Fukushima, D., Sassin, J., McGregor, P., Gallagher, T., Hellman, L. Effects of a prolonged three-hour sleep–wake cycle on sleep stages, plasma cortisol, growth hormone and body temperature in man. *J Clin Endocrinol Metab* 1974; **38**:1018–1030.
12. Carskadon, M., Dement, W. Sleep studies on a 90-minute day. *Electroencephalogr Clin Neurophysiol* 1975; **39**:145–155.
13. Webb, W.B., Agnew, W.H. Sleep efficiency for sleep–wake cycles of varied length. *Psychophysiology* 1975; **12**:637–641.
14. Lavie, P., Scherson, A. Ultrashort sleep–waking schedule. I. Evidence of ultradian rhythmicity in 'sleepability'. *Electroencephalogr Clin Neurophysiol* 1981; **52**:163–174.
15. Lavie, P., Zomer, J. Ultrashort sleep–waking schedule. II. Relationship between ultradian rhythms in sleepability and the REM–NONREM cycles and effects of the circadian phase. *Electroencephalogr Clin Neurophysiol* 1984; **57**:35–42.
16. Lavie, P. Ultrashort sleep–waking schedule. III. Gates and 'forbidden zones' for sleep. *Electroencephalogr Clin Neurophysiol* 1986; **63**:414–425.
17. Offenbacher, H., Korner, E., Reinhart, B., Wolf, R., Fritsch, G., Logar, C., Lechner, H. Mobile long-term EEG monitoring in generalized seizure disorders of different etiology. *Eur Neurol* 1986; **25**:146–153.
18. Torsvall, L., Akerstedt, T., Gillander, K., Knutsson, A. Sleep on the night shift: 24-hour EEG monitoring of spontaneous sleep/wake behavior. *Psychophysiology* 1989; **26**:352–358.
19. Schaefer, K.E., Clegg, B.R., Carey, C.R., Dougherty, J.H., Waybrew, B.E. Effect of isolation in a constant environment on periodicity of physiological functions and performance levels. *Aerospace Med* 1967; **38**:1002–1018.
20. Campbell, S.S., Zulley, J. Napping in time-free environments. In: Dinges, D.F., Broughton, R.J. eds. *Sleep and Alertness: Chronobiological, Behavioral, and Medical Aspects of Napping.* New York: Raven Press; 1989: pp 121–138.
21. Kripke, D.F. Biological rhythms disturbances might cause narcolepsy. In: Guilleminault, C., Dement, W.C., Passouant, P., eds. *Narcolepsy.* New York: Spectrum Publications; 1976: pp 475–483.
22. Baldy-Moulinier, M., Arguner, A., Besset, A. Ultradian and circadian rhythms in sleep and wakefulness. In: Guilleminault, C., Dement, W.C., Passouant, P. eds. *Narcolepsy.* New York: Spectrum Publications; 1976: pp 485–498.
23. Billiard, M., Salva, M.Q., De-Koninick, J., Besset, A., Touchon, J., Cadilhac, J. Daytime sleep characteristics and their relationships with night sleep in the narcoleptic patient. *Sleep* 1986; **9**:167–174.
24. Broughton, R., Dunham, W., Newman, J., Lutley, K., Duschesne, P., Rivers, M., Ambulatory 24 hour sleep–wake monitoring in narcolepsy–cataplexy compared to matched controls. *Electroencephalogr Clin Neurophysiol* 1988; **70**:473–481.
25. Pollak, C.P., Green, J. Eating and its relationships with subjective alertness and sleep in narcoleptic subjects living without temporal cues. *Sleep* 1990; **13**:467–478.
26. Pollak, C.P., Wagner, D.R., Moline, M.L., Monk, T.H. Cognitive and motor performance of narcoleptic and normal subjects living in temporal isolation. *Sleep* 1992; **15**:202–211.
27. Mitler, M.M., Gujavarty, K.S., Sampson, M.G., Browman, C.P. Multiple daytime nap approaches to evaluating the sleepy patient. *Sleep* 1982; **5**: s 119–s 127.
28. Lavie, P. To nap, perchance to sleep – ultradian aspects of napping. In: Dinges, D.F., Broughton, R.J. eds. *Sleep and Alertness: Chronobiological, Behavioral, and Medical Aspects of Napping.* New York: Raven Press; 1989: pp 99–120.
29. Richardson, G.S., Carskadon, M.A., Orav, E.J., Dement, W.C. Circadian variation in sleep tendency in elderly and young adult subjects. *Sleep* 1982; **5**: s 82–s 92.

30. Carskadon, M.A. Patterns of sleep and sleepiness in adolescents. *Pediatrician* 1990; **17**:5–12.
31. Castaigne, P., Lhermitte, F., Buge, A., *et al*. Paramedian thalamic and midbrain infarcts: clinical and neuropathological study. *Ann Neurol* 1981; **10**:127–148.
32. Markand, O.N., Dyken, M.L. Sleep abnormalities in patients with brainstem lesions. *Neurology* 1976; **26**:769–776.
33. Prigatano, G.P., Stahl, M.L., Orr, W.C., Zeiner, H.K. Sleep and dreaming disturbances in closed head injury patients. *J Neurol Neurosurg Psychiatry* 1982; **45**:78–80.
34. Peled, R., Lavie, P. Paroxysmal awakenings from sleep associated with excessive daytime somnolence: a form of nocturnal epilepsy. *Neurology* 1986; **36**:95–98.
35. Hanly, P., Zuberi-Khokhan, N. Daytime sleepiness in patients with congestive heart failure and Cheyne–Stokes respiration. *Chest* 1993; **107**:952–958.
36. Zarcone, V.P. Sleep and alcoholism. In: Chase, M.H., Weitzman, E.D., eds. *Sleep Disorders: Basic and Clinical Research*. New York: SP Medical and Scientific Books; 1983: pp 319–325.
37. Darko, D.F., McCutchan, J.A., Kripke, D.F., Gillin, J.C., Golshan, S. Fatigue, sleep disturbance, disability, and indices of progression of HIV infection. *Am J Psychiatry* 1992; **149**:514–520.
38. Mitler, M.M., Poceta, S., Menn, S.J., Erman, M.K. Insomnia in the chronically ill. In: Hauri, P.J. ed. *Case Studies in Insomnia*. New York Plenum, 1991.
39. Hench, P.K., Mitler, M.M., Fibromyalgia 1. Review of a common rheumatologic syndrome. *Postgraduate Med* 1986; **80**:47–56.
40. Kleitman, N. *Sleep and Wakefulness*. Chicago: University of Chicago Press; 1963.
41. Hoddes, E., Zarcone, V.P., Smythe, H., Phillips, R., Dement, W.C. Quantification of sleepiness: a new approach. *Psychophysiology* 1973; **10**:431–436.
42. Dement, W.C., Carskadon, M.A., Richardson, G.S. Excessive daytime sleepiness in the sleep apnea syndrome. In: Guilleminault, C., Dement, W.C. eds. *Sleep Apnea Syndromes*. New York: Alan R. Liss; 1978: pp 23–46.
43. Johns, M.W. A new method for measuring daytime sleepiness: the Epworth Sleepiness Scale. *Sleep* 1991; **14**:540–545.
44. Johns, M.W. Reliability and factor analysis of the Epworth Sleepiness Scale. *Sleep* 1992; **15**:376–381.
45. Lowenstein, O., Loewenfeld, I. Electronic pupillography – a new instrument and some clinical applications. *Arch Opthalmol* 1958; **59**:352–363.
46. Yoss, R.E., Moyer, N.J., Ogle, K.N. The pupillogram and narcolepsy. A method to measure decreased levels of wakefulness. *Neurology* 1969; **19**:921–928.
47. Schmidt, H.S., Fortin, L. Electronic pupillography in disorders of arousal. In: Guilleminault, C. ed. *Sleeping and Waking Disorders; Indications and Techniques*. Menlo Park, CA: Addison-Wesley; 1982: pp 127–143.
48. Carskadon, M.A., Dement, W.C., Mitler, M.M., Guilleminault, C., Zarcone, V.P., Spiegel, R. Complaint versus sleep laboratory findings in 122 drug-free subjects with a complaint of chronic insomnia. *Am J Psychiatry* 1976; **133**:1382–1388.
49. Richardson, G.S., Carskadon, M.A., Flagg, W., van den Hoed, J., Dement, W.C., Mitler, M.M. Excessive daytime sleepiness in man: multiple sleep latency measurement in narcoleptic and control subjects. *Electroencephalogr Clin Neurophysiol* 1978; **45**:621–627.
50. Mitler, M.M., van den Hoed, J., Carskadon, M.A., Richardson, G., Park, R., Guilleminault, C., Dement, W.C. REM sleep episodes during the Multiple Sleep Latency Test in narcoleptic patients. *Electroencephalogr Clin Neurophysiol* 1979; **46**:479–481.

51. Carskadon, M.A., Dement, W.C., Mitler, M.M., Roth, T., Westbrook, P.R., Keenan, S. Guidelines for the Multiple Sleep Latency Test (MSLT): a standard measure of sleepiness. *Sleep* 1986; **9**:519–524.
52. Mitler, M.M., Hajdukovic, R.M., Erman, M., Koziol, J.A. Narcolepsy. *J Clin Neurophysiol* 1990; **7**:93–118.
53. Thorpy, M.J. Report from the American Sleep Disorders Association. The clinical use of the Multiple Sleep Latency Text. *Sleep* 1992; **15**:268–276.
54. Carskadon, M.A., Harvey, K., Duke, P., Anders, T.F., Litt, I.F., Dement, W.C. Pubertal changes in daytime sleepiness. *Sleep* 1980; **2**:453–460.
55. Carskadon, M.A., Dement, W.C. Nocturnal determinants of daytime sleepiness. *Sleep* 1982; **5**: s 73–s 81.
56. Carskadon, M.A., Dement, W.C. Cumulative effects of sleep restriction on daytime sleepiness. *Psychophysiology* 1981; **18**:107–113.
57. Mitler, M.M., Seidel, W.F., van den Hoed, J., Greenblatt, D.J., Dement, W.C. Comparative hypnotic effects of flurazepam, triazolam and placebo: a long-term simultaneous nighttime and daytime study. *J Clin Psychopharmacol* 1984; **4**:2–13.
58. Diagnostic Classification Steering Committee, Thorpy, M.J., chairman. *International Classification of Sleep Disorders: Diagnostic and Coding Manual.* Rochester, MN: American Sleep Disorders Association; 1990.
59. Mitler, M.M., Gujavarty, K.S. Browman, C.P. Maintenance of Wakefulness Test: a polysomnographic technique for evaluating treatment in patients with excessive somnolence. *Electroencephalogr Clin Neurophysiol* 1982; **53**:658–661.
60. Hartse, K.M., Roth, T., Zorick, F.J. Daytime sleepiness and daytime wakefulness: the effect of instruction. *Sleep* 1982; **5**: s 107–s 118.
61. Poceta, J.S., Timms, R.M., Jeong, D., Ho, S., Erman, M.K., Mitler, M.M. Maintenance of Wakefulness test in obstructive sleep apnea syndrome. *Chest* 1992; **101**:893–897.
62. Sangal, R.E., Thomas, L., Mitler, M.M. Maintenance of Wakefulness Test and Multiple Sleep Latency Test. Measurement of different abilities in patients with sleep disorders. *Chest* 1992; **101**:898–902.
63. Sangal, R.E., Thomas, L., Mitler, M.M. Disorders of excessive sleepiness: treatment improves ability to stay awake but does not improve sleepiness. *Chest* 1992; **102**:699–703.
64. Department of Transportation. Sleep Apnea Evaluation Specifications. Federal Aviation Administration Specification letter dated 6 October 1992.
65. Doghrami, K., Mitler, M., Sangal, R.B., Shapiro, C., Taylor, S., Walsleben, J. MWT Normative Study Group. A normative study of the Maintenance of Wakefulness Test (MWT): preliminary report. Sleep Res 1996; **25**: 233.
66. Doghrami, K., Mitler, M., Sangal, R.B., Shapiro, C., Taylor, S., Walsleben, J., Belisle, C., Erman, M., Hayduk, R., Hosn, R., O'Malley, E., Sangal, J., Schutte, S., Youakin, J. A normative study of the Maintenance of Wakefulness Test (MWT). *Electroencephalogr Clin Neurophysiol* in press.
67. Erman, M., Beckham, B., Gardner, D., Roffwarg, H. The modified assessment of sleepiness test (MAST). *Sleep Res* 1987; **16**:550.
68. Borbely, A.A., Baumann, F., Brandeis, D., Strauch, I., Lehmann, D. Sleep deprivation: effect on sleep stages and EEG power density in man. *Electroencephalogr Clin Neurophysiol* 1981; **51**:483–493.
69. Hasan, J., Hirvonen, K., Varri, A., Hakkinen, V., Loula, P. Validation of computer analyzed polygraphic patterns during drowsiness and sleep onset. *Electroencephalogr Clin Neurophysiol* 1993; **87**:117–127.
70. Broughton, R., Aguirre, M., Dunham, W. A comparison of multiple and single

sleep latency and cerebral evoked potential (P300) measures in the assessment of excessive daytime sleepiness in narcolepsy–cataplexy. *Sleep* 1988; **11**:537–545.
71. *People* v. *Thompson, Thomas, M.* Orange County, California Superior Court; 1983; case no. 49758.
72. *Francisco R. Vasquez* v. *Southern Pacific Transportation Company*; 1988; Salt Lake City, Utah.
73. *Idilbi* v. *Domino's Pizza, Inc.*; Los Angeles County, California Superior Court; 1991; case No. EAC 78877.
74. *Natalia Gloria Miller* v. *Filippi's Pizza et al.*; 1992; San Diego, California Superior Court.

8

Pharmacological Aspects of Drowsiness

J.A.E. Fleming
Vancouver Hospital

The word 'drowsiness' is derived from the Old English word *drusian*, to become slow. It may be used figuratively to imply intellectual or moral dullness but more commonly it is used to denote sleepiness. Many synonyms for drowsy exist, including dozy, dreamy, somnolent and fatigued. Their gist is imprecise, often meaning different things to different people.

Although the sleepy state is accessible to introspection and can be discriminated from related feeling states such as physical and mental fatigue, depression and other dysphoria, the subjective nature of the assessment can also hinder its assessment. For example, insomniac patients often describe themselves as being sleepy although reliable and objective tests of sleepiness fail to confirm this subjective impression,[1] whereas some sleepy patients deny the existence of severe sleepiness either because it is psychologically unacceptable to them or because they have lost their frame of reference for true alertness and are simply unaware of their lapses into inattentiveness and sleep.

Additionally, the language used by patients to describe their experience can influence the detection of sleepiness. Many patients complain of being 'tired all the time' or that they have 'no drive, no energy' rather than emphasizing their sleepiness. It is this variability in word usage (criterion variance) that has been implicated, in part, for the range in the reported prevalence (from 0.3% to 13.3%) of excessive daytime sleepiness (EDS) in the general population.[2] Although it is widely recognized that specificity in terminology is desired and required, it still remains elusive.

Forensic Aspects of Sleep. Edited by C.M. Shapiro and A. McCall Smith.
© 1997 John Wiley & Sons Ltd.

Even though there may be uncertainty about the meaning and usage of terms used to describe EDS, there is an emerging consensus among sleep researchers and clinicians that drowsiness is a basic, and potentially dangerous, physiological need state,[3] similar to hunger or thirst and as basic to survival. Just as starvation increases the drive to eat and drink, sleep deprivation increases sleepiness which, in turn, is relieved by napping or sleeping.[4] However, sleepiness differs from hunger and thirst in that it can be more easily masked by factors such as encouragement, enthusiasm and exercise.[5] Consequently, behavioral and subjective indicators of drowsiness are not always accurate reflections of true sleepiness, making its subjective evaluation potentially unreliable. For example, patients with sleep apnea have been observed to fall asleep while completing a subjective assessment scale where they rate themselves as feeling alert, wide awake or functioning at a high level![6]

Because of the variability in the expression of sleepiness as well as the influence of instruction[7] and motivation[8] on sleep propensity, the clinician examining a sleepy patient may or may not observe the usual signs of sleepiness, which include yawning, drooping eyelids or ptosis, reduced activity, lapses in attention or concentration and mood changes such as a general dysphoria or irritability. Protracted observation of the patient over a number of hours and engaged in a variety of tasks may be required to reliably identify drowsiness.[9] Prior to sleep episodes, yawning, inattentiveness, ptosis and head nodding may become more apparent. Profound sleepiness, often associated with obstructive sleep apnea, may be marked by additional signs and symptoms, including witnessed blackouts, personality changes, intellectual deterioration, hallucinations or hypnagogic imagery and automatic behavior.[10]

Viewing sleepiness as occurring along a continuum from mild to severe is useful clinically and is the approach taken by the International Classification of Sleep Disorders,[11] which subdivides sleepiness into mild, moderate and severe forms (Table 1) and correlates these descriptors with values from the Multiple Sleep Latency Test (MSLT; see below for a description of this test).

Like occasional insomnia, episodic mild sleepiness is probably a universal phenomenon reflecting sleep loss associated with social or occupational demands. It may be more pervasive in special populations, for example university students, where the predisposition to daytime sleepiness is thought to be the result of sleep deprivation caused by a reduced nocturnal sleep time.[12]

Characteristically, involuntary sleep episodes (sleep attacks) do not occur with mild sleepiness, although sleep may occur in low demand situations such as watching television, attending lectures or while reading. Typically, those with mild sleepiness can choose when and where they will sleep and will often elect to nap in order to curtail it. However, even such mild sleepiness may become a safety issue whenever a sleep debt is superimposed on the two time periods where there is a natural, physiological tendency to

Table 1. Classification of mild, moderate and severe sleepiness*

Category	Circumstance	Example	Frequency	Impairment	MSLT result[†]
Mild	Only at times of rest; little attention required	Resting; watching TV; passenger in car;	Episodic; usually not every day	Minor	10–15
Moderate	Mild physical activity; at most moderate degree of attention required	Driving; attending movie, concert or theatre	Daily	Moderate	5–10
Severe	Physical activity requiring mild to to moderate attention	Eating: conversation; driving; walking	Daily	Marked	<5

* Adapted from reference 11.
† Mean value in minutes; see reference 3.

become sleepy – the early afternoon and during the night time.[13] Furthermore, sedative drugs, such as alcohol[14] and certain antihistamines,[15] increase sleepiness and the risk of falling asleep following sleep deprivation.

Moderate sleepiness is present when the person falls asleep against his or her wishes when engaged in passive, sedentary activities such as reading, attending performances or being the passenger in a vehicle. The loss of a choice and the frequency (usually daily) moves the sleepy subject from the mild to moderate level and often there is some associated impairment in occupational or social functioning. Again, moderate sleepiness super-imposed on the times of maximal circadian sleepiness increases the risk of sleep occurring.[11]

Severe sleepiness occurs when there are frequent (usually daily) unwanted sleep attacks occurring in circumstances where alertness is both required and expected. Persons with severe sleepiness fall asleep while performing activities requiring full alertness, such as driving and eating. They are often branded by others as being lazy or boring and suffer significant impairments in their working and social lives.[16] Severely hypersomnolent individuals can appear intoxicated or intellectually demented.

THE CLINICAL EVALUATION OF DROWSINESS

The episodic clinical examination, with its attendant anxiety, is unlikely to unmask mild to moderate sleepiness although if the sufferer has to wait he or she may fall asleep in the waiting or examination areas. Conversely, it is not uncommon for the severely sleepy patient to exhibit some or all of the behavioral indicators of sleepiness or even to fall asleep during the examination! Although dependent upon the subject's awareness of his or her alertness, a number of subjective tools are available to assist in the clinical evaluation of sleepiness.

The sleep diary is an indispensable tool for assessing any sleep disorder and its effect on daytime functioning.[17] Typically, patients fill out such diaries for periods varying between one and two weeks and note their sleep–wake pattern over each 24-hour period. In addition to the usual nocturnal sleep period, the patient records optional naps and involuntary sleep episodes, and may be asked to record caffeine intake or other personal strategies used to promote daytime alertness. The sleep diary is helpful to both the clinician and the patient. The former can see any patterns of voluntary or imposed sleep restriction or disorganization as well as sleep fragmentation associated with disorders that may assist in making a diagnosis; the latter may become more aware of his or her sleep patterns and their interrelationship with the complaint of daytime sleepiness.

There are a number of standardized self-rating scales available for the measurement of daytime sleepiness. The Stanford Sleepiness Scale (SSS) is a seven-point, Likert self-rating scale,[18] which has been cross-validated with performance measures before, during and after sleep deprivation.[19] Although easy to use and inexpensive, it remains a subjective measure, which may be inaccurate in those subjects habituated to their sleepiness or who, for a variety of reasons, must deny their lack of alertness.[6] Additionally, it generally does not predict individual performance *efficiency* and cannot act as a substitute for performance measures in studies involving chronic sleep loss.[20]

Visual analogue scales (VAS), which consists of a 100-mm line where one end represents the one pole of the dimension to be measured ('very sleepy') and the other is opposite ('very alert'), are easily and rapidly completed. The subject is asked to mark the line at the point which represents his or her current state of alertness.[21] Such tests measure the subject's feelings of sleepiness at a particular time point rather than the general level of daytime sleepiness and, not surprisingly, the sleepiness they measure is different from the objective sleepiness measured by the MSLT.[3] A validated self-report measure, utilizing visual analogue scales to assess sleep–wake activity, which correlates well with the MSLT is the Sleep–Wake Activity Inventory.[22] This measure identifies six factors (EDS, psychic distress, social desirability, energy level, ability to relax and nocturnal sleep) with the EDS factor being the best predictor of the average MSLT and being able to differentiate between degrees of sleepiness as measured by the MSLT.

The last validated self-report measure to be considered is the Epworth

Sleepiness Scale.[23] It is a brief, easily completed, questionnaire that asks the subject to rate on a scale from zero to three the chances, in recent time, of dozing (0 = never doze; 3 = high chance of dozing) in eight common life situations such as watching TV or being the passenger in a car. It is a retrospective evaluation of the subject's typical behavior in a variety of soporific situations and the subject is clearly asked to differentiate between sleepiness and tiredness. It enjoys good psychometric properties[24] and is conceptually unique in measuring the whole range of sleep propensities from very high (score = 24) to very low (score = 0). Furthermore, it appears to be sensitive enough to distinguish between mild sleep disorders (for example, snoring) and more severe forms (for example, obstructive sleep apnea).[20]

Although self-report measures of drowsiness are inexpensive and easy to use, their reliability fluctuates. Objective measures of sleepiness – developed for use in both diagnosing patients with sleep disorders and monitoring the effects of sleep loss and medications on daytime alertness – are more consistently reliable yet inconvenient for subjects and expensive. Briefly, we shall consider four objective measures of alertness: performance tasks, pupillometry, the Multiple Sleep Latency Test (MSLT) and the Maintenance of Wakefulness Test (MWT).

Performance tasks measure drowsiness as a decline in efficiency over a period of time on a given repetitive task, such as tapping. Additionally tests of cognitive functioning, mood and vigilance with other performance tasks of long duration are utilized in typical test batteries,[25,26] which have been shown to be sensitive to the effects of sleep loss and prophylactic napping[27] in a variety of experimental situations. By their nature, performance tasks are cumbersome, requiring the subject to spend long periods (often an hour or more per task) completing the test. Specific tests for assessing the 'carry over' effects of medications and drugs on performance are commonly used[28] as well as monitoring actual driving performance,[29] although these tests are rarely used clinically in unmedicated, sleepy populations.

An alternative strategy for measuring sleepiness is to move from measuring it by behavioral means to using physiological parameters. In 1969, Yoss and colleagues described the electronic pupillogram as a method of measuring sleepiness in narcoleptics,[30] and this procedure has been used in a number of studies of sleepy or potentially sleepy subjects.[31] The technique utilizes changes in autonomic functioning associated with states of arousal–excitation mirrored in the size of the pupil. A normal alert individual sitting quietly, in darkness can maintain a stable pupil diameter of more than 7 mm for at least 10 minutes whereas the pupil of the drowsy patient is unstable.[32] Although interpretation variance has been minimized by computerization,[33] significant problems and limitations remain.[34] Small initial pupil diameters, dark irises and lid closure in sleepy subjects all pose problems and limit the widespread acceptance of this procedure, which, none the less, is a sensitive measure of sleepiness.[15]

The first detailed electroencephalographic (EEG) description of the awake–sleep transition of drowsiness[35] was made by Loomis and colleagues in 1937[36] and these observations have been incorporated in the current electrophysiological 'gold standard'[37] in the sleep laboratory measurement of sleepiness: the Multiple Sleep Latency Test.[38] The MSLT, which is usually performed after an overnight sleep study, is a four or five 'nap opportunity' test in which the subject rests in a quiet, darkened room and latency to sleep is determined by standard electrophysiological means.[39] Its advantage over other measures of sleepiness is that it directly measures the functional consequences of sleepiness – the propensity to fall asleep – over two-hourly periods across the waking day. Although its sensitivity and specificity have not been fully assessed, it reliably detects sleepiness following sleep disruption,[3] sleep loss,[40] and the effects of hypnotic medications[41] and alcohol.[42] It has good test–retest reliability and is responsive to manipulations known to reduce sleepiness such as sleep extension[43] and the use of caffeine.[44] Its reliability in measuring sleepiness in some patients at some times is limited by the fact that if mentally stimulated by whatever means, severely sleepy individuals may have little evidence of sleepiness during the MSLT,[45] although it is a reliable indicator of sleep tendency in most patients.

The Maintenance of Wakefulness Test (MWT)[46] was developed as a modification of the MSLT; rather than measuring sleep propensity, it measures the ability to remain awake. The recording procedure differs from the MSLT in that the subject sits, semi-recumbent rather than lying down, and is instructed to remain awake (without using extraordinary techniques to do so) rather than to go to sleep. A systematic exploration of the relationship between the MWT and MSLT in 258 patients with EDS demonstrates a significant but small correlation between these two tests[47] with the MWT variance accounting for only about 16% of the MSLT variance. This finding supports other work showing low correlations between these two tests.[48] It is of interest that some patients may be discordant (e.g. have low sleep latency on the MSLT but high sleep latency on the MWT) on these two tests;[47] Sangal and colleagues showed that 15% of their patients with sleep apnea were in the bottom 50% of the MSLT (i.e. the sleepier half) yet in the top 50% on the MWT (i.e. the more alert half). The reason for this discordance, which has been noted in other syndromes causing EDS, is unclear but suggests that there may be benefit in completing both the MWT and the MSLT, rather than just one, in the assessment of the drowsy patient.

Clearly, both defining drowsiness and measuring it are difficult tasks. Although there are a variety of measures and methods for evaluating this complex state, none has yet shown predictive value – especially for complex tasks such as driving – and none is equally effective in all conditions.[49]

THE CONSEQUENCES OF DROWSINESS

Sleep deprivation experiments in healthy subjects demonstrate that excessive sleepiness accounts for performance deficits in tasks requiring vigilance and that these effects are reversed following 'catch-up' sleep.[50] Just as sleepiness shows a rapid recovery, the cognitive functions that are sensitive to various 'doses' of sleep loss – such as divergent or creative thinking, logical reasoning and auditory vigilance[51] – return to baseline after recovery sleep with only part of the sleep loss needing to be recovered for a full return of psychological performance and behavior.[52,53]

On moving from experimental studies in normal subjects to healthy individuals with unusual sleep–wake schedules or clinical populations with sleep disorders, the effects of sleep loss become more difficult to predict and are often more pervasive and potentially more lethal. For example, in the Space Shuttle Challenger accident of 1986 sleep deprivation, if not causal, was certainly contributory.[54] Prior to the fateful launch, key managers had obtained less than two hours of sleep the night before and had been on duty since 01:00 on the day of launch. The Report of the Presidential Commission on the accident states: 'time pressure . . . increased the potential for sleep loss and judgment errors.'[54] Other studies in healthy subjects exposed to sleep loss in occupational settings show that lapses of attention and increased reaction time cause increased error rates on performance tasks[55] and that, for traffic accident report data, peak effects coincide with the times of peak circadian sleepiness.[56]

In everyday life, sleep loss associated with social and occupational demands can have disastrous or potentially disastrous consequences:[57] A recent study comparing shift working nurses with nurses working only day or evening shifts, showed that the shift working group had twice the odds of nodding off while driving to or from work as well as twice the odds of a reported work accident or error related to sleepiness.[55] In addition to the transitory changes associated with sleep loss,[58] the shift worker must cope with the effects of circadian realignment[59] as well as the social demands imposed by a different work schedule.[60]

In clinical populations, the effects of EDS can be devastating,[57] affecting performance in all aspects of life but particularly within relationships and at work. Patients with narcolepsy (see below) have difficulty both in maintaining alertness and with their cognitive functioning.[61] The impaired psychomotor performance of narcoleptics is due to their excessive sleepiness rather that any specific deficits in brain functioning[62] but there is growing evidence that the neurocognitive deficits associated with obstructive sleep apnea (see below) – impaired intellectual functioning, attention, memory and executive functions[63] – are not simply manifestations of impaired vigilance but reflect the effects of nocturnal hypoxemia. Recent research suggests that hypoxemia contributes preferentially to the impairment of executive functions which, unlike the other cognitive deficits, may remain unchanged following treatment.[64]

The consequences of daytime sleepiness, regardless of its cause, are significant: night workers and rotating shift workers have a three- to five-fold increase in psychosocial problems such as an inability to find time for family obligations, community service or other routine activities, and over half of surveyed night workers report falling asleep on the job at least once a week.[57] Major, highly publicized, accidents such as Three Mile Island, the Space Shuttle Challenger and the Exxon Valdez[65] remind us of the productivity and safety issues inherently associated with EDS but, perhaps, it is on the public roadways where sleepiness can have the most disastrous results. In a recent study, 38% of commercial truck drivers reported disturbed nocturnal sleep and daytime sleepiness and 46% of 193 subjects had 10 or more oxygen desaturations per hour of sleep, indicating a significant degree of breathing disturbance during sleep.[66] Given that sleepiness or fatigue account for 57% of accidents leading to a truck driver's death[65] and that three or four other people are usually killed in such an accident[67] the cost – estimated at $2 700 000 when fatalities occur[68] – in financial and human terms is staggering.

Effective treatment strategies for clinical conditions causing EDS exist and are part of the solution to this serious problem. However, ignorance about sleep and sleepiness is widespread among both the public and the helping professions.[65] As noted in the National Commission on Sleep Disorders Research, over 90% of individuals in the United States did not have access to the benefits of sleep disorders medicine partly because of ignorance about sleep disorders at the primary care level but also because of the cost and availability of sleep specialists.[57] Just as awareness about the health dangers of environmental toxins and pollutants has changed the way we protect our environment and food chain, awareness about the effects of sleep disruption and deprivation – in concert with research into effective treatments and strategies for minimizing these effects – is likely to improve the quality and safety of our waking lives.

SLEEP DISORDERS ASSOCIATED WITH DROWSINESS

As daytime sleep propensity is related to the amount of nocturnal sleep,[5] pathological EDS can result both from the disruption of sleep by a sleep disorder and from elective sleep deprivation.[50] Most people, especially when young, curtail their nocturnal sleep for social reasons and, whether it is an acute and substantial sleep loss or a smaller and protracted one, EDS commonly results.[20] Obviously, those individuals suffering from elective sleep

Table 2. The dyssomnias*

Psychophysiological insomnia
Sleep state misperception
Idiopathic insomnia
Narcolepsy
Recurrent hypersomnia
Idiopathic hypersomnia
Post-traumatic hypersomnia
Obstructive sleep apnea syndrome
Central sleep apnea syndrome
Central alveolar hypoventilation syndrome
Periodic limb movement disorder
Restless legs syndrome

* See reference 11 for the complete classification of sleep disorders.

loss would not view themselves as being 'disordered' even though, in certain circumstances, they can show identical deficits to those with chronic sleep disorders.

A special population who suffer from involuntary, accumulative and often protracted sleep loss are shift workers.[69] Particularly vulnerable are mothers of young families, who commonly curtail their sleep time in order to meet the demands of their occupational and domestic lives.[70] It is likely that both those who voluntarily reduce their sleep and shift workers understand the cause of their sleepiness (sleep loss) but they are probably unaware that because of their increased sleep propensity,[71] they are at particular risk for inappropriate and dangerous drowsiness or unpredictable, frank sleep attacks. This risk is increased significantly by adding alcohol[72] or sedative medications[41] or by engaging in activities that require full alertness, such as driving, at the times of peak circadian sleepiness.[13]

Patient populations with clinical sleep disorders have varying degrees of EDS depending on the associated sleep disorder. Often, the EDS associated with a sleep disorder is proportional to the degree of sleep disruption caused by the disorder, with conditions such as obstructive sleep apnea having similar effects to experimentally induced sleep disruption.[73] An exception to this general rule is one of the dyssomnias (Table 2): psychophysiological insomnia. These chronic, poor sleepers experience mood disturbances as well as decrements in attention, vigilance, energy and concentration yet they are not excessively sleepy on objective measurement. They will complain of tiredness and fatigue but are rarely 'drowsy-tired' or sleepy despite substantially reduced nocturnal sleep times. Many will try to nap during the day to relieve their dysphoria and discomfort but will be unable to do so because they remain 'hyper-alert' even during the daytime.[74]

Sleep state misperception is a disorder where the complaint of insomnia or excessive sleepiness occurs without objective evidence of a sleep disturbance.[75] Although the etiology of this disorder is uncertain, a number of hypotheses have been suggested, including increased mentation or thinking during sleep or a distorted time sense[76] causing impairment in evaluating the subjective total sleep time.[77] As the sleep time is usually adequate in this patient group, objective evidence of EDS is not present.

Idiopathic insomnia is a sleep disorder which may run in families and which has its onset in childhood. It is characterized by a lifelong inability to obtain adequate sleep. An assumed biochemical or neurological process causing either hyperactivity within the 'arousal system' or hypoactivity within the 'sleep system' has been proposed but not proven and, in some cases, 'soft' neurological signs – such as dyslexia or hyperkinesis – confirm central nervous system (CNS) involvement.[11] No studies demonstrating EDS as a consequence of idiopathic insomnia have been reported, suggesting that, as in those patients with psychophysiological insomnia, hyperarousal may maintain alertness during the day.

Narcolepsy,[78] a disorder of unknown etiology, is the prototypical, clinical example of EDS. Narcoleptics experience repeated, intrusive sleep episodes in situations where drowsiness is commonly experienced such as travelling in public transport and while attending boring lectures but they also experience unpredictable sleep episodes (sleep attacks) in situations where alertness is fully expected, and required, such as when driving a car. These sleep attacks as well as the other symptoms of Narcolepsy – cataplexy (the loss of muscle power when experiencing strong emotions such as anger), sleep paralysis (waking from a sleep episode and being momentarily unable to move, caused by the extension of the voluntary muscle atonia associated with rapid eye movement (REM) sleep into wakefulness) and hypnagogic hallucinations (vivid, intense and often frightening dreams or nightmares at sleep onset) – significantly impair the sufferer.[79] Untreated patients with narcolepsy are severely sleepy by objective measures, having MSLT values of less than 5 minutes.[11]

Recurrent hypersomnia, of which the Kleine–Levin syndrome[80] is one form, is a rare disorder characterized by recurrent episodes of hypersomnia. The episodes usually occur weeks or months apart with sleepy periods lasting from several days to weeks and with a periodicity as frequent as 12 times per year. During the intervals between episodes the patient appears healthy. In the Kleine–Levin syndrome, an accompanying feature is episodic binge eating coinciding with the sleepy periods. There are no available data on the rates of psychosocial impairment or accidental injury associated with this group of disorders.[11]

Idiopathic hypersomnia (IH) is a disorder characterized by EDS but without the indicators of REM sleep intrusion (cataplexy, sleep paralysis and hypnagogic hallucinations) seen in narcolepsy. For this reason it has been known as non-REM narcolepsy.[11] Unlike narcoleptics, short naps are generally not refreshing in IH, and both the nocturnal sleep period, which is not interrupted as it is in narcolepsy, and the daytime naps tend to be longer in IH than in narcolepsy. MSLT values suggest that these patients are less sleepy than narcoleptics and are usually of less than 10 minutes.[11]

Post-traumatic hypersomnia is a sleep disorder where EDS follows a traumatic injury to the CNS, typically a closed head injury of moderate severity. Following the injury, the excessive sleepiness is part of a post-traumatic encephalopathic syndrome of headaches, fatigue, difficulty concentrating and memory impairment. In a less common variant, insomnia without daytime excessive sleepiness may be the major complaint.[11] The EDS is most prominent in the immediate post-traumatic period and resolves over weeks to months, although residual sleepiness and other sleep complaints may persist or even gradually worsen in the 6–18 months following the injury. Disabling degrees of sleepiness are seen in more severely injured individuals following long periods of coma and with other, objective, neurological deficits.[11]

Evaluations of patients with post-traumatic hypersomnia are limited and show that this is not a homogenous group.[81] Following traumatic injury, other sleep disorders, presenting as EDS, such as obstructive sleep apnea[82] and narcolepsy[78] may be 'uncovered' or caused by the initial injury, suggesting that the minimal evaluation of such patients should include a detailed sleep study, including an MSLT.[81]

Obstructive sleep apnea (OSA) syndrome[82] is a disorder characterized by repetitive episodes of upper airway obstruction, caused by the periodic collapse of the pharyngeal airway during sleep, usually associated with a reduction in blood oxygen saturation. Although the lives of millions of people each year are significantly impaired by the sequelae of OSA, often the symptoms and signs, which typically develop insidiously over a period of years, are initially overlooked. The population prevalence is estimated to be between 1 and 2%[11] and there is a strong association with obesity, neck circumference or shirt size, snoring and age.[83]

During apneas caused by airway obstruction, airflow is impeded by the collapsed pharynx despite continued efforts to breathe. This causes progressive asphyxia, which increasingly stimulates breathing efforts against the collapsed airway, typically until the person is awakened. Hypopneas predominate in some patients and are caused by partial pharyngeal collapse. The clinical sequelae of OSA relate to the cumulative effects of exposure to periodic asphyxia and to sleep fragmentation caused by apneas and hypopneas. Cardiac and vascular morbidity may include systemic hypertension, cardiac arrhythmias, pulmonary hypertension, cor pulmonale, left ventricular dysfunction, stroke and sudden death.[82] Some patients with frequent, brief apneas and hypopneas and normal underlying cardiopulmonary function may have considerable sleep disruption yet not experience nocturnal hypoxia. As the disorder progresses, sleepiness becomes increasingly irresistible and dangerous, and patients develop cognitive dysfunction, inability to concentrate, impairments in memory and judgment, irritability and depression. These problems may lead to family and social problems as well as job loss.[82]

The diagnosis of OSA is made with polysomnography, and the decision to treat is based on an overall assessment of the severity of sleep-disordered breathing, sleep fragmentation and associated clinical sequelae. The therapeutic options include continuous positive airway pressure (CPAP), the use of mechanical devices to maintain the patency of the upper airway, and corrective surgery, with effective treatment resulting in an improvement in EDS.[84] However, compliance with the most frequently used treatment – CPAP – is variable, with patients typically over-reporting their usage compared to an objective measure[85] and often using the device for less than the total sleep period.[86] A number of variables are associated with non-compliance[87] but, of note, sleeping without CPAP for just one night reverses virtually all of the sleep and daytime alertness gains derived from effective treatment.[88]

Snoring, one of the signs of OSA, is not a benign phenomenon.[89] Although not always associated with OSA, it can cause significant sleep disruption and fragmentation, resulting in daytime impairment.[90] Routinely, the clinician should ask about snoring – especially in obese patients – as well as the other signs and symptoms of OSA, including EDS, because sedative medications, which interfere with the arousal response to apneic events, worsen the condition and its morbidity.[91]

Two less common respiratory sleep disorders are central sleep apnea (CSA) syndrome and central alveolar hypoventilation syndrome.[11] Central sleep apnea is not a single disease but represents the final pathway in a large group of heterogeneous disorders, which can be classified into four groups: neurologic disorders, periodic breathing, upper airway abnormalities and idiopathic syndromes.[92] The associated clinical features result from the interaction between the underlying disorder and the control of respiration. Two different prototypes are seen: patients who are hypercapnic and those who are eucapnic or hypocapnic.[93] The common feature of these two groups is recurrent episodes of central apnea during sleep, related to the withdrawal of the drive to breathe associated with wakefulness. Although EDS has been identified in this patient group, it seems that patients with pure central sleep apnea less commonly complain of drowsiness than do patients with OSA.[94]

The final two intrinsic sleep disorders – periodic limb movement disorder (PLMD) and restless legs syndrome (RLS) – often occur together and may share common pathophysiological mechanisms.[95] In RLS, the sufferer experiences bilateral, disagreeable sensations typically in the lower limbs (the severely afflicted will be troubled by discomfort in the arms as well) just prior to sleep onset and accompanied by a compulsive drive to move the limbs.

Temporary relief from discomfort by movement is characteristic. The symptoms can last for a few minutes to hours and vary throughout the patient's lifespan.[96] The disorder peaks in middle age and increases with age so that about 34% of individuals over the age of 60 will be afflicted.[97] It is estimated to affect between 5 and 15% of the normal population yet be prevalent in a variety of other medical disorders such as uremia (20%) and rheumatoid arthritis (30%).[25]

PLMD also shows an age-related effect, with advanced age being associated with more severe findings.[98] It is found in 29% of subjects over 50 years and 44% of subjects aged 65 years and older.[28] Interestingly, even though the periodic movements cause arousals and awakenings from sleep the majority of sufferers experience insomnia without EDS. The treatment of RLS and PLMD emphasizes medications, and four groups[28] have been shown to be helpful: dopaminergic, benzodiazepine, opioids and a miscellaneous group which includes antidepressants such as trazodone.[99] As will be discussed in a later section, many medications given at night can have adverse, carry-over effects into the next day. Thus, in managing RLS and PLMD, two effects on daytime performance are to be expected: the effects of the disease process itself and the effects of the intervention, which in combination with the sleep disorder may have additive, deleterious consequences. Although there has been much research on the more morbid sleep disorders – such as OSA and narcolepsy – there are far fewer studies on RLS and PLMD, especially studies addressing long-term treatment outcome. Thus, knowledge of how these disorders, in their treated and untreated states, affect daytime performance and vigilance is scant.

MEDICAL AND PSYCHIATRIC SLEEP DISORDERS

Sleep disturbance is often a secondary symptom of a primary medical or psychiatric sleep disorder.[11] Thus, any disorder associated with discomfort or pain may cause sleep disruption and have potential, adverse consequences for daytime alertness. Most psychiatric disorders have, as an associated feature, a sleep disturbance; commonly this is insomnia but EDS is also seen.[100] Generally, when disturbed sleep has not been a problem prior to the illness episode, treatment of the primary medical or psychiatric disorder will result in an eventual return to normal sleep. However, in certain disorders – such as Parkinsonism[101] and the often chronic, usually recurrent, mood disorders[102] – a protracted sleep disturbance may persist and become a focus for additional treatment.

The secondary sleep disorders are a complicated and poorly understood group. For example, although the daytime symptoms of Parkinsonism have been recognized for almost 200 years, the nocturnal symptoms – which occur in up to 75% of patients – and their associated sleep abnormalities have only been systematically studied in the past 30 years.[101] Furthermore, differences between a disorder with and without a secondary sleep disorder are not well studied or delineated. For example, it is known that patients with mood disorders have increased accident rates but it is unknown if this rate is changed by the addition of a secondary sleep disturbance.[102]

The circadian rhythm sleep disorders

This group of disorders are clustered together as they share a common chronophysiological basis.[103] Their major feature is a misalignment between the patient's sleep pattern and that which is desired: the patient cannot sleep when sleep is desired, needed or expected.[11] Because sleep episodes occur at inappropriate times, wake periods can occur at undesired times and patients complain of insomnia or EDS.

In the time zone change or jet lag syndrome, depending on the number of time zones crossed, there will be varying degrees of difficulty in initiating and maintaining sleep, EDS, decrements in daytime alertness and performance as well as bodily symptoms that are largely related to gastrointestinal function. Other factors influencing the severity of the disorder include the direction of travel (eastward or westward, with westward travel being better tolerated than eastward), the time of the flight and individual susceptibility, including the age of the traveller.[104] Although the symptoms (such as fatigue) can be related to long flights, typically they result from sleep deprivation[11] and they usually abate within two or three days, occasionally lasting for as long as eight days. There are only a few studies on healthy young subjects affected by jet lag[105,106] and these demonstrate a variety of performance decrements. There are no systematic data on the effects of jet lag on patients with sleep or medical disorders although an additive effect on daytime performance would be expected.

Treatment of the jet lag syndrome includes attempting to facilitate sleep during 'off' times through the use of behavioral strategies,[107] sleep promoting medicines[108] or by changing the phase adjustment of the body clock through the use of chronobiotics such as light[109] or melatonin.[110] Hypnotics, which are the most commonly used intervention, are not – as discussed later – without risk, and longer acting hypnotics may increase daytime sedation rather than promote alertness.[108]

Shift work sleep disorder occurs in individuals required to work during the habitual hours of sleep. Typically, the sleep complaint is of difficulty sleeping, with unsatisfactory or non-restorative sleep, resulting in EDS. The condition usually persists for the duration of the work shift period.[11] Sleep loss results in reduced alertness, with consequent increases in accident proneness, and both occur during and after the work period.[57]

Individual differences in adaptation to shift work are well known;[60] 'night owls', coping better than 'larks' and the elderly, as with jet lag, doing less well than younger subjects. Shift work is known to have medical and psychiatric consequences,[111] but perhaps the largest health and safety issue arises from the loss of vigilance associated with the time on task.[112] There is debate over whether or not the disturbed sleep of shift workers is a disorder or just a problem;[113] none the less, there is consensus that the relative sleep deprivation and associated EDS cause significant morbidity and, even though there is no single panacea, a number of coping strategies may be helpful. Thus, education of both workers and shift schedule coordinators has been suggested and should include information about how circadian, sleep and domestic factors can influence the ability to cope with this type of work.[60] In some cases, educational and behavioral strategies will be insufficient and pharmacological interventions will be required. As for jet lag, the choice of drug is important to prevent the additional problem of sedation when maximal alertness is desired.[114]

The irregular sleep–wake pattern describes a temporally disorganized and variable sleep–wake schedule. Here, the average sleep time within the 24-hour period is normal but no single sleep period is of normal length and the timing of sleep is unpredictable.[11] Difficulty initiating and maintaining sleep as well as daytime napping are common but, unlike the remaining three circadian sleep disorders – advanced (ASPS) and delayed (DSPS) sleep phase syndromes and the non-24 hour sleep–wake syndrome – there are no recognizable ultradian or circadian patterns of sleep onset or wake times. Sleep is broken up into short blocks within each 24-hour period, with marked variability in the timing of sleep and wakefulness.

Although the prevalence is unknown, this syndrome is most common in patients with severe congenital, developmental or degenerative brain dysfunction, although rare cases have been seen in patients without brain damage who have ceased to adhere to a regular rest–activity pattern. Other factors predisposing individuals to this disorder include mood disorders and long convalescences with extensive bed rest.[11] The syndrome may be common in institutionalized patients and is responsive to treatment with melatonin,[115] although there have been no systematic, controlled studies of the management of the irregular sleep–wake pattern. In practice, a combination of behavioral[116] and chronobiological interventions are commonly used.[109,110] Care must be exercised to avoid compounding the problems of the cognitively impaired by over-sedating them with medications.

In the DSPS,[117] the major sleep episode is delayed in relation to the desired bedtime, resulting in difficulty in initiating sleep and in awakening at the desired time. When forced to get up at a normal time, patients with DSPS will be relatively sleep deprived and share the same symptoms as sleep deprived subjects,[50] including EDS. When allowed to sleep without constraint, such as at weekends, the sleep period of these patients is of normal duration but delayed in onset and, although varying from patient to patient, typically would run from late at night (e.g. 05:00) to the early afternoon (e.g. 13:00). DSPS is multi-factorial, dependent on lifestyle, mood and personality, as well as on familial factors but no single factor in isolation is sufficient to explain the delay in sleep timing.[118] Its prevalance is unknown but it probably accounts for between 5 and 10% of patients presenting to sleep disorders centers with the complaint of insomnia. Typically the disorder starts in adolescence after a period of late night studying, partying or shift work.[11] In about half of the cases psychopathology is present and when severe this may complicate recovery.[119] A variety of chronobiological strategies[120] have been employed to manage this disorder and currently melatonin is probably the easiest treatment regime to follow.[121] None the less, a comprehensive treatment addressing psychosocial issues as well as the disturbed timing of sleep is advised[120] to maximize the short-term benefit, although, in some cases, the long-term prognosis is poor.[118]

The ASPS is the opposite of the DSPS: there is a persistent early evening sleep onset (e.g. 20:00) and early morning awakening (e.g. 05:00), with attempts to retire and get up later usually being futile.[120] There are only a few cases of this syndrome reported in the literature, making it difficult to define its clinical course and treatment. As with other sleep disorders, if there is significant sleep disruption or deprivation then EDS may result, and should individuals with ASPS be required to work evening or night shifts marked sleepiness would result.[11] Because of the rarity of this disorder, definitive treatments have not been identified, although, as expected, one case has shown a response to evening light treatment.[122]

In the non–24 hour sleep–wake syndrome there is a chronic and consistent daily delay of about 1–2 hours in sleep onset and awakening times. The pattern is reminiscent of the free-running pattern seen in time isolation studies.[11] As the patient literally will sleep around the clock, there will be times when they will be in phase with normal social activity and there may be no complaint. When out of phase, there will be difficulty initiating sleep and the subsequent sleep deprivation may affect alertness and cause EDS. It is a rare disorder, with the majority of sufferers being blind; some have been retarded and others have had severe personality disorders of the avoidant or schizoid type.[11] Recent treatment studies have emphasized the use of melatonin[123] and bright light.[124]

To summarize this section, the sleep disorders associated with EDS represent a heterogeneous group where a common disturbance by a disease or circadian process changes the quality and length of the major sleep period. Usually their management focuses on treating the primary sleep disorder and, with a successful outcome, the EDS resolves. In some instances, less than optimal results occur and the EDS requires the use of additional treatments, notably the use of psychostimulants to promote daytime alertness.

RECREATIONAL DRUGS AND DROWSINESS

By understanding a drug's mechanism of action a variety of effects on both daytime functioning and sleep can be predicted. However, scientific knowledge about the direct effects of commonly used social or recreational drugs, such as caffeine, nicotine and alcohol,[125] on sleep is limited with these studies focusing on small numbers of subjects and acute, usually nocturnal, drug effects. Although the International Classification of Sleep Disorders identifies two drug related sleep disorders – the stimulant dependent and alcohol dependent sleep disorders[11] – no formal studies have been completed which assess changes in daytime sleepiness and performance caused by the direct effects of recreational drug use on nocturnal sleep.

Stimulant dependent sleep disorder is characterized by centrally acting stimulants causing a reduction of sleepiness or suppression of sleep during use and alterations in wakefulness following abstinence. The central stimulants encompass a variety of drugs, including phenylethylamines (e.g. amphetamines), cocaine, thyroid hormones and the xanthine derivatives, caffeine and theophylline. Many stimulants are used therapeutically for their peripheral sympathomimetic effects as decongestants and bronchodilators and others are used as appetite supressants and for the treatment of attention deficit disorder. As discussed later, in sleep disorders medicine stimulant medications are commonly used to treat EDS. The widely available and commonly used stimulants – caffeine, nicotine and cocaine – can all induce the stimulant dependent sleep disorder, causing insomnia and sleep loss. Following the cessation of high dose usage, a withdrawal syndrome is common and may be characterized by transient hypersomnolence.[11]

Caffeine

Caffeine, the most widely used drug in our society,[125] is a central nervous system stimulant often used to promote alertness.[44] Its effects are dose dependent and, for beverages, the dose varies according to the method of preparation.[126] Depending on whether it is brewed or percolated, a cup of coffee contains between 100 and 200 mg of caffeine, while tea and soft drinks, such as Pepsi and Coke, contain between 50 and 75 mg.[125] An often overlooked source of caffeine is certain foodstuffs (for example, chocolate and cocoa) and a number of over-the-counter medications, including cold remedies and pain killers.

Caffeine reaches its peak plasma level within an hour (usually 15–45 minutes) of intake and its elimination half-life, which shows great variability among individuals, ranges from 3 to 7 hours. Because it is widely known that caffeine can promote alertness, lessen fatigue and reverse the effects of sleep deprivation,[127] it is not surprising to find it being used frequently in chronically sleep deprived populations, such as students, travellers suffering from jet lag and shiftworkers.[128] However, because it is a potent sleep inhibitor, the gain in daytime alertness may be at the cost of the next night's sleep performance. This can result in a vicious cycle of caffeine being used to maintain alertness causing nocturnal sleep loss, which in turn causes next day fatigue, requiring further caffeine use for its management.

Caffeine's effect on sleep is dose and time dependent, with large doses taken close to bedtime having the worst effect.[125] Furthermore, previous exposure to caffeine and tolerance to its stimulant effect is important; non-consumers note more marked sleep disruption following caffeine intake than those who use it habitually and have developed tolerance to its stimulant effects.[129] An indirect effect of moderate caffeine use throughout the day on nocturnal sleep has also been noted: Withdrawal symptoms – such as headache – following the day's heavy use may delay sleep onset.[130]

Sleep laboratory studies have shown that when consumed within an hour of bedtime, caffeine increases the time taken to fall asleep (sleep latency) and the number of awakenings after sleep onset, and decreases the total sleep time and the amount of deep or delta sleep.[131] Thus, consumption of coffee or caffeine containing products in the evening can adversely affect sleep performance objectively, and this deterioration in sleep efficiency is often, but not always, discernible to the sleeper.[129] However, no study has shown that the sleep disruption associated with caffeine use alone results in objectively measurable changes, by the MSLT, MWT, or performance tests measuring next day alertness.

Although it can be concluded from clinical experience and research data that caffeine adversely affects sleep performance, there is only one study that has evaluated the impact of changing caffeine intake on sleep.[132] Edelstein and colleagues showed that eliminating caffeine in 10 psychiatric inpatients with sleep maintenance insomnia both decreased the number of awakenings and reduced the number of requests for sleep-promoting medications. These and other observations have led to the formulation of one of the golden rules of good sleep hygiene: curtail, or preferably eliminate, caffeine intake and never consume caffeinated products 4–6 hours before retiring.[125]

The alerting effect of caffeine which can be detrimental to nocturnal sleep can be helpful in situations where there is a voluntary or imposed sleep restriction.[133] Clinical experience suggests – and some studies support – that patients who are chronically sleep deprived attempt to maintain alertness through the use of caffeine.[127] Clearly, this can be a successful short-term strategy but there is a theoretical possibility that suddenly curtailing high caffeine doses will evoke a withdrawal syndrome (beginning within 12–24 hours of stopping and lasting for about a week), which, combined with a sleep debt, may result in significant EDS.[134]

Nicotine

Laboratory and survey studies show that nicotine has much the same effects as caffeine on nocturnal sleep, daytime performance and mood.[135] Nicotine has a biphasic effect producing, at low blood concentrations, a sedating and relaxing effect and, with higher blood levels, stimulation.[136] Like caffeine, the dose is important, with higher doses (i.e. smoking rates; nicotine content of smoked or chewed material) producing more stimulation and physiological arousal (i.e. increase heart rate, blood pressure and blood catecholamine levels).[125]

Smokers of one pack or more per day have significantly more difficulty in falling asleep than either non-smokers or those smoking less than one pack per day.[137] Generally, smokers take longer to fall asleep and have a lower sleep efficiency (time asleep divided by the time in bed) than non-smokers. A recent study on the use of the nicotine patch on non-smoking snorers[138] confirms the findings of previous studies on the effects of nicotine on sleep. In these 20 subjects, the patch caused a significant reduction in the total sleep time (by over half an hour), a lengthening of the sleep latency, a reduction in the amount of REM sleep and a reduction in sleep efficiency from 89.7% to 83.5%. Whether or not these changes would be seen in smokers using the patch to quit smoking awaits further study. A further impediment to sound sleep is the interrelationship between smoking and other drug use. Smokers are high users of caffeine and other recreational drugs,[139] and the resultant effects of this interaction are additive and are especially detrimental to sleep.[125]

The acute effects of smoking cessation are controversial, with one study demonstrating an improvement in sleep quality[140] and another finding a significant increase in nocturnal arousals and awakenings and increased sleepiness, as measured by the MSLT during withdrawal.[141] Conventional wisdom suggests that after the withdrawal period is over, sleep quality improves once patients stop smoking.[135]

Nicotine, like caffeine, is commonly used by smokers to promote alertness and it has been shown both to improve performance on tasks requiring sustained attention and, during acute withdrawal, to cause a deterioration in psychomotor performance.[142] Nonetheless, clinical experience has demonstrated that curtailing smoking can result, with time, in improved sleep quality, which may be related to both drug effects (decreased nocturnal arousal) and behavioral effects (decreased conditioned or learnt awakenings to smoke during the night). To promote sound sleep, smokers should preferably cease smoking or curtail their intake prior to the sleep period and avoid smoking when waking up during the night.[125]

Cocaine

Cocaine hydrochloride, derived from the coca plant *Erythroxylon coca*, is a potent stimulant causing a similar sleep disturbance to that seen with amphetamine:[139] delay in sleep onset, (prolonged sleep latency) and a reduction in the total sleep time, with REM sleep being profoundly affected (shortened onset to the first REM period and suppression of REM sleep).[143] Typically, cocaine abuse or dependence does not occur in isolation and – as with nicotine use – other drugs, frequently alcohol, are used concurrently.[144] Thus, the effects on sleep can be complex. There are no studies measuring the effects of cocaine use on daytime sleepiness although hypersomnolence ('crashing') during withdrawal is a well-known feature of abstinence from cocaine[145] and other stimulants.

During the withdrawal process, sleep remains disturbed.[146] There is a rebound of REM sleep and the REM latency remains short. By the third week of withdrawal a disrupted sleep pattern persists and is very similar to that seen in chronic insomnia – a long sleep latency, increased wakefulness after sleep onset and a low sleep efficiency – but, to date, no study has measured daytime sleepiness or performance decrements as a function of this sleep loss.

Alcohol

Just as caffeine and nicotine may be used as self-medication, alcohol is commonly used for its sedative properties and this use is frequently combined with other recreational drugs, complicating the clinical presentation of many drug users.[147] Even when used alone, the consumption of alcohol is prevalent: about 90% of adults drink alcohol containing beverages, and alcohol use becomes problematic for between 40 and 50% of men, who will develop a temporary alcohol induced problem. About 10% of men and 3–5% of women will go on to develop persistent and pervasive alcohol-related life problems.[148]

Alcohol has complex effects on sleep. At low to moderate doses it induces sleep (shortens sleep latency) and reduces wakefulness for the first three to four hours of sleep, but often sleep becomes fragmented for the remainder of the night.[149] Typically, it reduces the time spent in delta (deep) sleep and it also suppresses REM sleep, which may rebound – causing nightmares and wakefulness – once use is stopped.[135] Typically, with nightly administration, tolerance to the sleep promoting effect takes place and the user has to increase the dose to get the same, original effect. As alcohol exacerbates sleep related breathing disorders and sleep apnea by potentiating sleep related atonia in the upper airway,[150] self-medication with alcohol can expose the undiagnosed sufferer to significant medical risks, including EDS.

The International Classification of Sleep Disorders identifies an alcohol dependent sleep disorder characterized by the use of alcohol for its hypnotic effects. In this disorder, alcohol use occurs in the evening and is not associated with alcoholic patterns of drinking.[11] With sustained use, tolerance develops and the user will often need to increase consumption in order to obtain the original sedative effect. The amount of alcohol consumed may be sufficient to cause a withdrawal reaction on discontinuation and, typically, when the user stops the insomnia complaint returns with more marked disruption of sleep (delayed sleep onset, more awakenings and decreased total sleep time).

Recovered alcoholics experience disturbed sleep even after they have been abstinent for some years.[151] However, there are no studies indicating whether or not this disturbance results in daytime impairment although it is recognized that the continued presence of significant insomnia is a risk factor for restarting or continuing drinking.[152]

It is important to remember the significant interaction between sleepiness, caused by sleep deprivation, and the behavioral effects of drugs. Although this effect has been demonstrated experimentally for alcohol and caffeine, it is likely to occur with any drug possessing stimulant or sedating properties. For example, the sedative effects of ethanol taken in the morning after a person has spent 11 hours asleep and the stimulant effects of caffeine taken on arising after 5 or 8 hours asleep result in the same degree of objective sleepiness[153] despite the different effects of these drugs on the CNS. Of note, increasing nocturnal sleep time can protect against some of the sedating and performance effects of alcohol.[154] It can be inferred from these data that individuals who are sleep deprived from any occupational, social or medical cause may be at increased risk for EDS when sedative drugs, including alcohol, are taken. Furthermore, carry-over effects for alcohol have been demonstrated in healthy, young good sleepers following a moderate, nocturnal dose of alcohol.[155] This residual effect persisted even after ethanol had been nearly completely eliminated from the blood and suggests that there is a risk of a persistent, next morning effect on alertness – independent of impaired motor function or reaction time – which may cause impairments in complex tasks such as driving.

Cannabis

Δ^9-Tetrahydrocannabinol (THC), the main active component of cannabis, is a sedative capable of inducing sleep and causing performance deficits.[156] When used with alcohol the effects of both are greater than either drug used alone.[157] Cannabis causes a reduction in stage REM sleep and a slight increase in stage delta sleep, and this pattern is reversed (i.e. REM rebound and decreased stage delta) on withdrawal.[158]

When used alone, marijuana impairs psychomotor skills such as driving, with 94% of subjects failing a roadside sobriety test 90 minutes after smoking the drug.[159] Even though no studies have been performed on the effects of cannabis on daytime sleepiness, either alone or in combination with sleep loss, studies of other sedatives suggest that a combined interactive effect is likely.[153] As THC has been found in the blood of 13.4% of traffic fatalities, usually in combination with alcohol,[159] the sleepy driver or worker may be at increased risk for accidental injury when mixing sleep loss with these drugs.

The hallucinogens

There are very few studies on the effects of the psychotomimetics (e.g. lysergic acid diethylamide (LSD), phencyclidine etc.) on sleep, with most early studies focusing on acute sleep disturbances caused by psychotomimetic use.[160] There is a known association between these drugs and the subsequent development of major psychiatric disorders, and sleep disturbance, with or without EDS, may develop as part of the associated features of these conditions.[161]

In humans the acute effects of LSD on sleep predominantly affect sleep architecture, principally increasing REM sleep time and arousals.[162] As with the other hallucinogens and 'designer drugs,' there are no studies of daytime sleepiness as a consequence of the known sleep disturbance which occurs with these agents,[163] although EDS associated with sleep loss from social and drug related causes would be expected.

THERAPEUTIC DRUGS AND DROWSINESS

Often when using medications which affect the central nervous system there is a trade-off between the desired therapeutic effect and troublesome adverse effects such as sedation. When side effects outweigh benefit, they can place the patient at risk[164] or indirectly protract recovery through non-compliance with the treatment plan; either outcome adversely affects the patient's quality of life. Improving on the efficacy and side-effect profile of established medications is part of the drive to develop new drugs and, over the years, significant pharmacological advances have resulted in the marketing of new medicines which have changed substantially the management of common medical[165] and psychiatric disorders.[166]

How a given drug will influence the human organism depends on a number of factors, including the formulation of the drug, its mode of administration, pharmacokinetics and pharmacodynamics as well as the age, gender, race and health of the recipient. (A detailed consideration of these phenomena is outside the scope of this chapter and the interested reader is directed elsewhere for a comprehensive review of these matters.[167]) In evaluating the available data on the effects of medications on human performance, it is important to remember that there are relatively few reported studies, many of which focus on the acute effects of medicines on small numbers of usually healthy, young subjects. Useful as these studies may be, they are limited in informing us about drug effects on the major users of these drugs, the infirm elderly.[168] A further limitation is that there is no established consensus as to how centrally acting agents should be evaluated and it is unlikely that a variety of tests (for example, computerized performance batteries, simulated driving tasks, on-road driving tests) measure the same skill or impairment,[169] but the use of non-standardized tests has raised questions about the validity of some research studies evaluating the psychomotor effects of drugs.[170] Thus, for a variety of reasons, there are inherent difficulties in characterizing classes of drugs in terms of their effects on sleep and vigilance. Often the evidence is sketchy or contradictory and the clinical relevance unclear or uncertain.

The anxiolytic-hypnotics

The most commonly used anxiolytic-hypnotics belong to the benzodiazepine class or its congeners. This group of medications has seen its share of controversy[171] yet benzodiazepines continue to be widely used for the management of insomnia and anxiety. Within this class, studies on the effects of diazepam on performance far exceed any other drug studied,[164] with laboratory, driving simulator and on-road studies showing that diazepam impairs many aspects of performance in dosages as low as 5 mg and these acute, single-dose effects remain for up to 5 hours[164] and, in one study, even after 3 weeks of continuous treatment, tolerance to these behavioral effects did not occur.[172]

As other benzodiazepines were developed, it became apparent that factors such as the rate of absorption, distribution and half-life were related to a drug's capacity to produce the adverse side effect of EDS, and long half-life compounds (for example, flurazepam and diazepam) were shown to cause more EDS than shorter acting drugs (for example, triazolam and lorazepam).[173] For these reasons the preferred benzodiazepines for managing sleep related complaints, uncomplicated by concurrent psychiatric disorders, are the short to medium half-life compounds and, because higher doses may also produce sedation,[164] the lowest effective dose should always be used.

Three different molecules have resulted from the attempt to decrease the performance deficits seen with the benzodiazepine sedative-hypnotics: buspirone, zopiclone and zolpidem. The azapirone buspirone owes much of its anxiolytic activity to its ability to attenuate central 5-hydroxytryptamine neurotransmission without any effect on GABAergic mechanisms (the mode of action of the benzodiazepines).[174] Thus, it possesses a much lower sedative potential than the benzodiazepines[170] but, unfortunately, its anxiolytic effect develops slowly over several weeks[175] and it usually worsens the sleep of insomniac patients.[176] However, in performance tests at low dosages (10–20 mg) buspirone does not affect performance and, unlike the benzodiazepines, it has no significant interaction with alcohol.[177]

The cyclopyrrolone zopiclone[178] and the imidazopyridine zolpidem[179] are newer and extensively studied hypnotics. Even though their effects are mediated by GABAergic mechanisms, some studies have shown that they cause less next-day sedation and improved psychomotor performance when compared to benzodiazepine sedatives. However, like buspirone, both zopiclone and zolpidem show extended, next-day impairments in performance when used in higher dosages.[180,179] Both simulated[181] and real[182] driving studies show that these two new drugs are an advance on earlier drug treatments for insomnia but a consensus on how much better they are, in terms of psychomotor performance, remains elusive.[183,184]

The antidepressants

Centrally acting medications produce sedation by interacting with receptors involved in various neurotransmitter systems.[185] The tricyclic antidepressants affect a number of transmitter systems, including histaminic, noradrenergic, cholinergic and serotoninergic mechanisms. Their effects on both histamine and adreno receptors are thought to be responsible for their sedative effects.[186] Additionally most, but not all, antidepressants affect the timing and duration of REM sleep, an effect that has no known consequence for daytime alertness but which is thought to be a phenomenon associated with a drug's antidepressant effect.[187]

Typically, impaired performance and daytime drowsiness result from the sedative profile of the antidepressant,[188] and this is worst for the so-called sedative antidepressants, such as amitriptyline, doxepin and mianserin, and less problematic for more stimulating drugs, such as protriptyline, nortriptyline and desipramine.[156] However, some authorities consider that only one antidepressant, amitriptyline, has been studied with sufficient rigor to conclude that it unequivocally impairs psychomotor performance.[164]

The newer antidepressants – the specific serotonin re-uptake inhibitors[189] – are usually free of direct sedative effects although they can cause EDS through their initial effects on nocturnal sleep. Because of its relatively stimulating effect, fluoxetine[190] has been noted to improve performance on psychomotor tests, including those associated with driving skills.[191]

In patients with mood disorders (compared to healthy controls), there is a great variability in complex performance tasks such as driving.[192] When utilizing sedative antidepressants these patients show changes in performance similar to those seen with age and gender, and, generally, these effects do not rule out safe driving.[172] However, not uncommonly, combinations of sedative drugs (for example, diazepam and amitriptyline) are used to control severe symptoms and the chronic, combined effects of such usage on psychomotor performance is not well understood.

Mood disorders can feature marked sleep disturbance as one of the symptoms yet there are no studies of the daytime performance of recovering depressives who, even on medications, continue to have sleep disruption, although additive impairments may be anticipated. Additionally, patients often use socially sanctioned drugs such as alcohol in order to modify their symptoms and this interaction of two or more central sedatives, with or without sleep loss, may place the patient at particular risk.[193] The newer antidepressants[194] bring distinct advantages, which improve compliance with treatment and outcome and, particularly, free the patient from troublesome sedative effects which are known to interfere with the safe execution of a number of tasks of daily living, including driving.[195]

Lithium, used as a mood stabilizer in manic-depressive illness and, less frequently, as an alternative or supplement to antidepressants[196] has similar effects on sleep to those observed with antipsychotic drugs (see below). Therapeutic doses suppress REM sleep and increase the latency to REM sleep. Slow wave sleep is usually increased, with wakefulness being reduced, although changes in total sleep time are not always observed.[156] Drowsiness, fatigue and cognitive difficulties have been reported as side effects with lithium;[197] however, they are not a consistent feature and may reflect confounding contributions from the patient's affective disorder.[156] In complex performance tasks only a very small number of patients taking lithium alone have been studied.[192]

The antipsychotics

Several classes of drugs, including the phenothiazines, thioxanthines and butyrophenones, are used as antipsychotic or neuroleptic agents.[198] They share many pharmacological properties, with their antipsychotic action resulting from central blockade of dopamine but their sedative side effects being related to blockade of central adrenoreceptors.[156] Like the tricyclics, many antipsychotics affect more than one neurotransmitter system, including 5-hydroxytryptamine, muscarinic, acetylcholine and histamine receptors, and the ratio of alpha-adrenergic to dopaminergic receptor affinity may predict the severity of sedation.[199] Additionally, as for other centrally acting drugs, additive sedative effects may be seen when these medications are taken concurrently with other compounds such as antihistamines, alcohol, hypnotics and anxiolytics.

There is wide variability within the class of medications regarding sleep and their sedative profiles. As a class they tend to reduce wakefulness and increase slow wave sleep but their effects on REM sleep depend on their specificity for a particular receptor system.[156] For example, the relatively specific dopamine agonists (e.g. pimozide) have no effect on REM sleep. At low doses chlorpromazine's $alpha_2$-adrenergic blocking effect predominates causing an increase in REM sleep but, at higher dosages, chlorpromazine's action at postsynaptic, $alpha_1$ receptors predominates, causing a reduction in

REM sleep.[156] REM sleep may also be affected by the anticholinergic activity of the antipsychotic as muscarinic mechanisms are involved in REM sleep timing.[187] The butyrophenones (e.g. haloperidol) and the substituted benzamides (e.g. remoxipride) are less sedative than the phenothiazines (e.g. chlorpromazine) and tolerance to their sedative effects usually occurs quite rapidly.

In tests of psychomotor performance, inherent disturbances associated with the schizophrenic process influence the results in addition to the effects of any medication.[200] Schizophrenics, during the acute phases of their illness, find it difficult to concentrate on certain tasks which assess psychomotor performance and, therefore, the tests chosen must be sensitive to these issues. In addition to the effects of sedation, many antipsychotics affect movement due to actions on dopamine transmission, and these dyskinesias can affect daytime performance both directly and indirectly through disturbed sleep.[101] There are few studies on the effects of antipsychotics on complex performance tasks such as driving[200] but one study of 22 patients, receiving depot neuroleptics for chronic schizophrenia, showed a significant decrement in driving performance compared to the normal control group.[201]

The newer antipsychotics clozapine and risperidone have been significant additions to the treatment of psychosis.[202] Clozapine is currently recommended for treatment resistant schizophrenia and for managing the negative symptoms of that disorder. In a dose dependent manner, it is very sedating, affecting up to 40% of treated patients,[203] but tolerance to this effect develops within 4–6 weeks.[204] In the elderly, however, sedation is problematic.[205] Unlike clozapine, the benzisoxazole risperidone produces less sedation and is better tolerated[206] even though sedation and drowsiness are often the most frequently reported treatment-emergent adverse events.[207] Interestingly, compared with the newer hypnotics and antidepressants, there have been far fewer investigations into the psychomotor effects of these atypical antipsychotics even though sedation and drowsiness are known consequences of initial treatment. To date, the only observable difference between the effects of antipsychotics and benzodiazepines in healthy volunteers is that the benzodiazepines cause pleasant sedation while for the antipsychotics the sedation is usually considered unpleasant.[208]

Antihistamines

Allergic diseases are very common and affect one of every six persons in the United States.[209] The clinical use of antihistamines has expanded steadily since their introduction in the early 1940s and survey findings show that 30 million Americans took an antihistamine within a given year. In 1988 $2 billion worth of antihistamines (including antihistamine-decongestant combinations) were consumed.[210]

Antihistamines exert their primary pharmacological effect by blocking receptor sites and preventing the action of histamine on the cell but it is the drug's capacity to cross the blood–brain barrier that determines its effect on alertness and performance. Unlike the old, small, water-soluble anti-histamines, which enter the brain easily, the newer, non-sedating anti-histamines are large, lipophobic molecules with a charged side chain that are extensively bound to protein and, therefore, have difficulty crossing the blood–brain barrier.[210] Sedation is the most common side effect of the first generation antihistamines, affecting 10–25% of users,[210] with this effect being discernible on the MSLT.[211] Sedation has been attributed to a variety of mechanisms such as the inhibition of N-methyltransferase and blockade of central histaminergic receptors, although serotoninergic antagonism, anticholinergic activity and blockade of central alpha adrenoreceptors have been implicated.[156]

An epidemiological study of fatal automobile accidents demonstrates that sedation translates into risk: drivers responsible for the accident which killed them were 1.5 times more likely to have been using a first generation anti-histamine than drivers who were not responsible for the accidents in which they were killed.[212] As for other sedative drugs, tests of psychomotor performance, simulated driving studies and on-road assessments show decrements in performance related to the type of antihistamine used and its dosage. In one study where d-chlorpheniramine was used 60% of the subjects were deemed incapable of continuing the 2.5 hour driving task.[210] Fortunately, pharmacological research has provided a variety of H_1 anti-histamines which are free of central effect in certain dosages and these are now the medications of choice for those who require full alertness and anti-histaminic effects.[213]

Miscellaneous agents

A variety of different medications for varying disorders can adversely affect sleep and daytime functioning.[156] The opioids, such as morphine and heroin, have a well-known sedative effect, producing drowsiness and mental clouding in acute dosages.[214] Tolerance to these effects can develop and, with chronic use, the withdrawal syndrome may include sleep disturbance and daytime sleepiness. Therapeutic dosages of the less potent opioid analgesics (such as codeine and pentazocine) have limited effects on psychomotor performance but these drugs do affect mood, and car accidents involving heroin addicts are more likely to reflect mood changes than impairment in psychomotor functioning.[215] Because the opioids are CNS depressants it is probable that additive interactions with alcohol and other sedatives occur, especially in naive subjects, but this possibility has not received much attention.[216] Although acetylsalicylic acid (ASA) may have hypnotic activity mediated by inhibition of prostaglandin synthesis or body temperature,[156] it, like acetaminophen, does not impair psychomotor performance yet ASA is found frequently in the blood of drivers involved in motor vehicle accidents.[215] Sedation is a recognized side effect of the non-steroidal anti-inflammatory drugs[217] and indomethacin and phenylbutazone affect psychomotor performance in the 50 mg and 200 mg dosage, respectively.[215] In one case report, naproxen caused a sleep disturbance related to nightmares.[218]

A number of drugs that act on the cardiovascular system have effects on sleep. The lipophilic beta-blockers such as propanolol and pindolol are associated with insomnia and nightmares; theoretically, the associated sleep disturbance could affect daytime alertness. Additionally, drowsiness may be caused by a blockade of noradrenergic vigilance-enhancing pathways.[156] The antihypertensive, clonidine, is sedative, an effect thought to be mediated by reduced dopamine turnover and which can persist for up to one month after treatment is commenced.[156] Methyldopa rarely affects nocturnal sleep despite changes in sleep architecture (increased REM sleep; decreased delta sleep). Sedation is the most frequently reported adverse effect, with about 30% of patients complaining of drowsiness, fatigue and lethargy.[156] Calcium channel blockers are associated with sedation but nifedipine does not appear to affect psychomotor performance.[219]

It is clear that a variety of drugs – both recreational and therapeutic – can affect sleep and daytime performance. This can be a direct, central effect with measurable consequences or an indirect effect mediated through sleep loss or deprivation, the latter disturbance being more difficult to record and measure scientifically yet as likely as the former to jeopardize the safety of the user.

THE THERAPEUTICS OF DROWSINESS

The first essential step to managing the patient with EDS is a careful sleep, medical and psychiatric history, because this will help determine if the patient's complaints reflect inadequate sleep, a primary sleep disorder or a sleep disturbance secondary to a medical or psychiatric disorder. Despite the considerable advances made in the diagnosis and treatment of sleep disorders in the past two decades, inadequate clinical assessments continued to be an obstacle to securing effective treatments for patients suffering from these disorders.[220] Careful evaluation of the patient and, ideally, at least a three-day, 24-hour sleep–wake diary will assist in determining the correct diagnosis, although some patients will require monitoring of their sleep.

In reviewing the sleep history and the sleep diary, the cause of some cases of EDS immediately will become apparent. The middle-aged housewife, who must get up at 04:30 to complete a long journey to her workplace and who, because of family demands, cannot retire until 23:30 is likely falling asleep at her desk in the mid-afternoon because of chronic sleep deprivation. If reallocating the household duties and increasing her sleep time corrects the daytime complaint, no further action will be required, but if EDS continues then further investigations will be necessary before a rational treatment can begin.

After assessing the sleep history and the sleep diary, the clinician needs to review sleep hygiene with the patient.[135] Poor sleep hygiene can complicate the presentation and management of any sleep disorder, so the rules of good sleep hygiene[221] should always be applied. These ten, common-sense recommendations address the homeostatic drive for sleep, circadian factors, drug effects and arousal in the sleep setting:

(i) Do not go to bed until you are drowsy.

(ii) Get up at the same time each morning, including weekends.

(iii) Do not take naps (this rule may be modified as necessary for shift workers and jet travellers).

(iv) Curtail or eliminate the use of alcohol; do not drink alcohol later than 2 hours prior to bedtime.

(v) Curtail or eliminate the use of caffeine; do not consume caffeine containing beverages after about 16:00.

(vi) Curtail or eliminate the use of nicotine; do not smoke within four hours of bedtime and do not smoke on awakening during the night.

(vii) Exercise regularly but avoid strenuous physical exertion after 18:00 hours.

(viii) A light carbohydrate snack (for example crackers and milk) may help to promote sleep in those who tend to eat most in the second half of the day.

(ix) The sleep environment should be comfortably warm with minimal levels of light and noice.

(x) Do not clock-watch; turn the clock face away.

At times, the sleep disturbance will require the use of short courses of sleep promoting medications in order to consolidate sleep and prevent daytime impairment. To avoid next-morning sedation, the short acting medications such as temazepam, zopiclone and zolpidem are preferred.[222] These medications can also be used to manage the circadian sleep disturbances associated with time zone change or jet lag syndrome[223] and shift work sleep disorder.[224]

Even though melatonin is not yet as widely available as the sedative-hypnotics, recent research has shown that this chronobiotic is useful in managing a variety of circadian sleep disturbances. Melatonin improves the sleep performance and daytime alertness of those afflicted by jet lag,[225] as well as the sleep disturbance associated with shift work.[226] Additionally, it has been

Table 3. Commonly used psychostimulants

Medication	Dose (mg per day)	Comment
Dextroamphetamine	5–60	Available in some countries as a timed release capsule
Methamphetamine	20–25	Not available in some countries
Methylphenidate	10–60	Common initial treatment
Mazindol	4–8	Licensed in most countries as anorexiant
Pemoline	37.5	Generally considered 'milder' than other stimulants
Modafinil	200–400	Experimental drug; under development

helpful with the delayed sleep phase syndrome[227] and in managing sleep disturbances of blind subjects[228] and multiply disabled children.[115]

When EDS is secondary to a primary sleep disorder such as obstructive sleep apnea or periodic limb movement disorder then successful treatment of these disorders usually results in a return to full alertness. In rare cases it may be necessary to utilize stimulants (Table 3) to maximize the gains obtained by the primary intervention but usually these medications are reserved for the more severe hypersomnolent disorders such as narcolepsy and idiopathic hypersomnolence.

The most commonly used and widely available stimulant is caffeine, with six cups of strong black coffee having the same effect as 5 mg of dextroamphetamine.[229] It is available in beverages such as coffee and soft drinks, in foodstuffs and also as the major component of over-the-counter 'wake-up pills.' Within the relatively sleep deprived culture of North America,[57] it is likely that the stimulants caffeine and nicotine are used relatively erratically to countermand the daytime effects of sleep deprivation. When used alone[127] and in combination with naps[133] caffeine is effective in reducing some of the performance decrements caused by sleep deprivation. However, when the sleepiness is more constant and pervasive, as in narcolepsy, usually the psychostimulants must be used in combination with other non-pharmacological strategies[230] in order to maximize alertness.

HISTORY OF STIMULANT USE

The first known psychostimulant, cocaine, was isolated in the mid-eighteenth century, and in 1884 it was given to Bavarian soldiers, who noted that it decreased fatigue.[231] Amphetamine, first synthesized in 1887 and later studied extensively by Alles,[232] also had a military connection, being used extensively during the Second World War because of its ability to increase alertness, curb appetite and improve the physical and mental performance of fatigued soldiers.[231] In 1931, Doyle and Daniels[233] described the use of ephedrine in the treatment of narcolepsy, and four years later Prinzmetal and Bloomberg[234] reported using benzedrine for this disorder, which remained a favoured medication to manage EDS for the next fourteen years.[235] After the war, amphetamine was used to treat Parkinsonism, and in 1958 the piperazine derivative of amphetamine, methylphenidate, was introduced and later used to treat hyperactivity in children.[236]

In the 1960s, amphetamines were used quite widely in medicine as treatment for epilepsy, obesity, barbiturate poisoning and the lethargy and fatigue associated with alcohol and drug withdrawal.[237] Additionally, fairly simple modifications to the amphetamine molecule produced a wide range of medications with differing effects: decongestants, anorexiants, antidepressants and hallucinogens.[238] Likely because of its widespread availability and use, amphetamine abuse peaked in the United States in the late 1960s, encouraging a rationalization for its use and the development of non-amphetamine compounds, such as the anorexiant fenfluramine.[239] However, throughout the world controversy continues to surround the use of amphetamines and, because of their adverse effects, several European countries have banned their use.[240] Nonetheless, dextroamphetamine has remained the standard by which all other central stimulants are compared,[229] and it is widely used today in the treatment of narcolepsy and idiopathic hypersomnolence.

THE PSYCHOSTIMULANTS: MODE OF ACTION

Dextroamphetamine and methylphenidate, the two prototypic stimulants, exert their effects on the central nervous system through changes in catecholamine transport, causing an increase of dopamine and norepinephrine at the synapse.[241] Central norepinephrine systems are very heterogenous, with catecholamines participating in the control of wakefulness as well as affecting cerebral blood flow and energy metabolism.[229] Their central effect accounts for the side effects of sleeplessness, irritability, and mood and appetite changes, and their peripheral noradrenergic effects account for the hemodynamic side effects of increased heart rate and blood pressure.[231] Methamphetamine (commonly used in the United States for treating obesity and attention deficit disorder) has, because of its greater lipophilicity, more central than peripheral effects. Although more adverse effects on mood and mentation might be anticipated a small, well-controlled but short-term study of eight narcoleptics demonstrated that methamphetamine normalized sleep tendency and performance without unacceptable side effects.[242]

As a group, the psychostimulants produce behavioral activation characterized by increased arousal, motor activity and alertness. This group of drugs has been classified into three groups: (i) direct acting sympathomimetics such as the alpha-1 adrenergic stimulant phenylephrine hydrochloride, (ii) indirect acting sympathomimetics such as amphetamines, methylphenidate, pemoline and mazindol and (iii) stimulants such as caffeine that are not sympathomimetics and have different mechanisms of action.[235] Some sympathomimetics have both direct and indirect actions but the medications commonly used for combatting EDS belong to the indirect group.

Evaluating the psychostimulants

Numerous studies have confirmed the effectiveness of the psychostimulants in combatting EDS. The level of evidence varies from subjective measurement of sleepiness to confirmation by objective measures such as testing by pupillometry,[243] the MSLT[242] or the MWT.[244] Although there is no reliable objective test that is predictive of driving risk,[245] in the United States two Federal agencies have recommended that the MSLT and MWT, respectively, be utilized to assess the fitness to drive and fly in patients treated for sleep apnea.[345] The most systematic evaluations of the psychostimulants on alertness have been in studies of patients with narcolepsy and idiopathic hypersomnolence, and these have been of two basic types: retrospective patient surveys[229] and studies using subjective evaluations, standard performance batteries and the MSLT or the MWT.[244]

Amphetamine

The intensity of amphetamine's stimulant effect depends on the isomer being used, the dose and the route of administration, with intranasal absorption being faster and more intense than the usual oral route.[242] The CNS effects of the dextroisomer (dextramphetamine) is three to four times greater than those of the levoisomer. Following oral dosing dextroamphetamine's stimulant effect peaks at 2–4 hours after the dose,[246] with the half-life (about 12 hours) being influenced by the pH of the urine: an alkaline urine lengthens the half-life to over 16 hours; an acid urine shortens it to 8 hours.[247] In some countries dextroamphetamine is available as a 10 or 15 mg timed release spansule, which, taken on rising, provides a sustained response for 10–12 hours without the sudden peak and short effect which occurs with the traditional oral dose.[229] The usual dose range for dextroamphetamine is 5–60 mg per day[246] and there is little advantage to exceeding this dose.[240] Indeed, Dement and Guilleminault have reported a paradoxical effect, where increased sleepiness was found in 33 subjects taking 100 mg per day or more, with this effect disappearing when the dose was reduced.[248]

A number of clinical trials of the effects of dextroamphetamine have been undertaken, yet a relatively small number have included objective measures of EDS such as the MSLT or MWT. In the largest clinical case series of the effects of dextroamphetamine (5–150 mg) on sleepiness associated with narcolepsy,[249] 73% of 63 patients enjoyed a moderate to good response, with the major side effects being irritability (49%), headaches (48%) and palpitations (24%). Eleven percent of the group reported disturbed sleep as a consequence of treatment. In a study of the effects of 10, 30 and 60 mg on the MWT in five narcoleptics, Mitler demonstrated a dose related improvement in MWT for the 30 mg and 60 mg doses.[250]

Methamphetamine

Methamphetamine is unavailable in some countries and, where available, it is not widely used: a survey by the American Narcolepsy Association found that only 4% of narcoleptics were receiving treatment with this drug.[251] Because of its lipophilicity, methamphetamine is absorbed faster (peak effects 1 hour after ingestion) than amphetamine[252] and it has a half-life of 4–5 hours.[242] It has a dose dependent effect on nocturnal sleep, affecting sleep continuity and REM sleep. The usual dosage is 20–25 mg per day.[246]

In a case series reported in 1960, its efficacy in narcolepsy was demonstrated.[253] Recent interest in this drug re-emerged following the double-blind, placebo-controlled study in eight narcoleptics conducted by Mitler and colleagues, where improvement in performance and sleepiness, measured by a test battery, a driving simulation task and the MSLT, was demonstrated.[242] Furthermore, this group has followed more than ten patients maintained on methamphetamine for between 3 and 20 months at typical doses of 15 mg per day and shown that tolerance does not develop and that there are no significant adverse reactions.[249]

Methylphenidate

Daly and Yoss introduced methylphenidate as a treatment for narcolepsy in 1946[254] and later described their successful use of this drug, in over 60 patients, in doses ranging from 20 to 200 mg.[255] In a later summary of 28 years' experience with methylphenidate they recommended that patients be started at low dosages and that the dosage be titrated upward to prevent sleep attacks, to a maximum of 200 mg per day. Should patients not respond to methylphenidate, a trial of methamphetamine was suggested.[256]

Methylphenidate is rapidly absorbed, with peak plasma levels occurring within 2 hours in both adults and children. The half-life is 2.4 hours in children and 2.1 hours in adults.[257] The usual dose range for narcoleptics is

10–60 mg per day given in divided dosages.[246] Two early case series in 25[253] and 60 subjects[254] found a good to excellent response to methylphenidate in 84% and 68% of narcoleptics, respectively. Side effects were measured in the Yoss and Daly study, with nervousness and tremulousness affecting 35%; anorexia, 22%; insomnia, 17% and palpitations, 3%.[254] A later sleep lab study in 13 patients treated with doses ranging from 10 to 60 mg demonstrated an improvement in MWT scores.[243]

Compared with the amphetamines, the side effect profile is more favorable, with nervousness and insomnia being most frequently reported.[257] Methylphenidate is contraindicated in patients with tic disorders or a family history of Tourett's syndrome. It should not be used concurrently with the antidepressant monoamine oxidase inhibitors (causes hypertension) and it may inhibit the metabolism of a number of drugs, including coumarin anticoagulants, anticonvulsants and tricyclic antidepressants so it should be used cautiously with these compounds.[257]

Mazindol

Mazindol, a tricyclic imidazoline derivative, which reduces appetite, increases alertness and stimulates the sympathetic nervous system,[258] is a well-tolerated and effective treatment for the short-term management of obesity.[259] Compared to amphetamines, it has fewer central and sympathomimetic effects and is considered to have low abuse liability.[260] It has an REM supressant action on nocturnal sleep but, unlike the amphetamines, does not interrupt the sleep period and, because of these qualities, it has been suggested as the drug of first choice for narcoleptics requiring treatment.[261]

The plasma half-life of mazindol and its metabolites is longer than dextroamphetamine, at 30–50 hours, with the alerting effect of the 2 mg dose lasting for about 6 hours, slightly longer than that seen with 10 mg of dextroamphetamine.[261] In narcolepsy, the usual dose range is 4–8 mg per day in divided dosages.[246] In a placebo controlled clinical trial[262] and a retrospective case series[263] mazindol was well tolerated. In one study, with a dose range of 1–16 mg, mazindol provided a moderate to good response in 78% of patients, 39% of whom experienced adverse effects which were usually mild and related to the gastrointestinal tract.[263] In the other study, a fixed 4 mg per day dosage was used and there were no significant side effects.[262] With the exception of pregnancy, there are no absolute contraindications for its use although it should be used with caution in hypertensive patients.[257] Used most widely as an anorexiant, it has been well tolerated and without liability for abuse.[259] Depression associated with its use has been reported in two cases,[264] as has one case of reversible cardiomyopathy associated with concurrent use of fenfluramine and mazindol[265] which may be a drug interaction.

Pemoline

Pemoline, an oxazolidine derivative, is usually commenced at 37.5 mg per day,[246] with the effective dose ranging from 37.5 to 150 mg per day.[266] Peak serum levels are reached in 2–4 hours after dosing and the serum half-life is approximately 12 hours.[257] Well tolerated – insomnia is the most frequently reported side effect[257] – it is recognized as being less effective than the other psychostimulants.[267] Relatively high doses (mean of 113 mg per day) are required to bring about improvement in the MWT[244] although there may be a selective improvement in objective cognitive performance.[268] With this drug, a rare, idiosyncratic but serious adverse effect is liver (hepatocellular) damage. Young males (under 20 years) appear to be at particular risk within the first year of treatment[269] and liver function tests should be completed prior to and periodically during therapy, especially in the young. Abuse of pemoline is very rare but when it does occur a drug induced, usually paranoid, psychosis may complicate the clinical picture.[270]

Modafinil

Modafinil is an alpha-1 postsynaptic agonist which has a plasma peak 2–3 hours after oral ingestion and an elimination half-life of 8–10 hours.[271] Open studies have provided good results in 60–70% of subjects. A multicentre, double-blind, 12-week sleep laboratory study of modafinil in 50 narcoleptics[271] showed a significant improvement in the results of the MWT and replicated the findings of a previous double-blind study, which used self-report measures,[272] in showing no disruption of nocturnal sleep. There were no significant adverse events but only 56.8% of the subjects were considered to be good responders. In a study of 123 patients with EDS of mixed cause (76% narcoleptic; 19% idiopathic hypersomnia; 5% with disrupted nocturnal sleep) Laffont and colleagues[273] obtained, for the narcoleptic group, 'excellent' results for 10 patients (27%), 'good' results in 23 (63%) and 'fair' in 4 (11%). Side effects (gastric discomfort, hot flushes, dry mouth, headache and dizziness) were dose related and worst at 300 mg per day. They disappeared when the dose was reduced to 200 mg per day.

Evaluating the relative efficacy of these medications is difficult because different investigators use different outcome measures, and subject samples vary markedly in their degree of daytime sleepiness. Furthermore, some studies use multiple dose regimes whereas others use fixed doses. Using a normalization technique,[274] Mitler and colleagues[235] have attempted to compare the results of pemoline (112.5 mg), modafinil (300 mg), dextroamphetamine (60 mg) and methylphenidate (60 mg) using the MWT and with methamphetamine (40–60 mg) using the MSLT. They concluded that each drug caused a clinically significant improvement but dextroamphetamine, methampheta-mine and methylphenidate outperformed modafinil and pemoline, bringing alertness measurements to above 60% of normal values. No medication resulted in a normal level of alertness.

Miscellaneous stimulants

There are a number of miscellaneous medications which have been used to combat EDS but have been found wanting, and others which are in various stages of development. The beta blocker, propranolol, used in the manage-ment of hypertension and cardiac arrhythmias, was noted by Kales and col-leagues to eliminate the sleep attacks of narcolepsy in one patient.[275] Later, Meier-Ewert et al.[276] studied the effects of propranolol (80–240 mg per day) in 48 narcoleptic patients over an average period of 18.4 months. Initially all patients received single drug therapy; after 10 days or longer, 50% of patients also received tricyclics or stimulants because propranolol alone did not suffi-ciently suppress the narcoleptic symptoms. Vigilance testing, completed on 16 patients during the first four months of treatment, showed significant improvements in all test criteria, including a shorter reaction time. Sleep studies completed on 14 patients, on the eighth and ninth days of medication, showed that average total sleep time decreased by 5.7%, but other sleep characteristics did not change significantly. The initial effectiveness of pro-pranolol on daytime sleepiness was judged by 50% of the subjects to be good to very good, and in these patients the effects seemed equivalent to that of pemoline. However, within 6 months, effectiveness started to decrease, and after 26 months only 8% (2 out of 24) of those patients taking the single drug were satisfied with the propranolol treatment. Fifty-eight percent of the patients dropped out of the study after 26 months. Side effects included dis-turbed night sleep, decreased blood pressure, increased lethargy, allergic skin rash and asthma.

As abnormalities in central dopaminergic mechanisms are considered to be etiologically significant in narcolepsy, administering L-tyrosine, the natural precursor of dopamine, to narcoleptics makes theoretical sense.[277] In an open-label study, Mouret and his colleagues treated eight narcoleptics with oral tyrosine, and within six months all were free from daytime sleep attacks and cataplexy.[278] However, a randomized, double-blind, placebo-controlled study of L-tyrosine (9 g daily) in ten subjects with narcolepsy and cataplexy failed to show any difference in the ratings of daytime drowsiness, cataplexy, sleep paralysis, night-time sleep, overall clinical response, and the MSLT between the tyrosine treated and placebo control groups.[279] The authors of this report concluded that although dietary supplementation with tyrosine 9 g daily for 4 weeks had a mild stimulant action on the central nervous system, it was not clinically relevant for managing EDS associated with narcolepsy.

Gamma hydroxybutyrate, an experimental medication in many countries, is an endogenous neurochemical. It may be a sleep neurotransmitter or a neuromodulator, as, in both normals and narcoleptics, it rapidly induces sleep, increases sleep continuity as well as the amount of delta or deep sleep and does not suppress REM sleep.[280] By improving nocturnal sleep, it may improve cataplexy but it has minimal effects on increasing daytime alertness in narcoleptics.[235]

A number of stimulating antidepressants have been tried in open-label and single case studies. Protriptyline was thought to improve alertness in narcoleptics[281] but objective measurements of daytime alertness failed to show any significant change with doses up to 67 mg per day.[242] Other newer antidepressants (e.g. viloxazine hydrochloride and ritanserin) have been tested and although they can improve alertness the effect is slight and not considered clinically useful.[235] An exception is the new, selective, reversible monoamine oxidase inhibitor, selegiline. It enhances the dopaminergic tone within the brain and has been used in the management of Parkinson's disease.[282] As it is metabolized in the liver into L-methamphetamine and L-amphetamine[283] a trial in narcoleptics was inevitable. At low doses (5–10 mg) it was not effective[284] but a recent double-blind placebo-controlled study in 17 narcoleptics showed that a dose dependent improvement in narcoleptic symptoms was demonstrable.[285] However, there were no significant changes in the MSLT results. Patients maintained a tyramine free diet and overall the treatment was well tolerated. Whether or not it is cost effective and will become a preferred treatment requires further studies. A more recent report using higher doses showed positive results.[286]

CONCLUSION

Drowsiness is a measurable phenomenon which is usually related to sleep disruption or deprivation from elective, occupational or pathological causes. When associated with sleep disorders, the treatment often results in the amelioration of drowsiness, but in some cases of narcolepsy and obstructive sleep apnea continued impairment may persist, despite adequate treatment, making driving and other complex tasks potentially hazardous. To date, there is no test that can reliably evaluate an individual's capacity to drive an automobile although there are tests of psychomotor performance, inherent sleep propensity and the ability to resist falling asleep.

Throughout the world, caffeine is the most commonly used drug to combat fatigue and drowsiness. Despite a wide variety of pharmaceutical agents available to modify EDS, none has reached a preferred status. An ongoing search is required to improve on the 60% amelioration of EDS noted with the most potent of the psychostimulants. In clinical practice continued vigilance for, and management of, the causes of disrupted sleep along with careful evaluations and the use of complementary behavioral strategies will maximize the potential gains for patients afflicted with significant daytime sleepiness.

REFERENCES

1. Lichstein, K.L., Wilson, N.M., Noe, S.L., Aguillard, R.N. and Bellur, S.N. Daytime sleepiness in insomnia: behavioral, biological and subjective indices. *Sleep* **17**(8):693–702, 1994.
2. D'Alessandro, R., Rinaldi, R., Cristrina, E., Gamberini, G. and Lugaresi. E. Prevalence of excessive daytime sleepiness – an open epidemiological problem. *Sleep* **18**(5):389–391, 1995.
3. Carskadon, M.A. and Dement, W.C. The Multiple Sleep Latency Test: what does it measure? *Sleep* **5**: S67–S72, 1982.
4. Matsumoto, K. and Harada, M. The effect of night-time naps on recovery from fatigue following night work. *Ergonomics* **37**(5):899–907, 1994.
5. Roth, T., Roehrs, T.A., Carskadon, M.A. and Dement, W.C. Daytime sleepiness and alertness. In Kryger, M.H., Roth, T., Dement, W.C. (eds): *Principles and Practice of Sleep Medicine*, 2nd edn. Toronto, W.B. Saunders, 1994, pp 40–49.
6. Dement, W.C., Carskadon, M.A. and Richardson, G.S. Excessive daytime sleepiness in the sleep apnea syndrome. In Guilleminault, C., Dement, W.C. (eds): *Sleep Apnea Syndromes*. New York, Alan R. Liss, 1978, pp 23–46.
7. Hartse, K.M., Roth, T., Zorrick, F.J. Daytime sleepiness and daytime wakefulness: the effect of instruction. *Sleep* **5**: S107–118, 1982.
8. Alexander, C., Blagrove, M. and Horne, J. Subject motivation and the Multiple Sleep Latency Test (MSLT). *Sleep Res* **20**:403, 1991.
9. Wierwille, W.W. and Ellsworth, L.A. Evaluation of driver drowsiness by trained raters. *Accid Anal Prev* **26**(5):571–581, 1994.
10. Guilleminault, C., Milliard, M., Montplaisir, J. and Dement, W.C. Altered states of consciousness in disorders of daytime sleepiness. *J. Neurol Sci* **26**:377–387, 1975.
11. *International Classification of Sleep Disorders: Diagnostic and Coding Manual.* Diagnostic Classification Steering Committee, Thorpy, M.J. chairman. Rochester, Minnesota, American Sleep Disorders Association, 1990.
12. Carskadon, M.A., van den Hoed, J. and Dement, W.C. Sleep and daytime sleepiness in the elderly. *J Geriatr Psychiatry* **13**:135, 1980.
13. Richardson, G.S., Carskadon, M.A., Orav, E.J. and Dement, W.C. Circadian variation in sleep tendency in elderly and young adult subjects. *Sleep* **5**: S82–S94, 1982.
14. Roehrs, T.A., Zwyghuizen-Doorenbos, A. and Zwyghuizen, H. Sedating effects of ethanol and time of drinking. *Sleep Res* **18**:71, 1989.
15. Montgomery, L.C. and Deuster, P.A. Effects of antihistamine medications on exercise performance. Implications for sportspeople. *Sports Med* **15**(3):179–195, 1993.
16. Martikainen, K., Urponen, H., Partinen, M., Hasan, J. and Vuori, I. Daytime sleepiness: a risk factor in community life. *Acta Neurol Scand* **86**:337–341, 1992.
17. Moldofsky, H. Evaluation of daytime sleepiness. *Clin Chest Med* **13**(3):417–415, 1992.
18. Hoddes, E., Dement, W. and Zarcone, V. The development and use of the Stanford Sleepiness Scale (SSS). *Psychophysiology* **9**:150, 1972.

19. Carskadon, M.A. and Dement, W.C. Sleep tendency: an objective measure of sleep loss. *Sleep Res* **6**:200, 1977.
20. Herscovitch, J. and Broughton, R. Sensitivity of the Stamford Sleepiness Scale to the effects of cumulative partial sleep deprivation and recovery oversleeping. *Sleep* **4**(1):83–91, 1981.
21. Herbert, M., Johns, M.W. and Doré, C. Factor analysis of analogue scales measuring subjective feelings before and after sleep. *Br J Med Psychol* **49**:373–379, 1976.
22. Rosenthal, L., Roehrs, T.A. and Roth, T. The Sleep–Wake Activity Inventory: a self-report measure of daytime sleepiness. *Biol Psychiatry* **34**(11):810–820, 1993.
23. Johns, M.W. A new method for measuring daytime sleepiness: the Epworth Sleepiness Scale. *Sleep* **14**(6):540–545, 1991.
24. Johns, M.W. Reliability and factor analysis of the Epworth Sleepiness Scale. *Sleep* **15**(4):376–381, 1992.
25. Heslegrave, R.J. and Angus, R.G. The effects of task duration and work-session location on performance degradation induced by sleep loss and sustained cognitive work. *Behav Res Methods Instrum Comput* **17**:592–603, 1985.
26. Wilkinson, R.T. Methods for research on sleep deprivation and sleep function. *Int Psychiatry Clin* **7**:369–381, 1970.
27. Bonnet, M.H. The effect of varying prophylactic naps on performance, alertness and mood throughout a 52-hour continuous operation. *Sleep* **14**(4):307–315, 1991.
28. Hindmarch, I. Instrumental assessment of psychomotor functions and the effects of psychotropic drugs. *Acta Psychiatr Scand* **89** (suppl 380); 49–52, 1994.
29. Volkerts, E.R. and O'Hanlon, J.F. Hypnotics' residual effects on driving performance. In O'Hanlon, J.F., de Gier, J.J. (eds): *Drugs and Driving*. London, Taylor and Francis, 1986, pp 123–136.
30. Yoss, R.E., Mayer, N.J. and Ogle, K.N. The pupillogram and narcolepsy. *Neurology* **19**:921–928, 1969.
31. Lichstein, K.L., Wilson, N.M., Noe, S.L., Aguillard, R.N. and Bellur, S.N. Daytime sleepiness in insomnia: behavioral, biological and subjective indices. *Sleep* **17**(8):693–702, 1994.
32. Berlucchi, G., Moruzzi, G., Salva, G. and Stratta, P. Pupil behavior and ocular movements during synchronized and desynchronized sleep. *Arch Ital Biol* **102**:203, 1964.
33. Merritt, S.L., Keegan, A.P. and Mercer, P.W. Artifact management in pupillometry. *Nursing Res* **43**(1):56–59, 1994.
34. Schmidt, H.S. and Fortin, L.D. Electronic pupillography in disorders of arousal. In Guilleminault, C. (ed.): *Sleep and Waking Disorders: Indications and Techniques*. Menlo Park, CA, Addison-Wesley, 1981, pp 127–141.
35. Santamaria, J. and Chiappa, K.H. *The EEG of Drowsiness*. New York, Demos Publications, 1987.
36. Loomis, A.L., Harvey, E.N. and Hobart, G.A. Cerebral states during sleep as studied by human brain potentials. *J. Exp Psychol* **21**:127–144, 1937.
37. Walsleben, J. The measurement of daytime wakefulness. *Chest* **101**:890–891, 1992.
38. Thorpy, M.J. The clinical use of the Multiple Sleep Latency Test. The Standards of Practice Committee of the American Sleep Disorders Association. *Sleep.* **15**(3):268–276, 1992.
39. Carskadon, M.A., Dement, W.C., Mitler, M.M., Roth, T., Westbrook, P.R. and Keenan, S. Guidelines for the multiple sleep latency test (MSLT): a standard measure of sleepiness. *Sleep* **9**:519–524, 1986.

40. Carskadon, M.A., Harvey, K. and Dement, W.C. Sleep loss in young adolescents. *Sleep* **4**:299–312, 1981.
41. Bliwise, D., Seidel, W., Karacan, I., Mitler, M., Roth, T., Zorick, F. and Dement, W. Daytime sleepiness as a criterion in hypnotic medication trials: comparison of triazolam and flurazepam. *Sleep* **6**:156–163, 1983.
42. Zwyghuizen-Doorenbos, A., Roehrs, T., Lamphere, J., Zorick, F. and Roth, T. Increased daytime sleepiness enhances ethanol's sedative effects. *Neuropsychopharmacology* **1**(4):279–286, 1988.
43. Roehrs, T., Timms, V., Zwyghuizen-Doorenbos, A. and Roth, T. Sleep extension in sleepy and alert normals. *Sleep* **12**:449–457, 1989.
44. Zwyghuizen-Doorenbos, A., Roehrs, T., Lipschutz, L., Tims, V. and Roth, T. Effects of caffeine on alertness. *Psychopharmacology (Berl)* **100**:36–39, 1990.
45. Jahnke, B. and Aldrich, M.S. The multiple sleep latency test (MSLT) is not infallible. *Sleep Res* **19**:240, 1990.
46. Mitler, M.M., Gujavarty, K.S. and Browman, C.P. Maintenance of Wakefulness Test: a polysomnographic technique for evaluating treatment in patients with excessive somnolence. *Electroencephalogr Clin Neurophysiol* **53**:658–661, 1982.
47. Sangal, R.B., Thomas, L. and Mitler, M.M. Maintenance of Wakefulness Test and Multiple Sleep Latency Test – measurement of different abilities in patients with sleep disorders. *Chest* **101**: 898–902, 1992.
48. Sangal, R. and Thomas, L. Mean sleep latency and mean maintenance of wakefulness. *Sleep Res* **17**:245, 1988.
49. Johnson, L. Daytime sleepiness in good sleepers: measurements and correlates. In Broughton, R.J., Ogilvie, R.D. (eds): *Sleep, Arousal and Performance*. Boston, Birkhaüser, 1992, pp 220–229.
50. Bonnet, M. Sleep deprivation. In Kryger, M.H., Roth, T., Dement, W.C. (eds): *Principles and Practice of Sleep Medicine*, 2nd edn. Toronto, W.B. Saunders, 1994, pp 50–67.
51. Blagrove, M., Alexander, C. and Horne, J.A. The effects of chronic sleep reduction on the performance of cognitive tasks sensitive to sleep deprivation. *Appl Cogn Psychol* **9**(1):21–40, 1995.
52. Horne, J.A. Sleep loss and divergent thinking ability. *Sleep* **11**:528–536, 1988.
53. Johnson, L.C. Sleep deprivation and performance. In Webb, W.B. (ed): *Biological Rhythms, Sleep and Performance*. New York, Wiley, 1982, pp 111–142.
54. *Report of the Presidential Commission on the Space Shuttle Challenger Accident*, Vol. II, Appendix G. Washington, DC, US Government Printing Office, 1986.
55. Gold, D.R., Rogacz, S., Bock, N., Tosteson, T.D., Baum, T.M., Speizer, F.E. and Czeisler C.A. Rotating shift work, sleep and accidents related to sleepiness in hospital nurses. *Am J Public Health* **82**(7):1011–1014, 1992.
56. Horne, J.A. and Reyner, L.A. Sleep related vehicle accidents. *BMJ* **10**(6979): 565–567, 1995.
57. National Commission on Sleep Disorders Research *Wake Up America: A National Sleep Alert*, Vol. 1, Executive Summary and Executive Report, Report of the National Commission on Sleep Disorders Research. National Institutes of Health. Washington, DC, Sup. of Docs, US Government Printing Office, 1993.
58. Weitzman, E.D., Kripke, D.F., Goldmacher, D., McGregor, P. and Nogeire, C. Acute reversal of the sleep–waking cycle in man. Effect on sleep stage patterns. *Arch Neurol* **22**(6):483–489, 1970.
59. Folkard, S. and Monk, T.H. Shiftwork and performance. *Hum Factors* **21**:483–492, 1979.
60. Monk, T.H. Shift work. In Kryger, M.H., Roth, T., Dement, W.C. (eds): *Principles and Practice of Sleep Medicine*, 2nd edn. Toronto, W.B. Saunders, 1994, pp 471–476.

61. Broughton, R., Ghanem, Q., Hishikawa, Y., Sugita, Y., Nevsimalova, S. and Roth, B. Life effects of narcolepsy in 180 patients from North America, Asia and Europe compared to matched controls. *Can J Neurol Sci* 8(4):299–304, 1981.
62. Schulz, H. and Wilde-Frenz, J. The disturbance of cognitive processes in narcolepsy. *J Sleep Res* 4:10–14, 1995.
63. Bédard, M.A., Montplasir, J., Richer, F., Rouleau, I. and Malo, J. Obstructive sleep apnea syndrome: pathogenesis and neuropsychological deficits. *J. Clin Exp Neuropsychol* 13:950–964.
64. Montplaisir, J., Chicoine, A.-J., Rouleau, I. and Nielsen, T. Symposium: cognitive processes and sleep disturbances. Conclusion – Nocturnal sleep and its relation to diurnal cognitive functioning. *J Sleep Res* 4:21–22, 1995.
65. Mitler, M.M., Dinges, D.F. and Dement, W.C. Sleep medicine, public policy and public health. In Kryger, M.H., Roth, T., Dement, W.C. (eds): *Principles and Practice of Sleep Medicine*, 2nd edn. Toronto, W.B. Saunders, 1994, pp 453–462.
66. Stoohs, R.A., Guilleminault, C. and Dement, W.C. Sleep apnea and hypertension in commercial truck drivers. *Sleep* 16(8 suppl): S11–13, 1993.
67. US Congress Office of Technology Assessment *Gearing up for Safety: Motor Carrier Safety in a Competitive Environment*, OTA-SET-382. Washington, DC, US Government Printing Office, 1988.
68. US Department of Transportation *The Costs of Highway Crashes*, FHWA-RD-91-055. Washington, DC, Federal Highway Administration, 1991.
69. Monk, T.H. Shift work. In Kryger, M.H., Roth, T., Dement, W.C. (eds): *Principles and Practice of Sleep Medicine*, 2nd edn. Toronto, W.B. Saunders, 1994, pp 471–476.
70. Folkard, S., Monk, T.H. and Lobban, M.C. Short and long-term adjustment of circadian rhythms in 'permanent' night nurses. *Ergonomics* 21:785–799, 1978.
71. Rosenthal, L., Roehrs, T.A., Rosen, A. and Roth, T. Level of sleepiness and total sleep time following various time in bed conditions. *Sleep* 16(3):226–232, 1993.
72. Wilkinson, R.T. and Colquhoun, W.P. Interaction of alcohol with incentive and with sleep deprivation. *J Exp Psychol* 76:623–629, 1968.
73. Bonnet, M.H. Performance and sleepiness as a function of frequency and placement of sleep disruption. *Psychophysiology* 23:263–271, 1986.
74. Regestein, Q.R., Dambrosia, J., Hallett, M., Murawski, B. and Paine, M. Daytime alertness in patients with primary insomnia. *Am J Psychiatry* 150(10):1529–1534, 1993.
75. Fleming, J.A. The difficult to treat insomniac patient. *J Psychosom Res.* 37(suppl 1):45–54, 1993.
76. Edinger, J.D. and Fins, A.I. The distribution and clinical significance of sleep time misperceptions among insomniacs. *Sleep* 18(4):232–239, 1995.
77. Carskadon, M.A., Dement, W.C., Mitler, M.M., Guilleminault, C., Zarcone, V.P. and Spiegel, R. Self-report versus sleep laboratory findings in 122 drug-free subjects with the complaint of chronic insomnia. *Am J Psychiatry* 133:1382–1388, 1976.
78. Aldrich, M.S. Narcolepsy. *Neurology* 42 (7 suppl 6):34–43, 1992.
79. Broughton, W.A. and Broughton, R.J. Psychosocial impact of narcolepsy. *Sleep* 17 (8 suppl): S45–49, 1994.
80. Pike, M. and Stores, G. Kleine–Levin syndrome: a cause of diagnostic confusion. *Arch Dis Child* 71(4):355–357, 1994.
81. Guilleminault, C., Faull, K.F., Miles, L. and van den Hoed, J. Posttraumatic excessive daytime sleepiness: a review of 20 patients. *Neurology* 33(12):1584–1589, 1983.
82. Wiegand, L. and Zwillich, C.W. Obstructive sleep apnea. *Dis Mon* 40(4):197–252, 1994.

83. Guilleminault, C. Clinical features and evaluation of obstructive sleep apnea. In Kryger, M.H., Roth, T., Dement, W.C. (eds): *Principles and Practice of Sleep Medicine*, 2nd edn. Toronto, W.B. Saunders, 1994, pp 667–677.

84. Sullivan, C.E. and Grunstein, R.R. Continuous positive airway pressure in sleep-disordered breathing. In Kryger, M.H., Roth, T., Dement, W.C. (eds): *Principles and Practice of Sleep Medicine*, 2nd edn. Toronto, W.B. Saunders, 1994, pp 694–705.

85. Rauscher, H., Formanek, D., Popp, W. and Zwick, H. Self-reported vs measured compliance with nasal CPAP for obstructive sleep apnea. *Chest* **103**(6):1675–1680, 1993.

86. Engleman, H.M., Martin, S.E. and Douglas, N.J. Compliance with CPAP therapy in patients with the sleep apnoea/hypopnoea syndrome. *Thorax* **49**(3):263–266, 1994.

87. Edinger, J.D., Carwile, S., Miller, P., Hope, V. and Mayti, C. Psychological status, syndromatic measures, and compliance with nasal CPAP therapy for sleep apnea. *Percept Mot Skills* **78** (3 pt 2):1116–1118, 1994.

88. Kribbs, N.B., Pack, A.I., Kline, L.R., Getsy, J.E., Schuett, J.S., Henry, J.N., Maislin, G. and Dinges, D.F. Effects of one night without nasal CPAP treatment on sleep and sleepiness in patients with obstructive sleep apnea. *Am Rev Respir Dis* **147**(5):1162–1168, 1993.

89. Hillerdal, G., Hetta, J., Lindholm, C.E., Hultcrantz, E. and Boman, G. Symptoms in heavy snorers with and without obstructive sleep apnea. *Acta Otolaryngol* **111**(3):574–581, 1991.

90. Guilleminault, C., Stoohs, R. and Duncan, S. Snoring (I). Daytime sleepiness in regular heavy snorers. *Chest* **99**(1):40–48, 1991.

91. Hanly, P. and Powles, P. Hypnotics should never be used in patients with sleep apnea. *J Psychosom Res* **37** (suppl 1):59–65, 1993.

92. Hanly, P.J. Mechanisms and management of central sleep apnea. *Lung* **170**(1):1–17, 1992.

93. Bradley, T.D. and Phillipson, E.A. Central sleep apnea. *Clin Chest Med* **13**(3):493–505, 1992.

94. Bradley, T.D., McNicholas, W.T., Rutherford, R., Popkin, J., Zamel, N. and Phillipson, E.A. Clinical and physiologic heterogeneity of the central sleep apnea syndrome. *Am Rev Respir Dis* **134**(2):217–221, 1986.

95. Montplaisir, J., Lorrain, D. and Godbout, R. Restless legs syndrome and periodic leg movements in sleep: the primary role of dopaminergic mechanism. *Eur Neurol* **31**(1):41–43, 1991.

96. Montplaisir, J., Godbout, R., Pelletier, G. and Warnes, H. Restless legs syndrome and periodic limb movements during sleep. In Kryger, M.H., Roth, T., Dement, W.C. (eds): *Principles and Practice of Sleep Medicine*, 2nd edn. Toronto, W.B. Saunders, 1994, pp 589–597.

97. Lavigne, G.J. and Montplaisir, J.Y. Restless legs syndrome and sleep bruxism: prevalence and association among Canadians. *Sleep* **17**(8):739–743, 1994.

98. Krueger, B.R. Restless legs syndrome and periodic movements of sleep. *Mayo Clin Proc* **65**:999–1006, 1990.

99. Fleming, J.A.E., Isomura, T. and Rungta, K. The effects of trazodone hydrochloride on periodic leg movements. *Sleep Res* **17**:79, 1988.

100. Nofzinger, E.A., Thase, M.E., Reynolds, C.F., Himmelhoch, J.M., Mallinger, A., Houch, P. and Kupfer, D.J. Hypersomnia in bipolar depression: a comparison with narcolepsy using the multiple sleep latency test. *Am J Psychiatry* **148**(9):1177–1181, 1991.

101. Aldrich, M.S. Parkinsonism. In Kryger, M.H., Roth, T., Dement, W.C. (eds):

Principles and Practice of Sleep Medicine, 2nd edn. Toronto, W.B. Saunders, 1994, pp 783–789.

102. Hall, R.C. and Wise, M.G. The clinical and financial burden of mood disorders. Cost and outcome. *Psychosomatics* **36**(2): S11–18, 1995.

103. Kryger, M.E., Roth, T. and Carskadon, M. Circadian rhythms in humans: an overview. In Kryger, M.H., Roth, T., Dement, W.C. (eds): *Principles and Practice of Sleep Medicine*, 2nd edn. Toronto, W.B. Saunders, 1994, pp 301–308.

104. Moline, M.L., Pollak, C.P., Monk, T.H., Lester, L.S., Wagner, D.R., Zendell, S.M., Graeber, R.C., Salter, C.A. and Hirsch, E. Age-related differences in recovery from simulated jet lag. *Sleep* **15**(1):28–40, 1992.

105. Hill, D.W., Hill, C.M., Fields, K.L. and Smith, J.C. Effects of jet lag on factors related to sport performance. *Can J Appl Physiol* **18**(1):91–103, 1993.

106. Jehue, R., Street, D. and Huizenga, R. Effect of time zone and game time changes on team performance: National Football League. *Med Sci Sports Exerc* **25**(1):127–131, 1993.

107. Graeber, R.C. Jet lag and sleep disruption. In Kryger, M.H., Roth, T., Dement, W.C. (eds): *Principles and Practice of Sleep Medicine*, 2nd edn. Toronto, W.B. Saunders, 1994, pp 463–470.

108. Seidel, W.F., Roth, T., Roehrs, T., Zorick, F. and Dement, W.C. Treatment of a 12-hour shift of sleep schedule with benzodiazepines. *Science* **224**(4654):1262–1264, 1984.

109. Wetterberg, L. Light and biological rhythms. *J Intern Med.* **235**(1):5–19, 1994.

110. Redfern, P., Minors, D. and Waterhouse, J. Circadian rhythms, jet lag, and chronobiotics: an overview. *Chronobiol Int* **11**(4):253–265, 1994.

111. Poole, C.J., Evans, G.R., Spurgeon, A. and Bridges, K.W. Effects of a change in shift work on health. *Occup Med* **42**(4):193–199, 1992.

112. Cabon, P., Coblentz, A., Mollard, R. and Fouillot, J.P. Human vigilance in railway and long-haul flight operation.*Ergonomics* **36**(9):1019–1033, 1993.

113. Regestein, Q.R. and Monk, T.H. Is the poor sleep of shift workers a disorder? *Am J Psychiatry* **148**(11):1487–1493, 1991.

114. Kanno, O., Watanabe, H. and Kazamatsuri, H. Effects of zopiclone, flunitrazepam, triazolam and levomepromazine on the transient change in sleep–wake schedule: polygraphic study, and the evaluation of sleep and daytime condition. *Prog Neuropsychopharmacol Biol Psychiatry* **17**(2):229–239, 1993.

115. Jan, J.E., Espezel, H. and Appleton, R.E. The treatment of sleep disorders with melatonin. *Dev Med Child Neurol.* **36**(2):97–107, 1994.

116. Okawa, M., Mishima, K., Hishikawa, Y., Hozumi, S., Hori, H. and Takahashi, K. Circadian rhythm disorders in sleep–waking and body temperature in elderly patients with dementia and their treatment *Sleep* **14**(6):478–485, 1991.

117. Regestein, Q.R. and Monk, T.H. Delayed sleep phase syndrome: a review of its clinical aspects. *Am J Psychiatry* **152**(4):602–608, 1995.

118. Alvarez, B., Dahlitz, M.J., Vignau, J. and Parkes, J.O. The delayed sleep phase syndrome: clinical and investigative findings in 14 subjects. *J Neurol Neurosurg Psychiatry* **55**(8):665–670, 1992.

119. Ito, A., Ando, K., Hayakawa, T., Iwata, T., Kayukawa, Y., Ohta, T. and Kasahara, Y. Long-term course of adult patients with delayed sleep phase syndrome. *Jpn J Psychiatry Neurol* **47**(3):563–567, 1993.

120. Roehrs, T. and Roth, T. Chronic insomnias associated with circadian rhythm disorders. In Kryger, M.H., Roth, T., Dement, W.C. (eds): *Principles and Practice of Sleep Medicine*, 2nd edn. Toronto, W.B. Saunders, 1994, pp 477–481.

121. Oldani, A., Ferini-Strambi, L., Zucconi, M., Stankov, B., Fraschini, F. and Smirne, S. Melatonin and delayed sleep phase syndrome: ambulatory polygraphic evaluation. *Neuroreport* **6**(1):132–134, 1994.

122. Czeisler, C.A., Allan, J.S., Strogatz, S.H., Ronda, J.M., Sanchez, R., Rios, C.D., Freitag, W.O., Richardson, G.S. and Kronauer, R.E. Bright light resets the human circadian pacemaker independent of the timing of the sleep–wake cycle. *Science* **233**(4764):667–671, 1986.

123. Sack, R.L., Lewy, A.J., Blood, M.L., Stevenson, J. and Keith, L.D. Melatonin administration to blind people: phase advances and entrainment. *J Biol Rhythms* **6**(3):249–261, 1991.

124. Czeisler, C.A., Shanahan, T.L., Klerman, E.B., Martens, H., Brotman, D.J., Emens, J.S., Klein, T. and Rizzo, J.F. 3rd. Suppression of melatonin secretion in some blind patients by exposure to bright light. *N Engl J Med* **332**(1):6–11, 1995.

125. Morin, C.M. Sleep hygiene education. In Morin, C.M. *Insomnia – Psychological Assessment and Management.* New York, Guilford Press, 1993, pp 145–155.

126. van Dusseldorp, M., Smits, P., Lenders, J.W., Thien, T. and Katan, M.B. Boiled coffee and blood pressure. A 14-week controlled trial. *Hypertension* **18**(5):607–613, 1991.

127. Penetar, D., McCann, U., Thorne, D., Kamimori, G., Galinski, C., Sing, H., Thomas, M. and Belenky, G. Caffeine reversal of sleep deprivation effects on alertness and mood. *Psychopharmacology (Berl)* **112**(2/3):359–365, 1993.

128. Dekker, D.K., Paley, M.J., Popkin, S.M. and Tepas, D.I. Locomotive engineers and their spouses: coffee consumption, mood, and sleep reports. *Ergonomics* **36**(1–3):233–238, 1993.

129. Levy, M. and Zylber-Katz, E. Caffeine metabolism and coffee-attributed sleep disturbances. *Clin Pharmacol Ther* **33**(6):770–775, 1983.

130. Hughes, J.R., Higgins, S.T., Bickel, W.K., Hunt, W.K., Fenwick, J.W., Gulliver, S.B. and Mireault, G.C. Caffeine self-administration, withdrawal, and adverse effects among coffee drinkers. *Arch Gen Psychiatry* **48**(7):611–617, 1991.

131. Karacan, I., Thornby, J.I., Anch, M., Booth, G.H., Williams, R.L., Salis, P.J. Dose-related sleep disturbances induced by coffee and caffeine. *Clin Pharmacol Ther* **20**(6):682–689, 1976.

132. Edelstein, B.A., Keaton-Brasted, C. and Brug, M.M. Effects of caffeine withdrawal on nocturnal enuresis, insomnia, and behavior restraints. *J Consult Clin Psychol* **52**(5):857–862, 1984.

133. Bonnet, M.H. and Arand, D.L. The use of prophylactic naps and caffeine to maintain performance during a continuous operation. *Ergonomics* **37**(6):1009–1020, 1994.

134. Hughes, J.R., Oliveto, A.H., Helzer, J.E., Higgins, S.T. and Bickel, W.K. Should caffeine abuse, dependence, or withdrawal be added to DSM-IV and ICD-10? *Am J Psychiatry* **149**(1):33–40, 1992.

135. Zarcone, V.P. Sleep hygiene. In Kryger, M.H., Roth, T., Dement, W.C. (eds): *Principles and Practice of Sleep Medicine*, 2nd edn. Toronto, W.B. Saunders, 1994, pp 542–546.

136. Gillin, J.C. Sleep and psychoactive drugs of abuse and dependence. In Kryger, M.H., Roth, T., Dement, W.C. (eds): *Principles and Practice of Sleep Medicine*, 2nd edn. Toronto, W.B. Saunders, 1994, pp 934–942.

137. Kales, J.D., Kales, A., Bixler, E.O., Soldatos, C.R., Cadieux, R.J., Kashurba, G.J. and Vela-Bueno, A. Biopsychobehavioral correlates of insomnia: V. Clinical characteristics and behavioral correlates. *Am J Psychiatry* **141**:1371–1376, 1984.

138. Davila, D.G., Hurt, R.D., Offord, K.P., Harris, C.D. and Shepard, J.W. Jr. Acute

effects of transdermal nicotine on sleep architecture, snoring, and sleep-disordered breathing in nonsmokers. *Am J Respir Crit Care Med* **150**:469–474, 1994.

139. Budney, A.J., Higgins, S.T., Hughes, J.R. and Bickel, W.K. Nicotine and caffeine use in cocaine-dependent individuals. *J Subst Abuse* **5**(2):117–130, 1993.

140. Soldatos, C.R., Kales, J.D., Scharf, M.B., Bixler, E.O. and Kales, A. Cigarette smoking associated with sleep difficulty. *Science* **207**(4430):551–553, 1980.

141. Prosise, G.L., Bonnet, M.H., Berry, R.B. and Dickel, M.J. Effects of abstinence from smoking on sleep and daytime sleepiness. *Chest* **105**(4):1136–1141, 1994.

142. Koelega, H.S. Stimulant drugs and vigilance performance: a review. *Psychopharmacology (Berl)* **111**(1):1–16, 1993.

143. Watson, R., Bakos, L., Compton, P. and Gawin, F. Cocaine use and withdrawal: the effect on sleep and mood. *Am J Drug Alcohol Abuse* **18**(1):21–28, 1992.

144. Miller, N.S., Summers, G.L. and Gold, M.S. Cocaine dependence: alcohol and other drug dependence and withdrawal characteristics. *J Addict Dis* **12**(1):25–35, 1993.

145. Gawin, F.H. and Kleber, H.S. Abstinence symptomatology and psychiatric diagnosis in cocaine abusers. *Arch Gen Psychiatry* **43**:107–113, 1986.

146. Kowatch, R.A., Schnoll, S.S., Knisely, J.S., Green, D. and Elswick, R.K. Electroencephalographic sleep and mood during cocaine withdrawal. *J Addict Dis.* **11**(4):21–45, 1992.

147. Extein, I.L. and Gold, M.S. Hypothesized neurochemical models for psychiatric syndromes in alcohol and drug dependence. *J Addict Dis* **12**(3):29–43, 1993.

148. Schuckit, M.A. and Irwin, M.A. Diagnosis of alcoholism. *Med Clin North Am* **72**:1133–1153, 1988.

149. Williams, H.L. and Salamy, A. Alcohol and sleep. In Kissin, B. and Begleiter, H. (eds): *The Biology of Alcoholism*, Vol. 2. New York, Plenum Press, 1972, pp 435–483.

150. Stradling, J.R. and Crosby, J.H. Predictors and prevalence of obstructive sleep apnoea and snoring in 1001 middle aged men. *Thorax* **46**:85–90, 1991.

151. Adamson, J. and Burdick, J.A. Sleep of dry alcoholics. *Arch Gen Psychiatry* **28**:146–149, 1973.

152. Shinba, T., Murashima, Y.L. and Yamamoto, K. Alcohol consumption and insomnia in a sample of Japanese alcoholics. *Addiction* **89**(5):587–591, 1994.

153. Lumley, M., Roberts, T., Asker, D., Zorick, F. and Roth, T. Ethanol and caffeine effects on daytime sleepiness/alertness. *Sleep* **10**(4):306–312, 1987.

154. Roehrs, T., Zwyghuizen-Doorenbos, A., Timms, V., Zorick, F. and Roth, T. Sleep extension, enhanced alertness and the sedating effects of ethanol. *Pharmacol Biochem Behav.* **34**(2):321–324, 1989.

155. Walsh, J.K., Humm, T., Muehlbach, M.J., Sugerman, J.L. and Schweitzer, P.K. Sedative effects of alcohol at night. *J Stud Alcohol* **52**:597–600, 1991.

156. Nicholson, A.N., Bradley, C.M. and Pascoe, P.A. Medications: effect on sleep and wakefulness. In Kryger, M.H., Roth, T., Dement, W.C. (eds): *Principles and Practice of Sleep Medicine*, 2nd edn. Toronto, W.B. Saunders, 1994, pp 364–372.

157. Bird, K.D., Boleyn, T., Chesher, G.B., Jackson, D.M., Starmer, G.A. and Teo, R.K. Intercannabinoid and cannabinoid–ethanol interactions on human performance. *Psychopharmacology (Berl)* **71**(2):181–188, 1980.

158. Feinberg, I., Jones, R., Walker, J., Cavness, C. and Floyd, T. Effects of marijuana extract and tetrahydrocannabinol on electroencephalographic sleep patterns. *Clin Pharmacol Ther* **19**(6):782–794, 1976.

159. Hollister, L.E. Cannabis – 1988. *Acta Psychiatr Scand* **78** (suppl 345):108–118, 1988.

160. Smith, D.E. and Seymour, R.B. Dream becomes nightmare: adverse reactions to LSD. *J Psychoactive Drugs* **17**(4):297–303, 1985.

161. Wiesbeck, G.A. and Taeschner, K.L. A cerebral computed tomography study of patients with drug-induced psychoses. *Eur Arch Psychiatry Clin Neurosci* **241**(2):88–90, 1991.
162. Muzio, J.N., Roffwarg, H.P. and Kaufman, E. Alterations in the nocturnal sleep cycle resulting from LSD. *Electroencephalogr Clin Neurophysiol* **21**:313–324, 1966.
163. Beebe, D.K. and Walley, E. Substance abuse: the designer drugs. *Am Fam Physician* **43**(5):1689–1698, 1991.
164. Smiley, A. Effects of minor tranquilizers and antidepressants on psychomotor performance. *J Clin Psychiatry* **48**(12) (suppl 1):21S–26S, 1984.
165. Wiklund, I. Quality of life and cost-effectiveness in the treatment of hypertension. *J Clin Pharm Ther* **19**(2):81–87, 1994.
166. Lonnqvist, J., Sintonen, H., Syvalahti, E., Appelberg, B., Koskinen, T., Mannikko, T., Mehtonen, O.P., Naarala, M., Sihvo, S., Auvinen, J. *et al.* Antidepressant efficacy and quality of life in depression: a double-blind study with moclobemide and fluoxetine. *Acta Psychiatr Scand* **89**(6):363–369, 1994.
167. Schatzberg, A.F. and Nemeroff, C.B. (eds). *The American Psychiatric Press Textbook of Psychopharmacology.* Washington, DC, American Psychiatric Press, 1995.
168. Borchelt, M. and Horgas, A.L. Screening an elderly population for verifiable adverse drug reactions. Methodological approach and initial data of the Berlin Aging Study (BASE). *Ann NY Acad Sci.* **717**:270–281, 1994.
169. Sanders, A.F. Drugs, driving and the measurement of human performance. In O'Hanlon, J.F., de Gier, J.J. (eds): *Drugs and Driving.* London, Taylor and Francis, 1986, pp 1–16.
170. O'Hanlon, J.F. Review of buspirone's effects on human performance and related variables. *Eur Neuropsychopharmacol* **1**(4):489–501, 1991.
171. Gudex, C. Adverse effects of benzodiazepines. *Soc Sci Med* **33**(5):587–596, 1991.
172. Linnoila, M., Erwin, C.W., Brendle, A. and Simpson, D. Psychomotor effects of diazepam in anxious patients and healthy volunteers. *J Clin Psychopharmacol* **3**(2):88–96, 1983.
173. Bliwise, D., Seidel, W., Karacan, I., Mitler, M., Roth, T., Zorick, F. and Dement, W. Daytime sleepiness as a criterion in hypnotic medication trials: comparison of triazolam and flurazepam. *Sleep* **6**(2):156–163, 1983.
174. Tunnicliff, G. Molecular basis of buspirone's anxiolytic action. *Pharmacol Toxicol* **69**(3):149–156, 1991.
175. Rickels, K., Schweizer, E., Csanalosi, I., Case, W.G. and Chung, H. Long-term treatment of anxiety and risk of withdrawal. Prospective comparison of clorazepate and buspirone. *Arch Gen Psychiatry* **45**(5):444–450, 1988.
176. Manfredi, R.L., Kales, A., Vgontzas, A.N., Bixler, E.O., Isaac, M.A. and Falcone, C.M. Buspirone: sedative or stimulant effect? *Am J Psychiatry* **148**(9):1213–1217, 1991.
177. Seppälä, T., Mattila, M.J., Palva, E.S. and Aranko, K. Combined effects of anxiolytics and alcohol on psychomotor performance in young and middle-aged subjects. In O'Hanlon, J.F., de Gier, J.J. (eds): *Drugs and Driving.* London, Taylor and Francis, 1986, pp 179–189.
178. Wadworth, A.N. and McTavish, D. Zopiclone. A review of its pharmacological properties and therapeutic efficacy as an hypnotic. *Drugs Aging* **3**(5):441–459, 1993.
179. Fleming, J., Moldofsky, H., Walsh, J.K., Scharf, M., Nino-Murcia, G. and Radonjic, D. Comparison of the residual effects of short term zolpidem, flurazepam and placebo in patients with chronic insomnia. *Clin Drug Invest* **9**:303–313, 1995.
180. Lader, M. and Denney, S.C. A double-blind study to establish the residual effects

of zopiclone on performance in healthy volunteers. *Int Pharmacopsychiatry* **17** (supple 2):108, 1982.

181. Harrison, C., Subhan, Z. and Hindmarch, I. Residual effects of zopiclone and benzodiazepine hypnotics on psychomotor performance related to car driving. *Drugs Exp Clin Res* **11**(2):823–829, 1985.

182. Volkerts, E.R. and O'Hanlon, J.F. Hypnotic's residual effects in driving performance. In O'Hanlon, J.F., de Gier, J.J. (eds): *Drugs and Driving*. London, Taylor and Francis, 1986, pp 123–135.

183. Griffiths, A.N., Jones, D.M. and Richens, A. Zopiclone produces effects on human performance similar to flurazepam, lormetazepam and triazolam. *Br J Clin Pharmacol* **21**(6):647–653, 1986.

184. O'Hanlon, J.F. and Volkerts, E.R. Hypnotics and actual driving performance. *Acta Psychiatr Scand* **74**(suppl 332):95–104, 1986.

185. Linnoila, M., Guthrie, S. and Lister, R. Mechanisms of drug-induced impairment of driving. In O'Hanlon, J.F., de Gier, J.J. (eds): *Drugs and Driving*. London, Taylor and Francis, 1986, pp 29–49.

186. U'Prichard, D.C., Greenberg, D.A., Sheehan, P.P. and Snyder, S.H. Tricyclic antidepressants: therapeutic properties and affinity for alpha-noradrenergic receptor binding sites in the brain. *Science* **199**(4325):197–198, 1978.

187. Fleming, J.A.E. REM sleep abnormalities and psychiatry. *J Psychiatr Neurosci* **19**:335–344, 1994.

188. Deptula, D. and Pomara, N. Effects of antidepressants on human performance: a review. *J Clin Psychopharmacol* **10**(2):105–111, 1990.

189. Tollefson, G.D. Selective serotonin reuptake inhibitors. In Schatzberg, A.F., Nemeroff, C.B. (eds): *The American Psychiatric Press Textbook of Psychopharmacology*. Washington, DC, American Psychiatric Press, 1995, pp 161–182.

190. Beasley, C.M. Jr. and Potvin. J.H. Fluoxetine: activating and sedating effects. *Int Clin Psychopharmacol* **8**(4):271–275, 1993.

191. Amado-Boccara, I., Gougoulis, N., Poirier-Littre, M.F., Galinowski, A. and Loo, H. Incidence des antidépresseurs sur les fonctions cognitives. Revue de la litterature. *Encéphale* **20**(1):65–77, 1994.

192. Gerhard, U. and Hobi, V. Is the depressive patient under adequate pharmacological treatment fit for driving? In O'Hanlon, J.F., de Gier, J.J. (eds): *Drugs and Driving*. London, Taylor and Francis, 1986, pp 221–230.

193. Hindmarch, I. and Subhan, Z. The effects of antidepressants taken with and without alcohol on information processing, psychomotor performance and car handling ability. In O'Hanlon, J.F., de Gier, J.J. (eds): *Drugs and Driving*. London, Taylor and Francis, 1986, pp 231–240.

194. Rudorfer, M.V. and Potter, W.Z. Antidepressants. A comparative review of the clinical pharmacology and therapeutic use of the 'newer' versus the 'older' drugs. *Drugs* **37**(5):713–738, 1989.

195. van Laar, M.W., van Willigenburg, A.P. and Volkerts, E.R. Acute and subchronic effects of nefazodone and imipramine on highway driving, cognitive functions, and daytime sleepiness in healthy adult and elderly subjects. *J Clin Psychopharmacol* **15**(1):30–40, 1995.

196. Lenox, R.H. and Manji, H.K. Lithium. In Schatzberg, A.F., Nemeroff, C.B. (eds): *The American Psychiatric Press Textbook of Psychopharmacology*. Washington, DC, American Psychiatric Press, 1995, pp 303–350.

197. Lee, S. Side effects of chronic lithium therapy in Hong Kong Chinese: an ethnopsychiatric perspective. *Cult Med Psychiatry* **17**(3):301–320, 1993.

198. Marder, S.R. and Van Putten, T. Antipsychotic medications. In Schatzberg, A.F.,

Nemeroff, C.B. (eds) *The American Psychiatric Press Textbook of Psychopharmacology*. Washington, DC, American Psychiatric Press, 1995, pp 247–263.

199. Peroutka, S.J., U'Prichard, D.C., Greenberg, D.A. and Snyder, S.H. Neuroleptic drug interactions with norepinephrine alpha receptor binding sites in rat brain. *Neuropharmacology* 16:549–556, 1977.

200. Grübel-Mathyl, U. Effects of neuroleptics on aspects relevant to driving fitness (preliminary evaluation). In O'Hanlon, J.F., de Gier, J.J. (eds): *Drugs and Driving*. London, Taylor and Francis, 1986, pp 241–248.

201. Wylie, K.R., Thompson, D.J. and Wildgust, H.J. Effects of depot neuroleptics on driving performance in chronic schizophrenic patients. *J Neurol Neurosurg Psychiatry* 56(8):910–913, 1993.

202. Owens, M.J. and Risch, S.C. Atypical antipsychotics. In Schatzberg, A.F., Nemeroff, C.B. (eds): *The American Psychiatric Press Textbook of Psychopharmacology*. Washington, DC, American Psychiatric Press, 1995, pp 263–280.

203. Buckley, P.F. and Meltzer, H.Y. Treatment of schizophrenia. In Schatzberg, A.F., Nemeroff, C.B. (eds): *The American Psychiatric Press Textbook of Psychopharmacology*. Washington, DC, American Psychiatric Press, 1995, pp 615–640.

204. Marinkovic, D., Timotijevic, I., Babinski, T., Totic, S. and Paunovic, V.R. The side-effects of clozapine: a four year follow-up study. *Prog Neuropsychopharmacol Biol Psychiatry* 18(3):537–544, 1994.

205. Pitner, J.K., Mintzer, J.E., Pennypacker, L.C. and Jackson, C.W. Efficacy and adverse effects of clozapine in four elderly psychotic patients. *J Clin Psychiatry* 56(5):180–185, 1995.

206. Klieser, E., Lehmann, E., Kinzler, E., Wurthmann, C. and Heinrich, K. Randomized, double-blind, controlled trial of risperidone versus clozapine in patients with chronic schizophrenia. *J Clin Psychopharmacol* 15 (1 suppl 1): 45S–51S, 1995.

207. Vanden Borre, R., Vermote, R., Buttiens, M., Thiry, P., Dierick, G., Geutjens, J., Sieben, G. and Heylen, S. Risperidone as add-on therapy in behavioural disturbances in mental retardation: a double-blind placebo-controlled cross-over study. *Acta Psychiatr Scand* 87(3):167–171, 1993.

208. King, D.J. Psychomotor impairment and cognitive disturbances induced by neuroleptics. *Acta Psychiatr Scand* 89 (suppl 380):53–58, 1994.

209. Smith, J.M. Epidemiology and natural history of asthma, allergic rhinitis and atopic dermatitis (eczema). In Middleton, E. Jr., Reed, E.C., Ellis, E.F., Adkinson, N.F., Yunginger, J.W. (eds): *Allergy: Principles and Practice*. St Louis, C.V. Mosby, 1988, pp 819–829.

210. Meltzer, E.O. Comparative safety of H1 antihistamines. *Ann Allergy* 67(6):625–633, 1991.

211. Roehrs, T.A., Tietz, E.I., Zorick, F.J. and Roth, T. Daytime sleepiness and antihistamines. *Sleep* 7(2):137–141, 1984.

212. Warren, R., Simpson, H., Hilchie, J., Cimbura, G., Lucas, D. and Bennett, R. Drugs detected in fatally injured drivers in the province of Ontario. In Goldberg, L. (ed.): *Alcohol, Drugs and Traffic Safety*, Vol. 1. Stockholm, Almquist and Wiksell, 1981, pp 203–217.

213. Nicholson, A.N. New antihistamines free of sedative side effects. *Trends Pharmacol Sci* 8:247–249, 1987.

214. Banning, A., Sjogren, P. and Kaiser, F. Reaction time in cancer patients receiving peripherally acting analgesics alone or in combination with opioids. *Acta Anaesthesiol Scand* 36(5):480–482, 1992.

215. Chesher, G.B. Influence of analgesic drugs in road crashes. *Accid Anal Prev* 17:303–309, 1985.

216. Stramer, G.A. A review of the effects of analgesics on driving performance. In O'Hanlon, J.F., de Gier, J.J. (eds): *Drugs and Driving*. London, Taylor and Francis, 1986, pp 251–269.
217. Rummans, T.A. Nonopioid agents for treatment of acute and subacute pain. *Mayo Clin Proc* **69**(5):481–490, 1994.
218. Bakht, F.R. and Miller, L.G. Naproxen-associated nightmares. *South Med J* **84**(10):1271–1273, 1991.
219. McDevitt, D.G., Currie, D., Nicholson, A.N., Wright, N.A. and Zetlein, M.B. Central effects of the calcium antagonist, nifedipine. *Br J Clin Pharmacol* **32**(5):541–549, 1991.
220. Everitt, D.E., Avorn, J. and Baker, M.W. Clinical decision-making in the evaluation and treatment of insomnia. *Am J Med* **89**(3):357–362, 1990.
221. Hauri, P. *The Sleep Disorders*, 2nd edn. Kalamazoo, Upjohn Company, 1982.
222. Gillin, J.C. and Byerley, W.F. The diagnosis and management of insomnia. *N Engl J Med* **322**(4):239–248, 1990.
223. Redfern, P., Minors, D. and Waterhouse, J. Circadian rhythms, jet lag, and chronobiotics: an overview. *Chronobiol Int* **11**(4):253–265, 1994.
224. Moon, C.A., Hindmarch, I. and Holland, R.L. The effect of zopiclone 7.5 mg on the sleep, mood and performance of shift workers. *Int Clin Psychopharmacol* **5** (suppl 2):79–83, 1990.
225. Petrie, K., Dawson, A.G., Thompson, L. and Brook, R. A double-blind trial of melatonin as a treatment for jet lag in international cabin crew. *Biol Psychiatry* **33**(7):526–530, 1993.
226. Folkard, S., Arendt, J. and Clark, M. Can melatonin improve shift workers' tolerance of the night shift? Some preliminary findings. *Chronobiol Int* **10**(5):315–320, 1993.
227. Oldani, A., Ferini-Strambi, L., Zucconi, M., Stankov, B., Fraschini, F. and Smirne, S. Melatonin and delayed sleep phase syndrome: ambulatory polygraphic evaluation. *Neuroreport* **6**(1):132–134, 1994.
228. Folkard, S., Arendt, J., Aldhous, M. and Kennett, H. Melatonin stabilises sleep onset time in a blind man without entrainment of cortisol or temperature rhythms. *Neurosci Lett* **113**(2):193–198, 1990.
229. Parkes, J.D. and Dahlitz, M. Amphetamine prescription. *Sleep* **16**(3):201–203, 1993.
230. Garma, L. and Marchand, F. Non-pharmacological approaches to the treatment of narcolepsy. *Sleep* **17**(8): S97–S102, 1994.
231. Patrick, R.L. Amphetamine and cocaine: biological mechanisms. In Barchas, J.D., Berger, P.A., Ciaranello, R.D., Elliott, G.R. (eds): *Psychopharmacology: From Theory to Practice*. New York, Oxford University Press, 1977, pp 331–340.
232. Alles, G.A. The comparative physiological actions of *dl*-beta-phenylisopropylamines. *J. Pharmacol Exp Ther* **47**:339–354, 1933.
233. Doyle, J.B. and Daniels, L.E. Symptomatic treatment for narcolepsy. *JAMA* **96**:1370–1372, 1931.
234. Prinzmetal, M. and Bloomberg, W. The use of benzedrine for the treatment of narcolepsy. *JAMA* **105**:2051–2054, 1935.
235. Mitler, M.M., Aldrich, M.S., Koob, G.F. and Zarcone, V.P. Narcolepsy and its treatment with stimulants. ASDA standards of practice. *Sleep* **17**(4):352–371, 1994.
236. Anders, T.F. and Ciaranello, R.D. Pharmacological treatment of minimal brain dysfunction. In Barchas, J.D., Berger, P.A. Ciaranello, R.D., Elliott, G.R. (eds): *Psychopharmacology: From Theory to Practice*. New York, Oxford University Press, 1977 pp 425–435.

237. Connell, P.H. The use and abuse of amphetamines. *Practitioner* **200**:234–243, 1968.
238. Glennon, R.A. Psychoactive phenylisopropylamines. In Meltzer, H.Y. (ed.): *Psychopharmacology: The Third Generation of Progress*. New York, Raven Press, pp 1627–1634.
239. Foltin, R.W. and Fischman, M.W. Assessment of abuse liability of stimulant drugs in humans: a methodological survey. *Drug Alcohol Depend* **28**:3–48, 1991.
240. Guilleminault, C. Amphetamines and narcolepsy: use of the Stanford database. *Sleep* **16**(3):199–201, 1993.
241. Fawcett, J. and Busch, K.A. Stimulants in psychiatry. In Schatzberg, A.F., Nemeroff, C.B. (eds): *The American Psychiatric Press Textbook of Psychopharmacology*. Washington, DC, American Psychiatric Press, 1995, pp 417–435.
242. Mitler, M.M., Hajdukovic, R. and Erman, M.K. Treatment of narcolepsy with methamphetamine. *Sleep* **16**(4):306–317, 1993.
243. Yoss, R.E. Treatment of narcolepsy. *Mod Treat* **6**:1263–1274, 1969.
244. Mitler, M.M., Hajdukovic, R., Erman, M. and Koziol, J.A. Narcolepsy. *J Clin Neurophysiol* **7**:93–118, 1990.
245. Anonymous. Sleep apnea, sleepiness, and driving risk. American Thoracic Society. *Am J Respir Crit Care Med* **150**(5 pt 1):1463–1473, 1994.
246. Guilleminault, C. Narcolepsy syndrome. In Kryger, M.H., Roth, T., Dement, W.C. (eds): *Principles and Practice of Sleep Medicine*, 2nd edn. Toronto, W.B. Saunders, 1994, pp 549–561.
247. Davis, J.M., Kopin, I.J., Lemberger, L. and Axelrod, J. Effects of urinary pH on amphetamine metabolism. *Ann NY Acad Sci* **179**:493–501, 1971.
248. Dement, W.C. and Guilleminault, C. Sleep changes in drug dependency hypersomnia and insomnia: causes, manifestations and treatment. *Excerpta Medica* **296**:42–43, 1973.
249. Parkes, J.D., Baraitser, M., Marsden, C.D. and Asselman, P. Natural history and treatment of the narcoleptic syndrome. *Acta Neurol Scand* **52**:337–359, 1975.
250. Mitler, M.M. Evaluation of treatment with stimulants in narcolepsy. *Sleep* **17** (8 suppl): S103–106, 1994.
251. The American Narcolepsy Association, Stimulant medications: An examination of the issues. *The Eye Opener* January 1992, pp 1–4.
252. Baselt, R.C. *Disposition of Toxic Drugs and Chemicals in Man*. St. Louis, C.V. Mosby, 1989.
253. Honda, Y., Akimoto, H. and Takahashi, Y. Pharmacotherapy in narcolepsy. *Dis Nerv Syst* **21**:1–3, 1960.
254. Daly, D.D. and Yoss, R.E. The treatment of narcolepsy with methylphenylypiperidylacetate: a preliminary report. *Proc Staff Meet Mayo Clin* **31**:620–625, 1956.
255. Yoss, R.E. and Daly, D.D. Treatment of narcolepsy with Ritalin. *Neurology* **9**:171–173, 1959.
256. Daly, D. and Yoss, R. Narcolepsy. In Magnus, O., Lorentz de Haas, A.M. (eds): *The Epilepsies*, Handbook of Clinical Neurology Vol. 15. Amsterdam, North Holland, 1974, pp 836–852.
257. Canadian Pharmaceutical Association *Compendium of Pharmaceutical Specialities*, 24th edn. Ottawa, Canadian Pharmaceutical Association, 1994.
258. Gogerty, J.H. and Trapnold, J.H. Chemistry and pharmacology of mazindol. *Triangle* **15**:25–36, 1976.
259. Stahl, K.A. and Imperiale, T.F. An overview of the efficacy and safety of fenfluramine and mazindol in the treatment of obesity. *Arch Fam Med* **2**(10):1033–1038, 1993.

260. Pickworth, W.B., Klein, S.A., Bunker, E.B. and Henningfield, J.E. Assessment of mazindol for abuse liability. *NIDA Res Monogr* **105**:443, 1991.
261. Parkes, J.D. and Schachter, M. Mazindol in the treatment of narcolepsy. *Acta Neurol Scand* **60**:250–254, 1979.
262. Shindler, J., Schachter, M., Brincat, S. and Parkes, J.D. Amphetamine, mazindol, and fencamfamin in narcolepsy. *Br Med J (Clin Res Ed)* **290**(6476):1167–1170, 1985.
263. Alvarez, B., Dahlitz, M., Grimshaw, J. and Parkes, J.D. Mazindol in long-term treatment of narcolepsy. *Lancet* **337**:1293–1294, 1991.
264. Rihmer, Z., Revai, K., Arato, M. and Perenyi, A. Two case reports of mazindol-induced depression. *Am J Psychiatry* **141**(11):1497–1498, 1984.
265. Gillis, D., Wengrower, D., Witztum, E. and Leitersdorf, E. Fenfluramine and mazindol: acute reversible cardiomyopathy associated with their use. *Int J Psychiatry Med* **15**(2):197–200, 1985.
266. Guilleminault, C. Narcolepsy. In Chokroverty, S. (ed.): *Sleep Disorders Medicine: Basic Science, Technical Considerations and Clinical Aspects.* Boston, Butterworth-Heinemann, 1994, pp 241–254.
267. Honda, Y. and Hishikawa, Y. The effectiveness of pemoline in narcolepsy. *Sleep Res* **8**:192, 1970.
268. Mitler, M.M., Shafor, R., Hajdukovich, R., Timms, R.M. and Browman, C.P. Treatment of narcolepsy: objective studies on methylphenidate, pemoline, and protriptyline. *Sleep* **9** (1 pt 2):260–264, 1986.
269. Nehra, A., Mullick, F., Ishak, K.G. and Zimmerman, H.J. Pemoline-associated hepatic injury. *Gastroenterology* **99**(5):1517–1519, 1990.
270. Polchert, S.E. and Morse, R.M. Pemoline abuse. *JAMA* **254**(7):946–947, 1985.
271. Billiard, M., Besset, A. Montplaisir, J., Laffont, F., Goldenberg, F., Weill, J.S. and Lubin, S. Modafinil: a double-blind multicentric study. *Sleep* **17**(8 suppl): S107–112, 1994.
272. Laffont, F., Cathala, H.P., Waisbord, P. and Kohler, F. Effects of modafinil on narcoleptic patients. Double blind cross over study. 9th European Congress of Sleep Research, Jerusalem, 1988: 215 (abstract).
273. Laffont, F., Mayer, G. and Minz, M. Modafinil in diurnal sleepiness. A study of 123 patients. *Sleep* **17** (8 suppl): S113–115, 1994.
274. Mitler, M.M. and Hajdukovic, R.M. Relative efficacy of drugs for the treatment of sleepiness in narcolepsy. *Sleep* **14**:218–220, 1991.
275. Kales, A., Cadieux, R., Soldatos, C.R. and Tan, T.L. Successful treatment of narcolepsy with propanolol: a case report. *Arch Neurol* **36**:650–651, 1979.
276. Meier-Ewert, K., Matsubayashi, K. and Benter, L. Propranolol: long-term treatment in narcolepsy–cataplexy. *Sleep* **8**(2):95–104, 1985.
277. Roufs, J.B. L-tyrosine in the treatment of narcolepsy. *Med Hypotheses* **33**(4):269–273, 1990.
278. Mouret, J., Lemoine, P., Sanchez, P., Robelin, N., Taillard, J. and Canini, F. Treatment of narcolepsy with L-tyrosine. *Lancet* **2**(8626/8627):1458–1459, 1988.
279. Elwes, R.D., Crewes, H., Chesterman, L.P., Summers, B., Jenner, P., Binnie, C.D. and Parkes, J.D. Treatment of narcolepsy with L-tyrosine: double-blind placebo-controlled trial. *Lancet* **2**(8671):1067–1069, 1989.
280. Scrima, L., Hartman, P.G., Johnson, F.H. Jr., Thomas, E.E. and Hiller, F.C. The effects of gamma-hydroxybutyrate on the sleep of narcolepsy patients: a double-blind study. *Sleep* **13**(6):479–490, 1990.
281. Schmidt, H.S., Clark, R.W. and Hyman, P.R. Protriptyline: an effective agent in the treatment of narcolepsy–cataplexy syndrome and hypersomnia. *Am J Psychiatry* **134**:183–185, 1977.

282. Heinonen, E.H. and Rinne, U.K. Selegiline in the treatment of Parkinson's disease. *Acta Neurol Scand* **126**:103–111, 1989.

283. Reynolds, G.P., Elsworth, J.D., Blau, K., Sandler, M., Lees, A.J. and Stern, G.M. Deprenyl is metabolized to methamphetamine and amphetamine in man. *Br J Clin Pharmacol* **6**:542–544, 1978.

284. Schachter, M., Price, P.A. and Parkes, J.D. Deprenyl in narcolepsy. *Lancet* **1**:831, 1979.

285. Hublin, C., Partinen, M., Heinonen, E.H., Puukka, P. and Salmi, T. Selegiline in the treatment of narcolepsy. *Neurology* **44**:2095–2101, 1994.

286. Reinish, L.W., MacFarlane, J.G., Sandor, P. and Shapiro, C.M. REM changes in narcolepsy with Selegiline. Sleep **18**(5): 362–367, 1995.

Index

Note: Page numbers in *italic* refer to figures and/or tables

Index compiled by Caroline Sheard MSc ALA